100 THINGS
RED WINGS FANS
SHOULD KNOW & DO
BEFORE THEY DIE

100 THINGS
RED WINGS FANS
SHOULD KNOW & DO
BEFORE THEY DIE

Kevin Allen and Bob Duff

TRIUMPH
BOOKS

This book is available in quantity at special discounts for your group or organization. For further information, contact:

Triumph Books LLC
814 North Franklin Street
Chicago, Illinois 60610
(312) 337-0747
www.triumphbooks.com

Printed in U.S.A.
ISBN: 978-1-60078-766-9
Design by Patricia Frey
Photos courtesy of AP Images unless otherwise indicated

To the memory of my eighth grade teacher,
Sister Pat Hogan, who convinced me I could
do more than I believed I could.

—Kevin Allen

For all Red Wings fans.

—Bob Duff

Contents

Foreword

The best one-timer I ever struck in my life came against my childhood idol Mike Palmateer at the Winter Classic Alumni Game at Comerica Park on New Year's Eve 2013.

Growing up in the small Canadian town of Leamington, Ontario, I must have seen Palmateer reach up with his lightning-quick glove and rob an NHL forward of a goal a few hundred times during the 1980s on *Hockey Night in Canada*.

It was like living my dream when Kris Draper fed me a perfect pass and I sent the puck screaming toward the upper corner of the net.

When Palmateer grabbed the puck as if he was plucking an apple off a branch, I thought I had died and gone to heaven.

"That was the greatest thing ever," I said to Palmateer. "It was cooler that you stopped it than it would have been if I had scored."

When I was skating away, I was trying to figure out how old Palmateer was, and I concluded he might be 65- or 70-years old. It turns out he was only 60. But he made that save like he was 25 again. He made the save the same flashy way he used to make saves when I was a child watching NHL games on television.

It's still one of my memorable NHL highlights, even though it happened in an alumni game. It just brought back so many childhood memories. It was made more fun by the fact that Draper had set up the shot.

After Palmateer made this amazing save, Draper yelled at me just like he always did during our playing days. He probably yelled at me 100 times for passes I didn't convert.

"C'mon, you can't bury that?" Draper said. "I put it on a tee for you."

"I was just surprised you passed the puck," I replied.

If I had to list three reasons why Detroit fans remember my career, I would say my fight against Colorado's Claude Lemieux is

No. 1, my association with the Grind Line is No. 2, and my Stanley Cup–clinching goal in 1997 against the Philadelphia Flyers is No. 3. Most hardcore fans can describe the move I made to shift around defenseman Janne Niinimaa.

But my Grind Line experiences have the most special place in my heart because of my friendship with Kirk Maltby and Kris Draper. Joey Kocur was also part of the Grind Line during his days there.

It's cool when you are a member of a line that the hockey world remembers. It's rewarding to know that fans are going to be telling their grandchildren that they saw the Grind Line play.

Draper and Maltby played everyone the same way, whether he was a fourth liner or Wayne Gretzky or Mario Lemieux. We all relished the role of disrupting the other team by frustrating the players we played against. I always made sure I was there when Maltby and Draper found themselves in trouble because of their mouth or playing style.

The other factor in our success was our ability to play the game. We could check. We could hit. We could play defense. We could score. Maltby and I were 50-goal scorers in the OHL. All three of us scored some important goals at the NHL level.

We had an identity in the NHL because of our name. When it comes to Detroit hockey, people know the Production Line, the Russian Five, and the Grind Line.

Our reputation also extended beyond the boundaries of Detroit. If you asked a hockey fan in Dallas who the Grind Line was, he might say, "You mean those idiots in Detroit? I hated those fuckers."

We liked being the villains in opposing arenas. The hatred opponents felt for us fueled our passion. We could stir up trouble quicker than hornets at a company picnic.

These are two of my favorite Detroit stories, and this book is crammed full of stories about players who wore the winged wheel as proudly as the Grind Line. Hope you enjoy the read.

—Darren McCarty
July 2014

1 What if Gordie Howe Had Debuted on Broadway?

Gordie Howe can only wonder how the axis of the hockey world might have been altered were fate to have kept him on his original path toward the National Hockey League.

In 1943 New York Rangers scout Fred McCorry spotted Howe playing in Saskatoon and invited Howe, 15, to attend his first NHL training camp, in Winnipeg with the Rangers, one of 36 amateurs invited to the camp. What course might his life might have taken were the Rangers wise enough to get his name on a contract?

"I was there four days," Howe recalled.

Howe was a youngster during the Depression, when money was scarce. Growing up, catalogs replaced shin pads as hockey equipment.

"My first day in camp with the Rangers, I watched the guy beside me get dressed, to see where everything went," Howe said.

Another hockey legend, Lester Patrick—who was the Howe of his era, coming out of retirement to play goal during the 1928 Stanley Cup Finals—ran the Rangers when the young Howe showed up amidst dozens of other prospects.

"He spoke to me four times," Howe said. "At the start of camp, he asked, 'What's your name, son?' and then they wrote it on a piece of paper and pinned it to the back of my sweater.

"The first day, I hit [Rangers veteran forward] Grant Warwick with a pretty good body check, and Mr. Patrick called me over and asked, 'What's your name, son?' Two other times, when I did something on the ice, he called me over and asked, 'What's your name, son?' Finally, I said, 'It's on the back of my shirt, sir.'"

1

Unsigned, Howe went home to Saskatoon, where on October 26, 1943, he turned out with the new Saskatoon Lions junior club. The following fall, Howe was invited to the Red Wings' training camp in Windsor, where he immediately turned heads.

"In those days, the Red Wings had a scout in Saskatoon, Fred Pinckney," Detroit GM Jack Adams explained to the Associated Press in 1966. "He watched Gordie's progress for about three years and then recommended that we take a look at him at our training camp."

Talking to *New York Times* columnist Arthur Daley in 1966, Adams defended Patrick's decision not to sign Howe.

"I always felt Lester took a bum rap on that one and didn't deserve the criticism he got for missing out on the greatest star the sport has ever had," Adams explained. "Whatever year it was, the Rangers were pretty well loaded with young players. All were top class, and Gordie was given such little ice time that he never had a chance to impress anyone. Besides, he was a tall, gangly kid, only 14 years old."

Lynn Patrick, Lester's son, doesn't let his father off the hook so easily over the Rangers' gaffe with Gordie. "Dad took him aside after the workout and suggested he learn a trade or something, to forget about hockey," Lynn Patrick told the *Boston Daily Record* in 1953.

The following season, Howe showed up at the Wings' camp.

"We were training at Windsor, Ontario, and we had so many kids that I didn't work them with the pros," Adams recalled. "I had them scrimmaging among themselves, and so there was no way I could miss Howe. He was doing things on the ice that the other kids couldn't do. He was ambidextrous and could do everything better."

In camp with the veterans, Howe quickly turned heads, splitting the veteran Detroit defense pairing of Jack Stewart and Bill Quackenbush to score a slick breakaway goal.

He was assigned to Detroit's OHA junior club in Galt, but Howe wasn't allowed to play because the Saskatchewan Hockey Association wouldn't permit him a transfer. He practiced all season with the team and participated in exhibition contests, learning the game from coach Al Murray, a onetime NHL defenseman with the New York Americans.

"He came to me and said, 'I've got some news for you, and you're not going to like it,'" Howe remembered. "That's when he told me my transfer didn't come through. But he told me if I stayed the year in Galt, he'd make me into a hockey player, and he did."

Howe turned pro in 1945, playing for coach Tommy Ivan with Omaha of the United States League. The next spring, Ivan was promoted to coach Indianapolis of the AHL.

Gordie Howe holds up the puck with which he scored his 700th goal.

Before training camp that fall, Adams told Ivan that Howe would be joining him at Indianapolis.

"No," Ivan said. "He'll be playing for you."

He was right.

Howe never saw the minor leagues again, skating in 1,687 games as a Red Wing and scoring 786 goals over his 25 seasons with Detroit, all still club records.

To this day, Howe is held in reverence by Red Wings fans too young to have ever seen him play.

"My dad can't sit in the seats [at Joe Louis Arena], because he gets mobbed nonstop for autographs," explained Mark Howe, who, like his dad, is a Hall of Famer who played for the Wings. "It's not that he doesn't appreciate the attention, but he feels badly for the people sitting around him, who never get to see the game."

More than four decades since he wore his Red Wings sweater for the final time, the man they call "Mr. Hockey" is still Mr. Red Wing.

Detroit fans can only shudder at the thought of how easily Howe's star could have shone on Broadway.

Howie Young and Bob Probert, Detroit's Wild Men

The parallels of their careers, their downfalls, and their resurrections are shockingly similar.

Both started in Detroit. Both set penalty-minute records in a Red Wings uniform. After Detroit, each man moved on to play for Chicago. And both bottomed out into the world of substance abuse before doing some time in a jail cell helped them turn their lives around.

Each also carried an aura that was larger than life.

Bob Probert and Howie Young are as much remembered for their drug-and-alcohol-addled misdeeds as they are for the role they filled on the ice with the Wings, as the NHL's toughest players.

Young turned to alcohol when he was 16, after his grandmother, the woman who raised him, died. Just days after the death of his father, Al, Probert left to play for the Brantford Alexanders of the Ontario Hockey League, and that's when his troubles with the bottle began.

"Probie was 17," recalled former teammate and close friend Joe Kocur. "He lost the one guy who could have straightened him out. He started hanging with the wrong crowd."

A defenseman, Young arrived with the Wings during Detroit's 1960–61 run to the Stanley Cup Finals. His combination of skill and toughness led Detroit GM Jack Adams to compare Young to the legendary Eddie Shore.

"Sometimes a guy like that will pump new life into a club," Adams explained to the Associated Press in 1961. "That's what he has done for us."

On the ice, Young was a policeman, collecting 273 penalty minutes during the 1962–63 season, then an NHL record.

Off the ice, Young fought with policemen. He was fined for an altercation involving three Detroit police officers in 1963. Young's scraps, both between the boards and while bellying up to a bar, became the stuff of legend.

Going on benders, Young would disappear for days at a time, and in 1963, the Wings decided they'd seen enough and shipped him off to the Blackhawks.

"We bent over backward to help Young many times, but he has not shown any desire to help either the club or himself," Detroit coach/GM Sid Abel said.

Young seemed to understand his own downfall, not that he appeared able to do anything to prevent it. "I was sent to the minors because no one wanted a drunk on their team," Young told the AP. "John Barleycorn doesn't care what anybody thinks. John Barleycorn doesn't care about anyone."

After failing in Chicago, Young was sent to play for the Los Angeles Blades of the minor-pro Western Hockey League. At first, the trend continued. Young got a Mohawk haircut and began to run with Frank Sinatra and his entourage, appearing in Sinatra's 1965 World War II movie *None But the Brave.*

One night on Sinatra's boat, Young's foolishness again got the better of him. "He told Sinatra he wasn't so tough and picked him up and threw him overboard," Young's longtime friend former NHL defenseman Jim McKenny told the *London Free Press.* "Sinatra's toupee flew off.

"Some of his gunsels beat the crap out of Howie. They stuck a couple of hundred dollars in his pocket and left him lying on the beach. He woke up under swaying palms with 200 bucks in his pocket and thought he was in heaven. He didn't remember anything about throwing [Sinatra] in the water."

Young's day of reckoning finally came on May 4, 1965. Sitting in a Los Angeles jail cell for disturbing the peace, he met another man who'd tried Alcoholics Anonymous. The next day, Young enrolled in AA.

"I wasn't on skid road," Young later recalled. "I was on death road."

Young credited L.A. coach Fern Flaman and GM Lynn Patrick for helping to straighten him out and embrace sobriety.

"Without them, I don't know where I'd be right now. Dead, maybe. It was that bad," Young told the *Boston Traveler* in 1966. "Without the drink on my brain, I could listen and think."

Young made it back to the NHL for a second stint with both the Wings and Blackhawks and a short stay with the expansion Vancouver Canucks.

"I had no urge to go back to the gutter, back into the insanity," Young told *New York Times* columnist Dave Anderson. "I was out there long enough."

In 1985, at age 48, a sober Young tried out with the Flint Spirits of the International Hockey League, around the same time that Probert was first making his mark in Detroit.

Like Young, Probert was as tough as they came. In 1987–88, he set a Red Wings franchise record with 398 penalty minutes but also scored 29 goals that season and was selected to play in the NHL All-Star Game.

"I think he did a lot for the franchise," former Detroit coach Jacques Demers said. "Bob Probert changed the dynamic of the building. If you want to come play in Detroit, there's [Bruise Brothers] Probert and Kocur. That won us a lot of games. [Steve] Yzerman was great, no question, but those two guys, they helped us a lot."

Away from the rink, Probert was every bit as problematic as Young.

"Bob was in trouble every week," Detroit senior vice president Jimmy Devellano remembered.

In 1986 Probert was charged with impaired driving. In 1988 he was one of eight Wings players who broke curfew on the eve of a Western Conference Finals game in Edmonton to go drinking at a bar called Goose Loonies. In 1989 he was arrested crossing the border into Detroit from Windsor when cocaine was found in his underwear. Convicted, Probert served time in a US federal prison.

Kocur believes that most of Probert's off-ice issues stemmed from old relationships he'd formed in his hometown.

"With his NHL buddies, Probert was okay. We kept him out of trouble," Kocur said. "When he went back to Windsor to see his old friends, that's when he got messed up."

After another drunk driving charge in 1994, the Wings let Probert go, and he signed as a free agent with Chicago.

"I always looked at him as a very good person who had some demons," Demers said. "I saw a lot of good things about him."

Like Young, Probert eventually turned his life around. He married and became a family man, helping his wife, Dani, raise their four children.

"The adjustment from my last year of playing to my first year of not playing was pretty tough," Probert admitted after his NHL career ended in 2002. "Constantly finding things to do, that's the key for me. Don't get bored, because when I get bored, I get into trouble."

Sadly, both Young and Probert met early and untimely ends.

On July 5, 2010, Probert was boating with his family on Lake St. Clair when he died suddenly after experiencing chest pains. He was 45.

Young died of cancer in 1999 in New Mexico at the age of 63.

3 Visit the Scene of the Crime: The Detroit-Windsor Tunnel

An estimated 13,000 vehicles per day cross the Canada-US border via the Detroit-Windsor Tunnel, the second-busiest border crossing between the two nations. But it was a 1988 GMC Jimmy driven by Detroit left-winger Bob Probert at 5:15 AM on March 2, 1989, that made this particular border crossing forever known to every Red Wings fan.

Probert and three passengers, including his future wife, Dani, were in the vehicle coming back to Detroit from Probert's hometown of Windsor, when a US Customs inspector discovered Probert's entry visa had expired and opted to take a closer look at the SUV.

During his search, the officer spotted numerous empty beer and liquor bottles on the car's floor. The inspector also noted, in a signed affidavit presented to US federal court magistrate Paul Komives, that "Probert appeared to be disoriented."

During secondary inspection, another customs official discovered two amphetamine pills in the Jimmy. After patting down Probert, he found a black cocaine mill in the inside pocket of his jacket. A white residue evident on the mill later tested positive for cocaine.

That discovery led to a strip search of Probert, and 14.3 grams of cocaine were found "concealed in his underwear," Richard Hoglund, special agent in charge for US Customs, told the *Windsor Star*.

Probert was taken into custody and the vehicle was impounded. It began an odyssey that led to Probert's conviction on drug charges and his serving three months of jail time in a federal prison in Rochester, Minnesota, where his fellow prisoners included fallen televangelist Jim Bakker and reputed Detroit mobster Jack Giacalone, who had been linked to the disappearance of Jimmy Hoffa.

"When I was arrested, it was the low point of my career," Probert was quoted as saying in his biography, *The Bruise Brothers*. "The truth is, it was a long time coming. I remember thinking as I was coming across the border that night how invincible I was. On the one hand you're thinking, 'What if they catch me?' but on the other hand, you're figuring that if they do, they'll just look the other way because you're a professional athlete.

"I think now that on some level, I was relieved when I got arrested because I'd gotten to the point where I didn't care. My self-esteem was very low. I just feel lucky I didn't kill anybody. It could have been a lot worse than it was.

"I think it was good that I got sent [to prison]. At the time I was powerless to change anything, even if I had wanted to. I did an awful lot of thinking in there."

Probert was suspended from the NHL for a season, returning to the Detroit lineup for the final four games of the 1989–90 season. He was also unable to cross the border and play any road games in Canada for 1,461 days while his lawyers fought with US immigration officials to gain Probert the right to reenter the country if he left the United States.

"One of the hardest things during the four years I wasn't allowed into Canada was seeing Windsor across the Detroit River," Probert said of his birthplace and home. "I saw it every day when I went down to the rink to practice. It was a little tough knowing it was that close, yet it seemed so far away."

To Probert's credit, he never played the "Why me?" blame game during his troubles with drug and alcohol abuse.

"I don't blame hockey, only myself," Probert said. "I chose to do what I did, and I paid the price for it."

4 Red Kelly's Number Should Hang from the JLA Rafters

There's a sense of foreboding when some look up at the retired numbers hung from the Joe Louis Arena rafters. Or should that be four-boding?

Many veteran watchers of the team are convinced that there's been a huge oversight in terms of which sweaters have earned a place of honor in the Wings franchise. They are convinced that Red Kelly's No. 4 should also be up top, and they have a valid point.

During his 13 seasons as a Wing, all Kelly did was win four Stanley Cups, play in seven Cup Finals series, become the first defenseman ever to win the Norris Trophy and the second defenseman to capture the Lady Byng Trophy.

Hockey people viewed Kelly as Detroit's true catalyst, the one player they couldn't do without, even more so than Gordie Howe.

"He's the guy who makes them click," Boston Bruins coach Lynn Patrick told the *Springfield Union* in 1954, pointing out that the Wings won the Stanley Cup in 1949–50 minus Mr. Hockey but had never won a title during the 1950s without Kelly in the fold.

"Kelly's the best defenseman in the league," Detroit coach Tommy Ivan told the Associated Press in 1954, predicting great things for his star rear guard that season. "He should win the new Norris Trophy. And I can't see anyone better for the Hart and Lady Byng Trophies."

Perhaps it's the way that it ended for Kelly in Detroit and the bitterness that ensued that has played a role in his absence from the row of Red Wings legends in the rafters.

Angered over a magazine article that portrayed Kelly as suggesting the Wings forced him to play with a broken ankle as they fought for a playoff position late in the 1958–59 season, Detroit GM Jack Adams dealt his All-Star rear guard to the New York Rangers in February 1960. Kelly balked at the deal and announced his retirement, but reconsidered a few days later when this time the Wings shipped him to the Toronto Maple Leafs.

"It's just plain ridiculous," Adams told UPI. "We couldn't force a player to play while he's injured, and we certainly wouldn't even if we could. I'm really surprised and disappointed at Red."

Kelly was equally miffed at his old boss. "Adams called me into his office one day and said he was going to groom me to be his successor," Kelly told the Canadian Press. "But I was gone to Toronto."

When the Maple Leafs eliminated Detroit from the playoffs in the spring of 1960, Kelly couldn't resist getting in another jab. "It's nice to be with a winner," he told the *Ottawa Journal.*

Exactly how deep the hard feelings went at the time was evident when a reporter asked Andra Kelly, Red's wife, who was expecting twins, if she'd picked out any names.

"Well, if they're boys, we may call one Jack and the other Adam," Mrs. Kelly joked.

In the spring of 1960, the Leafs and Kelly defeated the Wings in the Stanley Cup semifinals.

"I never once looked up in that box where I knew Adams would be looking down at us," Kelly told *Sports Illustrated*. "I knew they'd be told to come after me, and they did, but it didn't bother me. The more they came, the harder I fought. I figure it made me play better. I liked it."

Converted to center by the Leafs, Kelly won four more Stanley Cups in Toronto, two at the expense of the Wings.

"He sulked and wouldn't play on the forward line for us," Adams told UPI, though in fact Kelly frequently played up front during his Wings career.

Eventually, the years took the edge off the antagonism, and today Kelly embraces all that Detroit has to offer. "It's a great city with great fans and a great sports town," Kelly said.

Isn't it time that the Wings embraced all that Kelly brought to the team and gave his number the recognition it deserves?

Lidstrom Takes a Backseat to No Defenseman Except Orr

Nick Lidstrom was a star player for 20 seasons in the NHL because he didn't play the same game that everyone else was playing.

"It's like in racquetball when there's a young guy chasing the ball while the experienced guy stands in the middle and waits for the ball to come to him," said former NHL player and team executive Steve Tambellini. "That's how Lidstrom [played] hockey."

Lidstrom was never dazzling like Paul Coffey or physically imposing like Zdeno Chara. He didn't hammer the puck like Al MacInnis or hammer opponents like Scott Stevens. What Lidstrom did was *think* the game at a much higher level than his adversaries.

It was as if he were playing three-dimensional chess while everyone else was playing checkers.

"In chess, they say you need to think three or four moves ahead," said Toronto Maple Leafs president Brendan Shanahan, who was Lidstrom's teammate from 1996 to 2006. "Nick would think eight or 10 moves ahead."

Columbus Blue Jackets president John Davidson said Lidstrom was a "hockey genius."

The word "incomparable" is often misused or overused, but it applies to Lidstrom in hockey because there was uniqueness to his game that cannot be duplicated.

To find an apt comparison for Lidstrom, you have to leave hockey and look to the baseball diamond. You can make a case that Lidstrom was hockey's version of Lou Gehrig in terms of presence and reputation.

Like Gehrig, Lidstrom was a humble, soft-spoken man who played his sport with dominance and dignity. Like Gehrig, Lidstrom was a team-first player, a leader who led with class and professionalism. Like Gehrig, Lidstrom was an iron man. Lidstrom played two decades in a physical contact sport and rarely missed games.

At 40, Lidstrom was playing like a 30-year-old. He won seven Norris Trophies, four of them after age 35.

For many years, Lidstrom was the best in the game at making the first pass out of his zone. He had an uncanny ability to keep the puck in the offensive zone when he was the point on the power play. Nobody could knock the puck out of the air like Lidstrom

Nicklas Lidstrom—the best defenseman since Bobby Orr—in action during a game between the Detroit Red Wings and the Dallas Stars on January 17, 2012.

could. Nobody was more accurate with his shot from the point than Lidstrom.

Lidstrom always found the net. When he missed the cage, it was on purpose. He occasionally liked to bank the puck off the boards like he was shooting pool. Other times he would carom the puck off Tomas Holmstrom's rear end.

Near the end of his career, when shot-blocking was the rage, Lidstrom still didn't get his shot blocked very often. He had a quick release, and he seemed to have a higher understanding of when to shoot the puck and when to hold it.

"He was the best two-way defenseman in the world," Red Wings general manager Ken Holland said. "No one had better hand-eye coordination, and no one had more patience with the puck."

Former NHL defenseman Tom Laidlaw said Lidstrom was the most efficient, effective defenseman he ever saw. "No matter who he was playing against, Lidstrom was going to find a way to get it done," he said.

Laidlaw recalled that everyone was predicting doom for Lidstrom when he was matched up against Philadelphia's Legion of Doom line of John LeClair, Eric Lindros, and Mikael Renberg in the 1997 Stanley Cup Finals.

"People thought Lidstrom was going to get killed against them," Laidlaw recalled. "But Lidstrom was so smart, playing his angles. He knows he's not going to run over Lindros, but he wasn't going to let Lindros run over him, either."

Penalty killers would think they had a path to clear the puck only to find Lidstrom sliding over to knock down the puck and keep it in play.

As a defensive player, Lidstrom was impeccably efficient. He finished his career with a plus-minus of plus-450. He had one roughing penalty over two decades. He averaged only slightly more than 25 penalty minutes per season. Nobody was better than Lidstrom at tying up opponents without drawing a penalty. You'd watch Lidstrom attack a puck carrier, and it resembled a game of Twister. He would be draped over an opponent without touching him.

Lidstrom always found a way to bring the game to him. It was as if he could employ Jedi mind tricks. A forward would think he had found a seam in Detroit's defensive coverage and suddenly discover Lidstrom was in front of him sweeping the puck away with his stick. The key for Lidstrom was always perfect positioning.

The debate over the No. 1 defenseman in NHL history starts and ends with Bobby Orr. He revolutionized the game with his dynamic puck-moving artistry. He made coaches redefine how defensemen should be used. Orr had unprecedented ability and the proper timing to be the defenseman for the ages.

But a strong case can be made for Lidstrom as the No. 2 defenseman behind Orr. Others would argue for Doug Harvey or Larry Robinson or Denis Potvin or Raymond Bourque. Those are all quality candidates.

The argument for Lidstrom over those great defensemen is that Lidstrom's overall game was the closest to perfection. His memorable plays were frequent, and his mistakes were rare.

His durability was second to no defenseman in NHL history, including Orr, whose career was cut short by knee injuries. Orr was finished by age 31, and Lidstrom played All-Star–caliber hockey until he was 42.

Over his career, Lidstrom appeared in 1,564 regular-season games and another 263 playoff games. Orr played less than half that many. His totals are 657 regular-season games and 74 postseason contests.

Lidstrom's teammates called him "the Perfect Human" because he always did the right thing, on or off the ice. Lidstrom played like Superman and lived his life like Clark Kent. That's another similarity he shared with Gehrig.

6 The Mystery of the Missing No. 6

Jack Adams could never say enough good things about Larry Aurie.

"He weighed 142 pounds and had more guts per pound than anybody else alive," Adams told the *Seattle Daily Times* of Aurie. "You have to love that kind."

Adams clearly loved Aurie.

In the rafters at Joe Louis Arena, you will see the No. 1 of Terry Sawchuk, Nicklas Lidstrom's No. 5, the No. 7 worn by Ted Lindsay, Gordie Howe's No. 9, the No. 10 of Alex Delvecchio, Sid Abel's No. 12, and Steve Yzerman's No. 19.

What you don't see, in either the rafters or on the back of a Red Wings sweater, is Aurie's No. 6. The only Detroit player to wear No. 6 since Aurie left the Wings was Cummy Burton from 1957 to 1959. He was Aurie's nephew.

Though up until 2001 it was listed among Detroit's retired sweaters in the *NHL Guide and Record Book*, the fact of the matter is that Aurie's No. 6 was never officially retired and to this day remains a digit in limbo.

"The papers were never filed with the league," onetime Red Wings director of media relations Bill Jamieson explained. "Jack just took it out of circulation."

The time is long overdue to change this situation. The Wings must either officially recognize Aurie's sweater as a retired jersey, or they should simply return the digit to active duty and end the confusion.

Aurie, a Sudbury, Ontario, native, played 11 seasons with Detroit. He joined the club in 1927, Detroit's second season in the NHL and the year the Olympia opened. It was also the season Adams took over as coach and general manager.

Detroit's Retired Numbers
1 — Terry Sawchuk (March 6, 1994)
5 — Nicklas Lidstrom (March 6, 2014)
7 — Ted Lindsay (November 10, 1991)
9 — Gordie Howe (March 12, 1972)
10 — Alex Delvecchio (November 10, 1991)
12 — Sid Abel (April 29, 1995)
19 — Steve Yzerman (January 2, 2007)

Often referred to as "Little Napoleon" or "the Ty Cobb of Hockey," Aurie was a 5'6" fireplug who backed down from no one. When the Wings were a man short, Aurie would be among the first over the boards to kill the penalty. When Detroit went to the man advantage, Aurie anchored the first power play unit.

"He's the best two-way player in the business," Adams told the Associated Press in 1937. "Pound for pound, he has more courage than any player hockey has ever known."

Aurie fractured his left hand in a 1931 preseason game but declined to get the injury checked out, playing the entire season without complaint.

"Aurie never played in a losing game in his whole life—to hear him tell it," Adams said. "The scorekeepers must have counted wrong, in Larry's opinion."

In 1935 Aurie opened a flower shop in Detroit just as his on-ice fortunes were also about to blossom. Prior to the 1935–36 season, Adams acquired center Marty Barry from the Boston Bruins and inserted him between right-winger Aurie and left-winger Herbie Lewis on Detroit's top line. They became the most dangerous forward unit in the NHL. With that trio leading the way, the Wings finished first overall in the NHL and won the Stanley Cup in both the 1935–36 and 1936–37 seasons, the first time an American-based NHL team had ever accomplished this feat.

"There may be smarter athletes individually, but never before have I seen three such brains on one team," Adams told the *Sault*

Ste. Marie (MI) Evening Standard. "They are the Tinker-to-Evers-to-Chance of hockey," he added, invoking the legendary double-play combination of the Chicago Cubs.

"Whenever they get together on road trips or during practice on the home ice at Olympia arena, they are busy figuring out new plays to get the puck into the opposition nets.

"Marty knows what Larry and Herbie will do under certain circumstances. Aurie knows what Marty and Lewis will do. Lewis knows what Marty and Larry will do. There is no lost motion. "I've never in all my life seen three men perform so harmoniously."

The 1936–37 campaign was Aurie's best. He was leading the NHL in scoring, netting his career-high 23rd goal of the year in the next-to-last game of the regular season, before breaking his leg later in the game in a collision with New York Rangers defenseman Art Coulter, ending Aurie's season and costing him the scoring crown.

In the dressing room, as they attended to the two fractures in his leg, Aurie pleaded with doctors to allow him to return to action. Adams had to forcibly remove Aurie's sweater from his back to keep him from seeking to rejoin the fray.

He came back the following year but wasn't the same player, scoring just 10 goals, and Aurie, who was taken off the top line and benched during the season, announced that he would retire at the end of the season.

Aurie played what he thought was to be his final game as a Red Wing on March 20, 1938, at the Olympia against the Rangers. Adams started Aurie with his old linemates Barry and Lewis that night, but he was held pointless in a 4–3 Detroit win.

After the game, Adams announced no one would ever again wear No. 6. "It wouldn't seem right for anyone else to wear it," Adams said.

Aurie finished his NHL career with 147 goals and 129 assists in 489 games and went on to be player/coach at Pittsburgh, Detroit's farm team in the International-American League.

Aurie played one more game in a Detroit uniform the following season when the Wings were hit with a rash of injuries, and he scored a goal in a 3–0 win over Montreal.

In the early 1990s, the Wings considered putting No. 6 back into use, then thought better of the idea.

"We were going to bring it back into circulation," Jamieson recalled. "Then we decided those were Jack's wishes and elected not to do so."

It's time, then, that the Wings heed those wishes and retire No. 6 once and for all.

7 Ted Lindsay Was the First to Hoist the Stanley Cup

Former Detroit Red Wings captain Ted Lindsay is rightfully celebrated as the player who founded the NHL Players' Association. At considerable risk to his own career, Lindsay convinced players around the NHL that owners were taking advantage of them.

However, Lindsay was also a trailblazer with another act that fans probably appreciate more.

On April 23, 1950, Lindsay became the first NHLer to raise the Stanley Cup over his head and skate around the ice. Today, that practice is a staple of the NHL championship celebration ritual.

"I knew who paid our salaries," Lindsay said. "It wasn't the owners. It was the people. I just wanted them to have a closer look."

Lindsay had not planned the event. He said it was impulsive. It just seemed natural to raise the Stanley Cup high for people to see, especially after winning a dramatic double-overtime game against the New York Rangers in Game 7 of the Finals.

Detroit's Stanley Cup–Winning Captains
1935–36: Doug Young
1936–37: Doug Young
1942–43: Sid Abel
1949–50: Sid Abel
1951–52: Sid Abel
1953–54: Ted Lindsay
1954–55: Ted Lindsay
1996–97: Steve Yzerman
1997–98: Steve Yzerman
2001–02: Steve Yzerman
2007–08: Nicklas Lidstrom

Pete Babando had scored at 8:31 of the second overtime to create bedlam at Olympia Stadium. The game had been tied at 3–3 since Detroit's Jim McFadden had scored at 15:57 of the third period.

"This [situation] is what we dream about as players, maybe from the time we are born, to be recognized as the best in the world," Lindsay said. "I wanted to share it with the fans."

The scene played out with NHL president Clarence Campbell presenting the Cup to owner James Norris and general manager Jack Adams. With photographers snapping pictures, Norris and Adams had a ceremonial handing off of the Stanley Cup to Detroit captain Sid Abel. When the photo opportunity was over, Lindsay just grabbed the Stanley Cup off its perch on a table and headed over to the stands.

"[My teammates] probably thought, *That idiot Lindsay is off on another tangent*," Lindsay said.

There was no Plexiglass in those days, just chicken wire at the end of the rinks.

"Along the boards, the people who had season tickets had their elbows up there when you came by," Lindsay said. "They would have to put their head out to see what was happening in the corner."

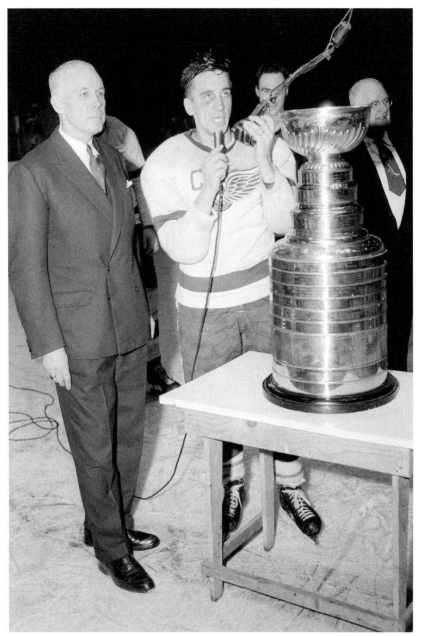

Ted Lindsay says a few words after receiving the Stanley Cup from National Hockey League President Clarence Campbell (left) in Detroit on April 14, 1955.

That meant that when Lindsay was skating around with the Stanley Cup, fans could reach out and touch it. "It was very loud," he said.

The Detroit fans had expected the championship because the Red Wings had the best record in the regular season. Plus, Lindsay, Abel, and Gordie Howe had finished one-two-three in the scoring championship.

But Howe had been severely injured in the opening game of the playoffs against Toronto, and the Rangers had played better than expected in upsetting the Montreal Canadiens in the semifinals. Detroit fans felt both relieved and excited that their team had delivered in the deciding game.

Babando was an unlikely Game 7 hero. He had only scored six goals in 56 games during the regular season. The game-winner was only his second goal of that postseason. "He was a shy guy," said the late Max McNab, who was on the Detroit squad. "He would have much preferred that anybody but him would have scored that goal."

Lindsay said it was the distribution of playoff money in 1950 and other championship seasons that cemented his belief that players needed a union. According to what he had been told, the Detroit players were supposed to receive $1,000 for winning the NHL regular-season title, $1,000 for winning the semifinal, and another $1,000 for capturing the Stanley Cup championship. But when players received their checks and paystubs, their total was $2,365 before taxes. "I could never find out where the other [money] went," Lindsay said.

Today, Stanley Cup championships are celebrated with parades through the city. But in those days, the Red Wings celebrated the championship only with a team party at the Book Cadillac hotel. It was dinner and drinks for players and their wives or girlfriends, and the event lasted until 3:00 AM. Champagne flowed. Adams passed out compliments like they were after-dinner mints. During the regular season, he was not free with his praise. But this was the one night, according to Lindsay, when management was generous.

"Our parade was, we all drove home after that," Lindsay said.

8 Igor Larionov and Slava Fetisov: The Russian Jackie Robinsons

It was August 1991. Viacheslav Fetisov stared down the barrel of the tank and didn't blink.

The battle between democracy and Communism in the former Soviet Union had reached a boiling point, and courage had replaced rhetoric as the weapon of choice.

"It was a very scary moment for all of us, but we didn't think the soldiers would shoot their own people," said Fetisov, whose family was among thousands of Russians who took to the Moscow streets, forming a human wall between the armed forces and the Kremlin.

"It was a situation which could have gone either way," Fetisov, the former Red Wings defenseman, remembered of the day when Soviet tanks fixed their gun turrets on the Kremlin.

Inside, Russian leader Mikhail Gorbachev was bringing an end to Communism as opposing Soviet forces fought back.

"There were some pretty big people behind the coup—the minister of defense, the KGB. The people had to do something," Fetisov said. "It was the kind of moment where you can feel it in the air that something will happen to change history."

A couple of years earlier, Fetisov had sat across a table from Dmitry Yazov, Russian defense minister and one of the men who would later lead the attempted coup, in an attempt to negotiate his release from the Soviet Union hockey program so that he could play in the NHL.

A major in the Russian Army, even though the only weapon he'd ever held in his hands was a hockey stick, Fetisov needed permission to resign his position in the armed forces in order to be allowed to leave the country. He'd served 15 years in the military, but his contract was for 25 years, and this did not sit well with Yazov.

"He said, 'Right now I can press the button and send you to Siberia, and tomorrow the whole of your family would follow you,'" Fetisov remembered.

It was Fetisov and Igor Larionov—the only men in hockey history to win the Stanley Cup, the Canada Cup, gold in the Olympics, and the World Championship and World Junior Championship titles—who risked their lives by challenging the Soviet Communist system in the late 1980s, demanding freedom for Russians to move to the NHL.

Those of us who have never lived under a totalitarian regime cannot comprehend the gamble they took. As a major in the Red Army, Fetisov could have been charged with treason.

"You never knew if that next knock at the door might be KGB, coming to take you to Siberia," Fetisov said.

Despite the potential for disaster, Fetisov felt it was something he had to do. "We had the hockey, and that was it," Fetisov said of his 15 years with Soviet national teams. "We lived in dormitories for 11 months of the year. We were robots. None of us had lived life."

An iron fist ensured these men would not escape from behind the Iron Curtain. "There was intimidation," Larionov explained. "We had a curfew, a fence around the camp."

Hockey was to be their only focus. "You practiced every day for 11 months of the year, always developing your skills," Fetisov said. "You were kept away from your family and all distractions, only to focus on hockey."

He continued, "As a coach, this is an ideal situation, but this is also why so many Russian players didn't play much past 30 or 31. You have to remember that there are two sides to every coin."

He would discover that there are two sides to every curtain—even an iron one—but not before taking some great personal risk along his journey to freedom.

Defection was an option, but Fetisov refused. He loved his country, his people, too much to betray them.

Fetisov was threatened with imprisonment for speaking out. His family was shunned. Friends stopped coming by. When the doorbell did ring, Fetisov feared that it would be KGB agents, coming to take him away.

"I was going up against a very scary monster," he said.

Other than his family and the New Jersey Devils, owners of his NHL rights, Fetisov's longtime friend and teammate Larionov and Russian chess master Garry Kasparov were the only voices to join his battle.

Fetisov teared up at this thought, saying, "They are my closest friends. They supported me all the way."

Standing up for what they believed in. Literally putting their lives on the line. Fetisov just shakes his head when he thinks about what he and Larionov did and then hears people with the gall to suggest Russian hockey players lack heart.

"We had enough bravery to go against the Soviet system," Fetisov said. "Believe me, there were some pretty scary moments for all of us."

Russian Recognition

The success of the Russian Five in Detroit's Stanley Cup triumphs in 1996–97 and 1997–98 turned many Russian people into Red Wings fans. One member of this Red Wings army was Russian center Andrei Loktionov.

"I liked to watch when Detroit had the Russian Five," said Loktionov, whose agent today is Larionov. "I am learning a lot from them, watching the way they played. I enjoy watching games from those times. I enjoy watching them play."

Fetisov and Larionov paid a price for the freedom they eventually earned. Privileges were taken away. The advantages offered to elite athletes were stripped from those who spoke out against the system.

"We were no longer allowed to go abroad for almost a year," Fetisov said. "It was a critical moment in our lives."

Larionov attacked national team coach Viktor Tikhonov and the Soviet Communist sports system in editorials and magazine articles, criticizing the rigorous training methods, inadequate compensation for players, and the lack of feedback offered to players in the methods employed by the team.

"I felt it was time to speak out," Larionov said. "You have to defend your human rights, even in the hockey business."

As far as the Soviet regime was concerned, the hockey players had no rights.

"They could have done anything they wanted to us, especially since we were in the army," Fetisov said. "The army could send us anywhere, anytime."

Fetisov gets emotional when speaking of Larionov, someone to whom he believes Russian players owe a huge debt of gratitude.

"There were many Russian players who came before us who never had this opportunity, and now they have nothing," Fetisov said. "There were many great players who wanted the chance that we have, but none were willing to go against the Soviet system, because they didn't have what Igor has here."

Fetisov gently tapped his heart and then said, "Igor Larionov is a very brave man. And he is my good friend."

In 1989 the two men won their battle to be allowed to come to the NHL.

"Finally, I belonged to myself," Larionov said. "It took a while to adjust to having so much freedom."

Detroit acquired Fetisov and Larionov in 1995, and in 1996–97 and 1997–98, they won back-to-back Stanley Cups with the Red Wings, completing their unique stockpile of hockey accomplishments.

"There's nothing missing from their résumés," former Detroit coach Scotty Bowman said.

Regardless, the true measure of what makes these men legendary is what they accomplished off the ice.

"When they gave me a passport and I got on that jumbo jet for the trip to North America for the first time in my life, I felt I had some freedom," Fetisov said.

"This," Larionov said, "was one of the greatest moments of my life."

More than the Stanley Cups, the Olympic and world titles, and numerous individual achievements, that moment provided them with the greatest joy.

"This is my biggest accomplishment," Fetisov said, trying to explain the sensation but understanding that it can't possibly register with the same resonance to someone who has never lived under the rule of a totalitarian regime.

"You have had your freedom your whole life. I waited 31 years for freedom," he said.

The Jackie Robinsons of Russian hockey, Fetisov and Larionov brought down an Iron Curtain and engineered the assembly of a bridge for Russian players to cross to the NHL.

"Russian people are resilient," Larionov explained.

Fetisov and Larionov put their lives on the line, and hockey was better for it.

9 Gordie Howe Won the NHL's Most Famous Fight

When Gordie Howe fought New York Rangers tough guy Lou Fontinato at Madison Square Garden on February 1, 1959, the story became big enough that it escaped the confines of the sports pages.

Life magazine, boasting a circulation of more than 7 million in those days, published a photo spread on the fight that included a memorable shot of Fontinato's badly broken nose.

The headline read: DON'T MESS AROUND WITH GORDIE.

Appearing in *Life* magazine was the equivalent of going viral in the post–World War II era. *Life* chronicled what Americans were talking about or should be talking about.

What made the fight interesting is that the NHL's top offensive star, Howe, had recorded a unanimous decision against the player considered to be the game's toughest fighter.

"If you didn't believe Fontinato was the heavyweight champ, all you had to do was ask him, because Louie was quite full of himself at that time," said famed reporter and broadcaster Stan Fischler.

Fontinato was a beloved player in New York. Rangers public-relations guru Herb Goren had given him the nicknames "Louie the Leaper" and "Leapin' Louie," and that had helped heighten Fontinato's popularity.

Fischler watched the fight from the Eighth Avenue side of the MSG press box, putting him right above the bout.

According to eyewitnesses, including Fischler, the underlying cause of the fight was Eddie Shack disturbing the peace, as he often did.

"Shack had been giving Howe a hard time for a couple of years," Fischler recalled. "If there was anyone who got under Howe's skin, if that was possible, it was Shack."

Detroit's First No. 9

It's quite possible that what first drew Johnny Sheppard to the rink might have been the chance to warm up a bit.

Sheppard's off-season job also involved working with ice. He ventured into the Arctic area of northern Canada to work as a fur trapper, and all reports indicated he was very successful at it.

Sheppard, who always hugged a lucky rabbit's foot for good luck, also wasn't too shabby on a pair of skates. The original No. 9 in Detroit franchise history, this fur trapper came east to join the Cougars in 1926 after appropriately starring for the Western League's Edmonton Eskimos.

A beautiful stickhandler who played the game at tremendous pace, during the 1926–27 season—Detroit's first campaign—Sheppard led the club in goals (13), assists (8), points (21), and penalty minutes (60), the only time this quad has been landed in franchise history. The following season, Sheppard garnered the honor of scoring the first Detroit goal at Olympia Stadium in a 2–1 loss to the Ottawa Senators on November 22, 1927.

Called "the Littlest Rebel," Sheppard was also a shrewd businessman. In 1933, unhappy with his ice time playing for the Boston Bruins, he paid the team to acquire his release from his contract and two days later signed a pact with the Chicago Black Hawks. An inventor, in his spare time Sheppard allowed that he was working on devising an automatic transmission for automobiles, but he was beaten to the punch by another Canadian, Alfred Horner Munro of Regina, Saskatchewan, who patented the first automatic transmission in 1923.

Fischler said Howe and Shack both got their sticks up, and it looked as if they could end up fighting. News accounts said Shack's cut needed three stitches to close.

"And Louie did what he always did; he butted in," Fischler said. "He came skating in full speed from the left point."

Fontinato did connect on a couple of punches against Howe. "Then [Howe] just destroyed Fontinato," Fischler said.

Red Wings defenseman Marcel Pronovost recalled that Howe switched hands with his punches. His uppercuts delivered the most damage. "That's when he nailed Fontinato on the nose," Pronovost said. "You could hear the smack from the bench where I was. Fontinato went splat, splash. His knees buckled. He never recovered."

The late Johnny Wilson, in a 2006 interview, recalled that Howe held up Fontinato to prolong the fight.

"Lou would be going down, and Gordie would grab him by the back of the sweater and whack him again," Wilson recalled.

Through the years, estimates about the length of the fight have varied greatly. Some say the fight lasted less than a minute, and others say it went on for three or four minutes.

Art Skov was the linesman who broke up the fight, and in a 2004 interview, he recalled that the players formed a half circle around Fontinato and Howe to give them room to fight. He recalled that Rangers center Andy Bathgate was the first to tell Skov he had better intervene.

"Louie was tired from getting hit, and Howe was tired from hitting him," Skov said.

A *Hockey Digest* account of the fight said Fontinato did open a gash above Howe's eye with one of his punches.

But Skov said, "It was the most one-sided fight I ever saw."

Fischler said he doesn't recall Fontinato being defeated in a fight before that night.

"And he wasn't just beaten, he was destroyed," Fischler said. "It was an embarrassment."

Fischler said when the reporters arrived at the Rangers' dressing room after the game, they could hear shouting and loud banging behind the door.

Bill Gadsby was playing for the New York Rangers then, and he admitted to Fischler that Fontinato had thrown a fit in the dressing room.

"He was humiliated," Fischler said. "He was throwing skates off the wall and doing crazy things."

Goren, according to Fischler, made the rounds with reporters to spin the idea that Fontinato had actually held his own in the fight.

"[He said we] had failed to notice all the good body blows that Louie got into Howe," Fischler said.

Fischler still laughs about Goren's efforts more than a half century later. "The picture in *Life* magazine of Fontinato's bloodied face ended that alibi," Fischler said.

Hockey Digest reported that Fontinato's nose "looked like a rudder swung hard to starboard" after the fight with Howe. Fontinato entered the hospital after the game to have surgery on it. According to the same report, Howe suffered a dislocated finger.

The fight seemed to have a devastating impact on the Rangers. "In a sense, Gordie Howe helped end the New York Rangers' playoff run," Fischler said. "The Rangers choked in the homestretch. The Rangers were seven points ahead of the Leafs with two weeks to go, and the Leafs caught them on the final night. A lot of things went wrong, but one of the key things was that Fontinato was useless."

In a 1964 *Sports Illustrated* story, writer Mark Kram said that 1959–60 Rangers coach Phil Watson "claimed dejectedly that [the fight] had shattered the spirit of his club for the entire season."

In a 2006 interview with Wilson, he said that he had become friends with Fontinato when they played together later in their careers.

"He told me, 'I had to fight Gordie because he was the king,'" Wilson said. "If I beat him, I would have been the king. I was a half inch from being the king until he got a hold of me."

Perception often becomes reality, and the story of Howe pummeling Fontinato enhanced Howe's reputation as a ferocious, terrifying competitor. Over his next 13 seasons in the NHL, Howe only fought three more times. It was clear that no one wanted to mess with Gordie.

10 Fifteen Hundred Times Three Equals One

In the history of the National Hockey League, just 14 players have skated in 1,500 games. But only three of those 15 did so while playing their entire careers with one team, and all three of them were Red Wings.

Nicklas Lidstrom (1,564), Alex Delvecchio (1,549), and Steve Yzerman (1,514) form this unique triumvirate. In 2012 Lidstrom shattered Delvecchio's NHL record for the most games played by a one-team player, but Delvecchio still holds forth as the one-team player who skated the most seasons in that team's uniform, 24 in total from 1950–51 through 1973–74.

Delvecchio held the one-team games-played mark for 32 years until he was surpassed by Lidstrom, though this was news to the unassuming man who wore No. 10 for the Wings for so many years.

"To be truthful, I didn't even know I had any record for playing games," Delvecchio said at the time. "All I wanted to do was play hockey. But I can't think of a better person to beat it than Nick.

"He's a great hockey player. He's not that rough and tough on the ice, but he handles himself, checks well, great shot. He's just a leader out there."

In fact, Lidstrom and Delvecchio are a lot alike in the way they played the game—clean, steady, reliable, and often overlooked.

A three-time Lady Byng Trophy winner, Delvecchio picked up just 383 penalty minutes in his entire NHL career, or 15 fewer than Bob Probert's club-record total in 1987–88.

"I think I had maybe five fights my whole career," Delvecchio said.

While guys like Ted Lindsay and Gordie Howe, often Delvecchio's linemates in his early NHL days, brought ruggedness to the ice, Lindsay felt Delvecchio's poise and polish were equally significant to the team's success. "That's what made our hockey club so successful. We had the right mix of styles and personalities," Lindsay said.

Delvecchio was the picture of consistency. He scored at least 20 goals in 13 of his 24 campaigns. He registered 50 or more points 17 times. He missed just 43 games in that span, and he captained the Wings from 1962 to 1973, longer than any player in team history other than Yzerman.

The man they called Fats was also a versatile sort. Delvecchio was named an NHL second-team All-Star in 1952–53 at center and in 1958–59 at left wing. He skated in the NHL All-Star Game 13 times (1953–59, 1961–65, 1967), a total surpassed by only six players in league history.

Howe often referred to Delvecchio as "an All-Star without a title," but there were plenty of milestones flecked all over Delvecchio's résumé.

In 1966 he became the fifth player to collect 100 points in Stanley Cup play, and on December 5, 1968, with a helper against the Minnesota North Stars, Delvecchio was the third NHLer to garner 600 assists. A couple months later, Delvecchio followed Howe and Montreal Canadiens captain Jean Beliveau as the third NHL player to post 1,000 career points with an assist February 16, 1969, against the Los Angeles Kings. He was also the sixth NHLer to ascend to the 400-goal plateau.

He retired in 1973 as the NHL's second–all-time scoring leader, trailing only Howe. Delvecchio was Howe's center in 1968–69 when he became the first Red Wing to collect 100 points in a season and was Mickey Redmond's center in 1972–73 when Redmond posted Detroit's first 50-goal campaign.

"Alex deserved a lot of the credit for any success I had," Redmond said. "He got you the puck; he laid in right there on your stick. He was terrific."

In his final full NHL season, Delvecchio posted 71 points, the third-highest total in NHL history by someone past their 40th birthday.

On November 10, 1991, the Wings retired Delvecchio's No. 10 jersey.

"I've been inducted into the Hall of Fame, I've won Stanley Cups, but this is better," he said.

The club also commissioned artist Omri R. Armany to sculpt a statue of Delvecchio, which was unveiled on October 16, 2008, at Joe Louis Arena.

11 GM Jack Adams Broke Up the Band in 1955

Ted Lindsay won the Stanley Cup with the Detroit Red Wings in 1950, 1952, 1954, and 1955, and yet he still feels shortchanged.

He believes Detroit general manager Jack Adams cost the team a few more championships by trading away key players. He is not alone in that thinking.

"I still believe to this day that the five Stanley Cups that Montreal won [from 1956 to 1960] should have been ours," Lindsay said. "At worst, we should have won three of those five. We had the team. We had the talent. We had the chemistry."

On May 27, 1955, Adams dealt forwards Johnny Wilson, Tony Leswick, Glen Skov, plus defenseman Benny Woit, to the Chicago Blackhawks for Dave Creighton, Gord Hollingworth, John McCormack, and Jerry Toppazzini.

All of the players Adams moved in the deal were important contributors to the 1955 championship team. Leswick and Skov played on a checking line with Marty Pavelich. Skov had scored 14 goals, and Leswick chipped in 10. Wilson had netted 12. Woit had been a regular defenseman, but Adams always seemed to find fault with him.

On June 3, 1955, Adams traded goalie Terry Sawchuk, Vic Stasiuk, Marcel Bonin, and Lorne Davis for Ed Sandford, Real Chevrefils, Norm Corcoran, Gilles Boisvert, and Warren Godfrey.

"It was truckload trade," former Red Wings player Marty Pavelich said years later. "Adams sent over Cadillacs and got back Chevettes."

Trading away Sawchuk seemed like an odd decision. At the time of the trade, Sawchuk was 25 and had been an All-Star for five consecutive seasons. He owned 56 shutouts during that period and boasted three Vezina Trophies and a Calder Trophy. Plus, Stasiuk was a young player on the rise. He developed into a consistent 20-goal scorer in Boston.

It was well known among the players that Adams wasn't particularly fond of the temperamental Sawchuk.

"Adams didn't want to trade Sawchuk to Montreal because he thought he would make Montreal too strong," Lindsay remembered.

Lindsay felt the Red Wings lost their chemistry in the 1955 deals. "We were a machine that was running efficiently, and Adams disrupted everything," he said.

Lindsay's view of the Red Wings that summer was that the Red Wings needed only to start thinking about replacing shot-blocking defenseman Bob Goldham, who was 32 at the time. But Lindsay felt that Goldham still had two good seasons left in him.

If Adams wasn't going to change his mind about trading Sawchuk, Lindsay believed he should have moved him to Montreal.

"We could have received a doggone good defenseman from Montreal," Lindsay theorized. "Maybe Montreal would have given up Tom Johnson or Doug Harvey."

Lindsay said some of the players Adams acquired were solid players. "But they weren't winners," he added.

Years later, Jimmy Skinner, coach of the 1954–55 Red Wings team, revealed that Adams was forced to make the deal with the Blackhawks.

"He had to trade those players to Chicago because the Norris family owned the Chicago team too, and he had to give them some players," Skinner said. "If you ask me, Jack kept the league going. He made trades that would help other teams, even though he was hurting himself. He wanted the league to be strong."

Adams probably knew that he should not have traded Sawchuk, because he reacquired him in 1957. But Adams gave up Johnny Bucyk to re-land Sawchuk. Bucyk ended up becoming a Hall of Fame player in Boston.

"I remember him calling Boston GM Lynn Patrick and telling him he should take Johnny Bucyk," Skinner said before he died in 2007. "He had to talk him into it."

Montreal won five consecutive Stanley Cup championships from 1956 to 1960. They had a star-studded team led by Jean Beliveau, the aging Rocket Richard, plus Dickie Moore, Bernie "Boom Boom" Geoffrion, Jacques Plante, and Harvey and Johnson. Montreal had a championship-caliber roster.

But Howe was in his prime, and imagine how strong the team would have been had it kept Sawchuk, Stasiuk, Bucyk, Skov, Leswick, etc. It's easy to believe that this Detroit group could have kept winning.

12 You Can Still Visit the Red Wings' First Arena

Olympia Stadium met the wrecking ball in 1987. Now, with the Red Wings marching toward a deal for a new downtown arena, Joe Louis Arena will soon be on the endangered species list.

But it is not too late for fans to see the arena where the franchise's first NHL games were played.

Windsor Arena, located at 334 Wyandotte Street East, was home to the Detroit Cougars during the 1926–27 season while Olympia Stadium was being constructed.

Now 90 years old, Windsor Arena is still standing, although it wasn't used for hockey during the 2013–14 season. But it is the same building where Howie Morenz, Frank Boucher, George Hainsworth, and Eddie Shore played against the Cougars.

The Detroit franchise was born on May 15, 1926, when a group led by Charles Hughes, Wesley Seybourn, and John Townsend founded the team that would join the NHL along with the New York Rangers and Chicago Blackhawks to give the league 10 teams. Art Duncan was the team's first coach.

The Cougars' ownership group paid $100,000 to receive the players from the financially troubled Victoria Cougars of the Pacific Coast League. The new owners were happy with the purchase because the Victoria Cougars had won the Stanley Cup in 1925.

Windsor Arena, then called Border Cities Arena, was renovated to accommodate NHL crowds. It held about 6,000 fans.

The Cougars lost their home opener 2–0 to the Boston Bruins on November 18, 1926, before a capacity crowd at Border Cities Arena. The *Boston Herald* reported the arena "was packed to the doors."

Detroit Home Arena Debut Games

Windsor Arena (November 18, 1926)	Boston Bruins 2 at Detroit Cougars 0
Olympia Stadium (November 22, 1927)	Ottawa Senators 2 at Detroit Cougars 1
Joe Louis Arena (December 27, 1979)	St. Louis Blues 3 at Detroit Red Wings 2

Future Hall of Famer Hap Holmes was supposed to be Detroit's goalie, but he became ill and Herb Stuart was his substitute.

News accounts of the game said fans were miffed by what they considered high ticket prices ($1.65 to $3.75). American fans also complained that they had to pay both Canadian and American taxes.

Even without Holmes playing, there were eight future Hall of Fame members on the ice that night. Hall of Famer Cooper Smeaton was the referee. Boston's team included defensemen Sprague Cleghorn and Eddie Shore, plus forwards Harry Oliver and Gordon (Duke) Keats. It was only the second game of Shore's career, and he didn't play much.

Detroit's lineup included Frank Fredrickson, Jack Walker, and Frank Foyston.

Keats scored the first goal against the Cougars just 1:45 into the game. He also set up the second goal by Archie Briden.

Border Cities Star writer Dick Gibson said it was clear why the Bruins were "picked as the potential league champions."

"From the goal, every man fitted into the machine, one set of forwards going just as good as the one it relieved," Gibson wrote.

Gibson graded the Cougars poorly in his newspaper column. "Almost as speedy as their opponents, the Detroiters did not show the same smart teamwork. They missed passes and got out of position frequently, while every man was marked by his check wherever he moved."

It is interesting to note that 88 years ago sportswriters were already complaining about coaching tactics taking the excitement and offensive flow out of the game.

"We admire the flawless Boston defensive system, but it was so perfect that the average spectator would not appreciate it," Gibson penned. "He only realized that the final stages of the affair lacked in thrills."

Despite high expectations brought on by the presence of Victoria players, the Cougars' only season in the Windsor Arena didn't go well. The Cougars finished last in the NHL, with a record of 12–28–4.

One oddity of the season was that Keats, who scored the first goal against the Cougars, was traded, along with Briden, to Detroit by Boston on January 7, 1927, for Fredrickson and Harry Meeking.

Keats ended up scoring the franchise's first hat trick on March 10, 1927, in a 7–1 win against the Pittsburgh Pirates. Keats ended up being a player/coach and posted a 2–7–2 record as the franchise's second coach.

13 Pavel Datsyuk Can Do the Happy Gilmore Drive

Each fall, when the Detroit Red Wings gather for their annual golf tournament during training camp in Traverse City, Michigan, they look forward to an afternoon of fun and games.

At the same time, they also can't wait to see the magic man at play. On the ice, Detroit center Pavel Datsyuk can make the puck dance at the end of his stick. Apparently, he possesses equally uncommon skills with a golf club in his hand. Datsyuk, it seems, can do the *Happy Gilmore* drive.

Like the Adam Sandler character in the 1996 film about a frustrated hockey player who turns to the PGA Tour to find success, Datsyuk can stand in the tee box, pace off 10 yards back, and then turn and run toward the golf ball and whack it with his driver like he is taking a slap shot.

Oh, other Wings have tried to emulate this feat over the years, but only Datsyuk possesses the unique hand-eye coordination capable of allowing him to smack the little white orb 250 yards down the middle of the fairway.

"You look at each other and say, 'Wow, did you see that?'" Detroit defenseman Niklas Kronwall said.

Often, they make similar remarks during games when Datsyuk does something dazzling on the ice. He's been turning heads and leaving opponents shaking theirs in disbelief ever since he came to the NHL from his native Russia in 2001, joining the Wings in time to win a Stanley Cup as a rookie.

"He makes unbelievable moves that we've never seen before," former Detroit defenseman Mathieu Dandenault said.

"He's the smartest player I've ever played with," said Brett Hull, Datsyuk's linemate for the first three years of his NHL career.

The shifty pivot could stick-handle past an opponent in a phone booth, and hitting him is like trying to check a rope.

"I don't know of a player in the NHL who handles the puck as well as Pavel and does the creative things that he does," former Detroit teammate Brendan Shanahan said. "It's a part of the game we're losing, because most coaches don't allow their players to try the things that Pavel can do."

Detroit general manager Ken Holland believes Datsyuk could be even more dangerous were he not such a responsible defensive player.

"He's a player who probably doesn't fulfill his offensive potential because he's so committed defensively," Holland said. "He's as hard on the back-check as he is chasing the puck on offense.

"His hockey IQ is off the charts. He has incredible will and determination. He's maybe the best one-on-one player in the world. He's a world-class player. He's irreplaceable."

The kids would label Datsyuk's abilities with the puck as "sick," but Phoenix Coyotes defenseman Keith Yandle willingly ups the adjective ante on Datsyuk's dangling efforts.

"The guy is disgusting," Yandle said with admiration. "It is fun to watch him but not fun to play against him."

Another Russian marvel can only marvel at the deft dekes Datsyuk frequently deals out to fool opponents. "He's a good one," Washington Capitals three-time Hart Trophy winner Alexander Ovechkin said of Datsyuk.

At the rink, no one's capable of mimicking the moves mastered by Datsyuk.

"He has the puck all night, and he's making his Pavel Datsyuk moves," teammate Johan Franzen said.

What's a Datsyuk move, you ask?

"You can't understand, really," Franzen explained.

At the end of practice, Datsyuk tends to experiment with new dangles before trying them out in games, and other Detroit players form a captive audience as he works out the kinks.

"It's funny sometimes," Kronwall said. "Maybe the average Joe doesn't see the small things he does out there [because] he makes it look easy. It's a lot of fun to watch."

When he brings those moves to game night, everyone in the building is captivated. Even Datsyuk's linemates aren't sure what he's going to do next when he has the puck on his stick.

"What he's capable of on the ice, it's remarkable," said former Detroit forward Kris Draper, an occasional Datsyuk linemate. "You don't know what he's going to do. You don't know where he's going to go. All you try to do when you play with him is get open and stay out of his way."

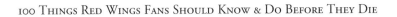

Pavel Datsyuk reacts to his shot on September 13, 2007, at the Grand Traverse Resort and Spa in Acme, Michigan, during his third year playing in the annual golf tournament to benefit Centre Ice.

Draper still vividly recalls the morning he arrived at the rink to discover he'd be skating alongside Datsyuk in that night's game for the first time.

"I felt like I'd won the lottery," Draper said.

Linemates can't figure out Datsyuk's deftness of hand, so pity the poor goaltenders who make their living attempting to stop Datsyuk dazzlers. Datsyuk tries to vary his breakaway bids so that netminders can't get a read on him.

"I don't want them to know my moves," he said.

He's not nearly as guarded about his unique tee-off talent. "You come to the golf course, I will show you," he said of his Happy Gilmore–like prowess with a driver.

Those who've seen him turn this one-of-a-kind feat on the links can only shake their heads in disbelief.

"It's entertaining," Shanahan said, before paying Datsyuk the ultimate compliment: "I'd buy a ticket to watch him play."

Golf or hockey?

In Datsyuk's case, either one is worth the price of admission.

14 Mud Bruneteau's Clear History

One thing was clear about Modere "Mud" Bruneteau—when the Red Wings needed a big goal, they could often count on him.

His original nickname was fashioned after his given name was shortened to Mod and then morphed into Mud, but the name he gained during his Detroit days was well earned. They called Bruneteau "Mr. Clutch."

Detroit signed Bruneteau, whose parents hailed from the southern Pyrenees mountains in France and whose father spoke no

English, out of the Winnipeg senior ranks in 1934, where, curiously, he'd been employed as an office worker by the Norris Grain Company, the business operated by Red Wings owner James Norris.

"He's a fine boy and a hard worker," Norris Grain Company secretary C.A. Babbitt told the Canadian Press of Bruneteau, who in his downtime would admire the Red Wings team photo that hung in Babbitt's office and proclaim that he'd play for the Wings one day.

Bruneteau's dream came true during the 1935–36 season, and he made a Stanley Cup debut that spring that has yet to see its equal.

The rookie right-winger saw limited ice time as the Wings opened the playoffs at the Montreal Forum against the Montreal Maroons. Through three periods the teams were scoreless, so off to overtime they headed.

One overtime period passed without an outcome. Then another. And another. And another. And another.

As the teams took the ice for the sixth overtime period, the crowd of 9,500 had thinned considerably. Some of those who stayed had lost the battle to keep their eyes open.

On the benches, both teams turned to seldom-used players as the regulars grew leg weary. Late into the sixth extra frame, four Maroons crashed the net of Detroit goalie Normie Smith, but when he turned them aside, one Montreal defender was caught up ice, leaving Archie Wilcox alone to defend as Hec Kilrea broke down the ice with the puck alongside Bruneteau.

Bruneteau slipped behind Wilcox, took the feed from Kilrea, and deked around Montreal goalie Lorne Chabot to slip home the only goal of the game.

The puck wedged between the twine and the back bar in the net and never fell to the ice. "You know, to this day that goal judge still hasn't put the light on," Red Wings forward Pete Kelly, another member of the 1935–36 squad, said in a 2001 interview.

The elapsed time was 176 minutes and 30 seconds, an NHL record for the longest game that remains on the books today, and it was 2:25 AM when Bruneteau, who'd only been recalled from the Wings' Detroit Olympics farm team two weeks earlier, netted his record tally.

"I always knew that boy Bruneteau had the stuff, and he sure came through with a nice effort there," Adams told the *Calgary Daily Herald*.

In a gesture of true sportsmanship, Chabot fished the puck out of his net and had it sent over to the Detroit dressing room for Bruneteau to savor. "I guess the kid will always remember that goal and would like to have it as a memento," Chabot told people in the Maroons' dressing room, according to reports in the *Montreal Gazette*.

Bruneteau was almost left speechless when Detroit coach Jack Adams presented the puck to him. "Gee whiz, gee whiz, that's swell," was all he could say.

After the game, Jim Norris Jr., son of the Wings owner, wired news of the game to *Ripley's Believe It or Not!* For Bruneteau, if the story had ended there, he still would have been remembered forever, but he would accomplish much more before his hockey days were done.

When Detroit repeated as Stanley Cup champs in the spring of 1937, Bruneteau became the first player in NHL history to win a Cup in each of his first two seasons in the league. And he generally saved his best performances for the postseason.

During the 1942–43 season, Bruneteau led the Wings with 23 goals, playing on a line with Sid Abel and Carl Liscombe. In the opener of Detroit's Stanley Cup Finals series with Boston, Bruneteau beat Bruins goalie Frank Brimsek three times in a 6–2 victory for the first playoff hat trick in Red Wings history. Detroit went on to win the Cup, and Bruneteau registered five goals and nine points in nine postseason games.

Ow, Quit It

During the Stanley Cup–record six-overtime, 176:30 game between the Wings and Montreal Maroons on March 24–25, 1936 (it ended after midnight on the 25th), Detroit defenseman Bucko McDonald was credited with 26 hits.

Prior to the game, a boisterous Red Wings fan promised McDonald five dollars for every body check he dished out during the game.

A year later, Bruneteau and linemates Liscombe and Syd Howe rewrote the record book. They combined to score 103 goals, shattering the NHL mark for goals in a season by a forward line of 102, set by the Boston unit of Cooney Weiland, Perk Galbraith, and Dit Clapper in 1929–30. Bruneteau also set a Wings single-season mark, netting 35 goals.

Detroit opened the playoffs against the Bruins, and in Game 5 of the series, Bruneteau beat Paul Bibeault 17:12 into overtime to give the Wings a 3–2 victory and a similar series edge.

Bruneteau's NHL days ended in 1946 when he was named player/coach of Detroit's Omaha USHL franchise, and the conclusion came with Bruneteau having never been assessed a major or misconduct penalty.

As a coach, Bruneteau continued to score big for the Wings. Among the proteges he sent along to Detroit were future Hall of Famers Gordie Howe, Terry Sawchuk, and Marcel Pronovost. It's why Adams found him just as clutch as a teacher as he had been as a scorer.

"Bruneteau is much too important to us in Omaha," Adams told the *Windsor Star*. "He's done a tremendous job with the kids we have there, and the fans worship him."

For years, Detroit had its eye on Mud.

15 Terrible Ted's Redux: A Comeback for the Ages

In the summer of 1960, after three seasons with the Chicago Blackhawks, former Red Wings captain Ted Lindsay announced his retirement as an NHL player.

"Either I'm slowing up or these players are getting faster," Lindsay told the Canadian Press at the time.

It turned out that Lindsay wasn't done. In the fall of 1964, he heard from his old club, and Lindsay opted to see if he could once more answer the call of the Red Wings.

Sid Abel, Lindsay's old Production Line center, had become coach/GM of the Wings, and after seeing Lindsay perform alongside him and Gordie Howe when their famous unit was reunited for a charity game, Abel figured the man known as "Terrible Ted" was far from terrible as a player.

In fact, Abel was certain Lindsay could help his club and invited him to training camp on a tryout basis.

"If I improve to the point where I think I have been an asset to the team, I'll stick," Lindsay said as he arrived for camp. "If not, I'll pack it up, because I don't need the money.... I just wanted to end my career as a Red Wing."

Abel offered his reasoning to the *Boston Record-American*: "Actually, Lindsay wasn't completely out of hockey," Abel explained. "You see, he'd been running a hockey school in Detroit all the time he was retired. He also had been working out with the Wings whenever we practiced at home. So his legs were in shape and he hadn't gone to any weight."

Quickly, Lindsay showed he still had some of the old skills that made him the NHL scoring champion in 1949–50 and a three-time All-Star.

"In training camp, Lindsay skated better than some of our rookies," Abel said. "It was just a question of whether or not he'd give it a try.

"I was afraid that maybe he wouldn't feel he could get himself into good enough physical condition to take all the bumping around. He had to prove it to himself, and he did."

While many famous athletes have flopped when coming out of retirement, Lindsay never doubted that he'd be successful at his comeback attempt.

"Sid said, 'Come back and play,'" Lindsay recalled. "It was something I wanted to do. I wanted to end up a Red Wing."

Lindsay earned a spot on the team, and Abel made a cash deal with Chicago to reacquire the left-winger's NHL rights. There was a sense of symmetry to it all. Lindsay's first tenure as a Red Wing had begun two decades earlier in the fall of 1944.

Wearing No. 15 instead of his normal No. 7, which now belonged to Norm Ullman, Lindsay proved immediately he hadn't mellowed. In his first NHL game in four years, the season opener against the Toronto Maple Leafs, Lindsay was handed a 10-minute misconduct and a $25 fine for verbal abuse of referee Vern Buffey.

"Lindsay's command of the English language is quite startling," remarked Leafs defenseman Bob Baun to the Associated Press.

Lindsay's wife and former teammate Marty Pavelich had both tried to talk him out of his comeback attempt, and NHL president Clarence Campbell, long Lindsay's foil over his miscreant on-ice deeds as a player, scoffed at the notion that anyone could return to hockey's best league after four years in retirement.

All were proven wrong, as Lindsay defied the odds.

"When you are doing something you love, it's never hard," Lindsay explained. "You're doing it because you want to do it. I knew for sure I could play."

Abel was excited to be proven right as Lindsay helped lead the team to a spectacular season.

"He's still a live wire on the bench, and the inspirational effect he's had on our many young players has been tremendous," Abel told the *Boston Herald*. "He's simply fantastic."

One of only two men in NHL history to lead the league in scoring and in penalty minutes during his career, Lindsay surrendered none of his ruggedness to Father Time, collecting a team-leading 173 penalty minutes. In another game against Toronto, Lindsay was fined $75 after being assessed misconduct and game misconduct penalties by Buffey. He refused to pay his fine, insisting that he wouldn't stand for Campbell's "kangaroo court."

After being suspended indefinitely by Campbell, Lindsay ultimately stepped off his stand, paid his fine, and was reinstated. "I didn't want to hurt the club," he explained.

Displaying little rust, Lindsay earned admiration from his peers.

"He can skate and he's smart," Montreal Canadiens forward Dick Duff told the *Ottawa Journal*.

"It certainly is a remarkable feat," Boston Bruins GM Lynn Patrick said of Lindsay's return, in the *Boston Traveler*.

For the first time since 1956–57, Lindsay's previous season with the Wings, Detroit topped the regular-season standings. Lindsay finished with 14–14–28 totals and played in all 70 games, winning over even his harshest critics with a comeback for the ages.

"This is one of the most amazing feats in professional sports," Campbell told the *Boston Traveler*. "I know I was among the many knowledgeable hockey people who expressed skepticism when it was first announced that Lindsay would try a comeback after being away from the game for four years. But now I know I was wrong. Ted has done what I thought was impossible."

At the end of the season, after Detroit was upset by Chicago in the Stanley Cup Semifinals, Lindsay retired again, this time for good.

"This won't mean a lot to everyone, but I ended up a Red Wing, and that means a lot to me," Lindsay said.

Lindsay was inducted into the Hockey Hall of Fame in 1966, one of the rare times that the Hall waived its three-year waiting period, but he displayed that he'd lost none of his irascibility when he refused to show up for the induction ceremony after he learned the rules of the day prohibited his wife and children from attending.

"Ted's making it tough on the Hall committee," fellow inductee Babe Pratt joked during his acceptance speech. "Now they can only induct bachelors."

16 Konstantinov Was Detroit's Ultimate Warrior

When he thinks back on that fateful day, Brendan Shanahan recalls that it was Friday the 13th.

He also is haunted by the memory that as their limousine was getting ready to leave, he'd tried unsuccessfully to talk teammates Vladimir Konstantinov and Viacheslav Fetisov and team masseur Sergei Mnatsakanov into staying for a game of cards.

"Slava got out and asked me to sign a couple of sweaters for him," Shanahan said. "I poked my head in the window and saw where Vladdie was sitting and where Mnatso was sitting.

"I said, 'Why are you guys going home? Stay and play cards.' They said, 'No, we're tired.' Slava got in and they drove off."

The next time Shanahan spoke to Konstantinov and Mnatsakanov, both men were hooked up to life support.

Around 9:00 PM on June 13, 1997, the limousine carrying the three men veered off Woodward Avenue in Birmingham, Michigan, and slammed into a tree at an estimated 50 mph.

Konstantinov and Mnatsakanov were both comatose after suffering closed head injuries. Konstantinov also suffered severe nerve and muscle damage to one arm. Mnatsakanov was left paralyzed in both legs and one arm.

Richard Gnida, the driver of the limo, suffered minor injuries. He had a lengthy record of traffic violations, including a suspended license. Gnida received a nine-month jail term for his offenses. Mnatsakanov and Konstantinov received life sentences in the permanent brain damage each man suffered.

"We only celebrated for six days," Shanahan said.

Less than a week removed from savoring their Stanley Cup triumph over the Philadelphia Flyers, the Wings found themselves in a hospital room where Konstantinov, the meanest, toughest warrior on their team, was being kept alive by a respirator.

Konstantinov's icy stare, intensity, and dogged determination earned him a reputation as the NHL's most difficult opponent.

"If you had 20 guys like him in your lineup, you'd win the Stanley Cup every year," former NHL power forward Keith Tkachuk said of Konstantinov. "He was just a great competitor. He never let up. He was always looking to hit you.

"I can't say that I looked forward to our meetings, but I always relished the challenge."

The Konstantinov who patrolled the blue line for Detroit was a contradiction in terms. On the ice he was unyielding, a man who asked no quarter and gave none. Away from the rink he was as warm and as friendly as a man could be.

"Vladdie liked everybody," Detroit senior vice president Jimmy Devellano said. "And he had time for everyone."

"Great guy. Big heart. Easygoing," Fetisov said of Konstantinov.

As they defended their Stanley Cup title in 1997–98, the Wings maintained Konstantinov's locker in their dressing room as a symbol and tribute to their fallen teammate.

"I think the memory kind of helped us to be a more united team, to play our best hockey," Detroit center Igor Larionov remembered. "We thought about how tough those guys are and how tough we have to be."

The locker included a Curious George doll in a Red Wings sweater. That was Konstantinov's nickname because, just like the cartoon monkey, he was always sticking his nose in where it didn't belong. A pet rock left-winger Slava Kozlov received in the mail during the 1997 playoffs, inscribed with the word *Believe*, rested on the shelf.

"I was in the same car," Fetisov said. "Just inches away from the same fate.

"Sometimes, I'd look at Vladdie's locker and I'd want to cry. But you couldn't cry. You had to stand up and play your best again and again—like Vladimir did."

The players also wore their hearts on their sleeves. A patch with both men's initials and the word *believe*, in English and Russian, adorned each Detroit sweater.

The Red Wings believed. They hoped. And years later, they've never forgotten the man known as "the Vladinator."

"How could you ever forget a guy like Vladdie?" asked former Wings goalie Chris Osgood.

17 Detroit Traded Away Its First True Superstar Forward

When the Detroit Cougars debuted as an NHL franchise in 1926–27, they thought they had their version of Steve Yzerman.

He was Frank Fredrickson, then 31, an Olympic gold medalist, a Stanley Cup winner, and a two-time Pacific Coast Hockey Association scoring champion when he signed with the Cougars.

In 1920 Frederickson served as captain and scored 12 goals in three games to lead Canada to the hockey gold medal at the Olympic Games in Antwerp, Belgium. Three years later, Fredrickson netted 39 goals and registered 16 assists for 55 points in 30 games to run away with the 1922–23 PCL scoring title.

Montreal Canadiens center Howie Morenz was the NHL superstar of that era, and there were people who believed Fredrickson was in Morenz's class as an offensive catalyst.

"[Morenz] is faster than Fredrickson," Detroit defenseman Harold "Slim" Halderson told the *Ottawa Journal*. "But I really do not think that he has the finish that Frank possesses."

Fredrickson and Halderson had played together for Team Canada at the Olympics and for Victoria when the team defeated Morenz's Canadiens for the 1925 Stanley Cup championship.

Fredrickson was a very complex man whose enjoyment of hockey may have been secondary to his love of music. If being an accomplished violinist paid more, it's possible that Fredrickson might not have played pro hockey. His wife, Bea, was a concert pianist.

When Fredrickson returned from the Olympics, Victoria Aristocrats owner Lester Patrick wanted to sign him. But Fredrickson rejected his offer to accept a violinist job with a five-piece orchestra at the Fort Garry Hotel in Winnipeg.

Undaunted, Patrick traveled to Winnipeg to listen to Fredrickson play. Between sets, Patrick and Fredrickson negotiated a deal that paid Fredrickson much more than Patrick originally offered.

Fredrickson received $2,500 for 22 games, making him the highest-paid player in the Pacific Coast Hockey Association. Fredrickson proved he deserved that deal, scoring 20 goals in his first 21 games in the league.

"For natural talent and all-around skills, I can compare him only to Fred ["Cyclone"] Taylor and Mickey MacKay," Patrick said.

Taylor said Fredrickson was "as fine a player I've ever seen," adding, "He is fast, shifty and smart and has a wonderfully quick shot."

In those days, Fredrickson was probably considered a high-maintenance player because he had a variety of interests and concerns. His background was also quite unique. His family was from Iceland, and he didn't even speak English until he was five.

When World War I broke out, Fredrickson enlisted in the military and was assigned to the Royal Flying Corps in 1916. He trained as a pilot in Egypt and then received orders to be a flight instructor and test pilot in Scotland.

En route to Britain, his troop ship, *Leasowe Castle*, was torpedoed and sunk by Germans 104 miles off the coast of Alexandra; 94 soldiers were killed in the sinking. Fredrickson was sitting in a raft, clutching his violin, when he was rescued by a Japanese destroyer.

After the war, Fredrickson went to Iceland, where he became the country's second pilot. He helped develop the country's airfields and also helped the fishing industry develop techniques for spotting schools of fish from the air.

While playing in Victoria, he announced he was retiring to open a music store in 1923. He did have the shop for a year, although he kept playing hockey.

Fredrickson also had the gift of gab, so much so that Patrick used to place a 30-minute time limit on his trips to Patrick's office.

When the PCHA player contracts were sold to the NHL after the league folded in 1926, no one was surprised that Fredrickson ended up with the most complicated negotiations.

The Cougars believed they would receive Fredrickson, but he didn't initially sign with them. The Boston Bruins cut a deal with Patrick for Fredrickson's services, but Fredrickson didn't go there either. The Bruins threatened to have him banned for the rest of his career.

"So I signed with Detroit and got $6,000, which was a lot of money," Frederickson told famed hockey writer Stan Fischler in 1970.

That made him the NHL's highest-paid player. But his joy over the new deal was short-lived. "When I got off the train from the West and picked up a paper in Detroit, I saw a lead story entitled, 'Fredrickson Gets $10,000,'" Fredrickson told Fischler. "Can you imagine how my teammates must have felt? They were getting only $2,000 and $2,500. But that newspaper story was the same old bunk. They always have to add a little."

Fredrickson told Fischler there was immediate "dissension" on the Cougars upon his arrival. The players, bitter over Fredrickson's large contract, would not pass him the puck. That led to Fredrickson starting very slowly, by his standards. He only had four goals and six assists for 10 points in his first 16 games.

Unable to get players on the same page, the Cougars decided trading Fredrickson was their best option. They moved him to Boston in a deal for another premium player, Duke Keats.

Fredrickson was his usual self in Boston, registering 14 goals and 21 points in his final 28 games. When he played his first game against Detroit, he scored both goals in a 2–0 Boston win. He finished fourth in the scoring race and helped Boston reach the Stanley Cup Finals, where they lost to the Ottawa Senators.

As might have been expected, Fredrickson didn't last long in Boston. Bruins GM Art Ross, still miffed that Fredrickson wouldn't sign with him before the season, banned him from playing the violin on team train trips.

In 1928 Ross then traded Fredrickson to the Pittsburgh Pirates, who were the NHL's worst team. Fredrickson blew out his knee in Pittsburgh and retired in 1931 after a brief comeback attempt with Detroit.

Fredrickson ended up coaching at Princeton in 1939 where he befriended a mathematics and physics professor who lived next door. As it turned out, the man also loved to play the violin. The hockey coach and the professor played duets for anyone who cared to listen. The neighbor was Albert Einstein.

Fredrickson might have been the NHL's most interesting man of that era.

18 Buy an Octopus from Superior Fish and Make It Fly

You may not remember who the No. 6 defenseman was on the Detroit Red Wings' 1997 Stanley Cup team.

But you know who Al Sobotka is. He's the barehanded octopus twirler, a key figure in all four of the Red Wings' Stanley Cup championships of the past 17 years.

How many photographs have you seen of Zamboni driver and arena manager Sobotka picking an octopus off the ice and spinning it overhead to the delight of a packed house at Joe Louis Arena?

Octopus tossing is as much of a Red Wings' tradition as the Captain, Bloody Wednesday, the Joe, the Grind Line, Scotty, Shanny, Ozzie, Jimmy D, and radio personality Art Regner screaming "Go, Wings!"

The octopus tradition started during the 1952 playoffs when brothers Pete and Jerry Cusimano, working at the family fish store in Detroit's Eastern Market, came up with the idea of throwing an octopus on the ice as a lucky charm for the Red Wings in the midst of their playoff march.

Their logic was that an octopus had eight tentacles and the Red Wings needed eight wins to earn the Stanley Cup. It made perfect sense to the Cusimano boys. They boiled the octopus before the first game in Detroit, figuring it made it easier to throw. They even strategized on the proper form for cephalopod hurling.

"If you try to throw it like a baseball, you'll throw your arm out," Pete Cusimano told the *Washington Post* in a 1997 interview. "I would fling it sidearm like a hand grenade. One time I missed and knocked a man's hat off. When he spotted what hit him, he left and never came back to his seat. They don't smell too pretty, either."

According to the *Post* story, when the Cusimano boys tossed that first octopus, the Olympia public-address announcer said, "Octopi shall not occupy the ice. Please refrain from throwing same."

The *Washington Post* said a referee picked up the octopus, not having any idea why it had been tossed.

However, Detroit Red Wings Hall of Fame defenseman Marcel Pronovost said the referee didn't want anything to do with the dead creature. It was Pronovost who made it go away.

"I scooped it up and skated over to the penalty box with it, but nobody there wanted to touch it, either," Pronovost said in his book *A Life in Hockey*. "I didn't think about it. I just picked it up. Oh yeah, you better believe I wondered why they were throwing the octopus on the ice."

The important aspect of the story is that the Red Wings went on to sweep the Toronto Maple Leafs and Montreal Canadiens in one of the most dominant postseason performances in NHL history. A tradition was born.

During the back-to-back Detroit Stanley Cup championships in 1954 and 1955, team member Bill Dineen said, "There were a lot of the octopuses flying."

Although there is no official octopus record book, it is known that 54 octopuses hit the ice during a game at Joe Louis Arena during the 1995 Stanley Cup Finals.

On the Red Wings' website is a story of Bob Dubisky and Larry Shotwell, coworkers at a meat and seafood retail company near Detroit, tossing a 38-pound octopus onto the ice during the

National Anthem prior to Game 1 of the Western Conference Finals. The following year Dubinsky and Shotwell upped the ante with a 50-pounder in the Western Conference Finals. The record octopus was proudly displayed on the hood of Sobotka's Zamboni between periods.

Superior Fish Company in Royal Oak keeps a supply of octopus ready in the spring to accommodate the octopus-tossing desires of devoted fans. It seems like the store has become part of the octopus tradition. On its website, Superior Fish offers Octoquette's rules for playoff octopus tossing.

Two of the main rules are that tosses should be made only after a Red Wings goal, and the toss should be made in a direction away from players.

Superior Fish Company employees will tell you what size octopus you should buy based on how far you are away from the rink. We are not making this up.

Octopus tossing is an expensive hobby. The cost of an octopus is four dollars per pound. Newspaper accounts from the 1990s said Superior would sell $1,000 worth of octopus on some game days.

There can be collateral damage when an octopus is thrown. Red Wings fan Nate Brown recalled sitting in the sixth row in Game 5 of the Western Conference Finals when a big one hit the ice.

"Right before the final line of the anthem, a guy dashed down the steps and hurled a 20-pounder on the ice," Brown recalled. "The thud of it hitting the ice and the roar of the crowd was unbelievable."

Brown high-fived the octopus thrower and then immediately realized his mistake.

"The smell was indescribable," Brown said. "Think rotten eggs and a baby's full diaper."

Brown caught a puck in the stands later in the game and attributed it to the slime on his hands. "The puck was like glued to my hand," Brown said.

The next day, Brown and his brother attended a wake and could not shake hands with anyone because of the stench. "My mother and grandmother swear by Lava soap, and not even that could get the smell out," Brown said.

Although the tradition is fully entrenched in Detroit, it surprises opposing players now and then.

In 1994 then–San Jose Sharks goalie Arturs Irbe was stunned to see 12 octopi going splat in front his net.

"I am not laughing, but thinking that this felt like a joke," he said. "These people, they are throwing seafood on the ice."

When the Cusimano brothers' eight tentacles for eight wins story was told to Irbe, he said, "Then, should they not throw two of them…since it now takes 16 wins?"

During the 1995 Stanley Cup Finals, New Jersey Devils defenseman Ken Daneyko had a stake in a restaurant, and that colored his thoughts about the octopus' garden that landed on the ice every game.

"I was thinking about scooping a couple of them up and taking them home," Daneyko said. "Do you know what I pay for calamari by the pound?"

During the same Stanley Cup Finals, then–Devils forward Claude Lemieux said, "The octopus, they're really smelly and slimy…they're disgusting."

That was okay, because Detroit fans thought Lemieux was disgusting after he hurt Kris Draper the following season.

The octopus tradition remains strong. But the volume of octopuses has been reduced in recent years, especially since the league office issued an edict against Sobotka swinging the octopus overhead.

In 2008 the NHL threatened to fine the Red Wings $10,000 if Sobotka twirled the octopus overhead while on the playing surface.

"Our main concern—and I don't know what you call the stuff that flies off the octopus when you swing it, so I'm going to call it gunk—is the condition of the ice when this gunk is spread in different places," said NHL commissioner Gary Bettman. "We don't want some of that gunk getting on the ice and one of our players blowing out a knee when he hits it."

To get around this edict, what Sobotka did was remove the octopus, transport it one foot off the ice, and then twirl it from the Zamboni entrance. Most fans could still see it. The octopus tradition remains strong. The first one will hit the ice as soon as anthem singer Karen Newman is near the end of her performance.

Sobotka is still a key figure, maybe more memorable in your mind than Aaron Ward, who was the team's No. 6 defenseman in the 1997 playoffs.

19 Yzerman Was the Greatest Captain in NHL History

When Detroit Red Wings captain Steve Yzerman was essentially playing on one leg in the 2002 NHL Playoffs, his concerned teammates often had conversations with him about his health.

"How are you doing?" someone would ask.

"I'm fine," Yzerman would answer.

To Yzerman, that was a full medical report. Everyone knew his knee was a mess, but no one knew how bad the situation was until it was announced that Yzerman would undergo an osteotomy, a surgical procedure where a bone is cut to realign the knee. A shim is placed underneath the knee to remove pressure on the hinge. When Yzerman had the surgery, one medical expert pointed out that the procedure is done primarily to allow senior citizens the mobility to go to the bathroom in the middle of the night. It wasn't usually done on world-class athletes.

When Steve Yzerman spoke, the team listened. His ability to gut it out in the face of injury, find success on the ice, and inspire his teammates with his level head and calm demeanor made him the ideal captain.

The truth that Yzerman was playing on a knee that far gone would appear to be irrefutable evidence that his willingness to make sacrifices in the name of competing and leading his team are second to none.

It doesn't take a trained litigator to make a case that Yzerman is the greatest captain in NHL history. Some argue that Mark Messier or Bobby Clarke were the best. Clarke is synonymous with the Philadelphia Flyers' success in the 1970s. He was a warrior, known for his ability to inspire his teammates. Messier was a ruthless captain, known for doing whatever it took to ensure his team had the best chance of winning the Stanley Cup. Edmonton Oilers fans will never forget how he single-handedly won a game in Chicago Stadium that turned out to be the turning point of the Oilers' 1990 Stanley Cup run. New York Rangers fans won't forget his guarantee of a victory against the New Jersey Devils in the 1994 postseason.

But Yzerman matched their inspirational value and surpassed those two great players in longevity at his post. Yzerman wore the *C* in Detroit for 1,303 games over 20 seasons. He was 21 when coach Jacques Demers gave him the job.

"I never hesitated on that decision," Demers said. "I knew from day one that Yzerman would be my captain…he carried that team by himself for years. All he needed was to be surrounded by good players."

Demers said Mike Ilitch and general manager Jim Devellano both supported his decision, even though Yzerman was young.

"Healthy, injured, or sick, Steve competed hard every night," Demers said. "He was very consistent in his desire to win."

Fans saw that demonstrated more and more as Yzerman grew older and injuries mounted.

General manager Ken Holland said he never saw anyone play in more pain than Yzerman when he led Detroit to their third Stanley Cup in 2002. "He got shot up before every game," Holland said. "He could hardly walk. He had a knee that was bone on bone. He was in such incredible pain."

Yzerman couldn't practice. He just played games. "If you watch clips of the 2002 playoffs, Steve would fall down, and he would have to use one knee and his stick to pop himself back up," Draper said.

In that Stanley Cup run, the Red Wings' third under Yzerman's command, they lost the first two games of the playoffs against the Vancouver Canucks at home.

"Before Game 3, Yzerman addressed the team," former Red Wings player Darren McCarty remembered. "He didn't yell or anything. It was Stevie being Stevie. He said that we were better than the way we had been playing. He said we needed to relax and play the way we know how to play. He said we needed to take charge."

The Red Wings won four consecutive games and were off and running toward the 2002 Stanley Cup championship.

"I can only remember him making about three major captain's speeches," McCarty said. "So when he spoke, we listened. But we were inspired more by Steve's actions than his words."

Yzerman could win a big faceoff, block a shot, or make a major defensive play. By the end of Yzerman's career, he was such a warrior that it was almost forgotten that he started his career as one of the most dynamic offensive stars in league history.

In 1988–89, Yzerman scored 65 goals and added 90 assists for 155 points. Only Mario Lemieux was more dangerous on a breakaway than Yzerman in that period.

"The only problem Steve ever had in his career was that Lemieux and Wayne Gretzky were in the league at the same time he was," Demers said. "Otherwise, he would have been considered an even greater player."

McCarty recalled that doctors would carefully try to time the numbing of Yzerman's knee to give him the maximum amount of relief during the game. "But if the game went to overtime, the relief would wear off," McCarty recalled.

Anyone who watched Yzerman play in those moments would support the idea that he was the greatest captain in NHL history.

Nicklas Lidstrom, One-Team Player: The Last of His Kind?

When it comes to long-standing tradition in sports, no city has carried a torch for its stars more than Detroit.

When defenseman and team captain Nicklas Lidstrom took the ice for the Red Wings' 2011–12 season opener, he became the sixth Detroit athlete to have played at least 20 seasons in his chosen sport and spent them all in the Motor City.

"Sometimes I think about it, but having been with such a good organization for 20 years, and being part of a winning tradition here, you almost take it for granted," Lidstrom said at the time.

In fact, later that season, Lidstrom surpassed another legendary Red Wings captain, Alex Delvecchio (1,549) to establish a new NHL mark for games played by a one-team player. Lidstrom, who retired at the end of that season, finished with 1,564 games played in a Detroit uniform.

"It's something that I'm proud of, to be able to play at a high level for a long period of time and reach 1,500 games," Lidstrom said.

In essence, Lidstrom was simply carrying on a Detroit tradition.

Lidstrom is the sixth athlete to play 20 seasons all with a Detroit team. The Red Wings (Delvecchio 24, Steve Yzerman 22, Lidstrom 20) have produced half of this record tally, while the Detroit Tigers (Al Kaline 21, Alan Trammell 20) added two to this rare group. Detroit Lions kicker Jason Hanson (21) completes this unique sextet.

Beyond Detroit, Chicago has four 20-season men—Stan Mikita (22) of the Blackhawks, and Ted Lyons (21), Red Faber (20), and Luke Appling (20) of the White Sox. After Chicago, Montreal (Jean Beliveau 20 and Henri Richard 20, of the Canadiens) and

Players Who Played 1,000 Games in a Red Wings Uniform

Player	Seasons	Games Played
Gordie Howe	1946–71	1,687
Nicklas Lidstrom	1991–2012	1,564
Alex Delvecchio	1951–73	1,549
Steve Yzerman	1983–2006	1,514
Kris Draper	1993–2011	1,137
Tomas Holmstrom	1996–2012	1,026

Baltimore (Brooks Robinson 23 and Cal Ripken 21, of the Orioles) are the only other cities to sport more than one of these unique athletes.

Many prominent Detroit athletes of today and yesterday wonder whether, with salary caps and expansion, there will be another player like Lidstrom, able to stay in one home and play for two decades in the same city.

"I'm well aware that the new CBA is going to make it more difficult for older players to stay with their teams," Yzerman acknowledged.

Players from other sports also see the rarity of what Lidstrom was able to accomplish and are curious to see if there will be another who will follow along his unique and singular path.

"I think with the way all of the leagues have expanded, there's a lot less emphasis on tradition," Trammell said. "I had chances to leave for more money, but you get to a point in your career, when you've started a family and settled into an area, that you really don't want to move."

In today's games, not many players are afforded that option, and even fewer will be, as economics continues to play a greater role in the way teams operate.

"I think if you look at this area's sports teams, tradition has always been a big part of it," said Lomas Brown, who played his first 11 NFL seasons as a tackle with the Detroit Lions, then split his final seven seasons in the league between four different teams. "You look at guys like Kaline, Lou, and Tram with the Tigers and Steve Yzerman with the Wings. People see that loyalty to one team and identify with those players.

"If that goes away and athletes become sort of like traveling vagabonds, I don't think that can be a good situation for any sport."

A Red Wing from 1983 to 2006, Yzerman remains hopeful that one-team players aren't going to go the way of the maskless netminder. He said, "For whatever reason, it worked out for me, and I believe there's always going to be guys who stay with their teams forever.

"I kind of like the idea that Alex Delvecchio played his whole career in Detroit. I think there's still going to be those special guys. I look at Al Kaline. It's very interesting when you see him walk around a golf course. People really respect him and admire him, but they also leave him alone and let him be a Detroiter just like them."

Yzerman has an ally in this belief in Red Wings legend Gordie Howe, who played 25 of his 26 NHL seasons with Detroit.

"Don't say never," Howe said. "There's a lot of Stevie Yzermans and Nicklas Lidstroms that are not made yet. There's always going to be somebody new that comes along."

21 J.C. Tremblay Was Injured Over a Card Game Insult

On November 27, 1965, Gordie Howe skated into a Montreal Forum corner with Canadiens defenseman J.C. Tremblay. Only Gordie skated out.

"Tremblay dropped like a sack of potatoes," former Red Wings player Bill Gadsby remembered.

That was also the night Howe scored his 600th career NHL goal, and the great fans of Montreal stood and applauded Howe like he was one of their own.

Suddenly they were booing Howe like he was the son of Satan.

This was in an era when few games were televised, and Gadsby is convinced that officials never saw what happened.

"The referee probably just looked at Tremblay lying on the ice and knew Gord had done something," Gadsby said.

Howe received a five-minute major for intent to injure, even though no one seemed to know what he did or why he did it. Howe offered no explanation as he skated to the penalty box with Montreal fans spitting fire and rage over his actions.

Gadsby and Howe were best friends and roommates, and Gadsby was comfortable interrogating Howe during their post-game dinner. "What the hell did you do to Tremblay?" Gadsby said he asked Howe.

Howe shrugged and said he wasn't sure. "Maybe the thumb of my glove stuck him in the eye," Howe told Gadsby.

Gadsby accepted the explanation, knowing he had seen that happen a few times during his career.

The next morning, Gadsby went to breakfast with Howe and was startled by the headline in the Montreal newspaper. He recalled that he turned the newspaper around to allow Howe to see a headline that stated that Tremblay had suffered a broken jaw.

"Gordie, you must have some powerful thumb," Gadsby recalled saying to Howe.

The true story came out over time. Howe was merely settling a score, exacting revenge for a Tremblay misdeed that had not come on the ice.

Some time before, Howe's Red Wings were out of the play-offs and he was working as an analyst for the radio broadcast of a Chicago-Montreal playoff series. He was riding the train between cities and had paused in one of the cars to watch the Canadiens play bridge.

At one point, Howe had commented that Montreal player Dick Duff had made a nice play.

According to Howe, Tremblay turned to him and said, "What's a dummy like you know about bridge?"

That night at the Forum, Howe was simply clearing his ledger of a debt owed.

Howe always had his own sense of what was fair and just. If you left Howe alone, he left you alone. If you crossed him in any way, he didn't forget.

Blackhawks great Stan Mikita recalled that when he was a young player, he once got his stick up in Howe's face. Mikita's teammates started looking at him like he was a dead man walking.

"I said, 'What's that old man going to do?'" Mikita recalled saying.

When nothing happened during that game, Mikita said he told his teammates that they had overstated Howe's reputation. Howe did nothing in their next meeting, either.

In Detroit's third meeting that season, Mikita found that Howe's reputation for ruthlessness was not overstated. Howe cut Mikita and TKO'd him with an elbow. Mikita said he never saw Howe coming.

Mikita said when he asked Howe if they were even, Howe said he hadn't decided. A few games later, Howe told Mikita that they were even but said if Mikita ever gave him a cheap shot again, he would "end his career."

Mikita said he never again gave Howe a cheap shot.

"People feared Gordie," former St. Louis player Bob Plager said in the book *Crunch*.

Plager recalled that Tim Ecclestone was playing his first NHL game for the St. Louis Blues and Howe elbowed him three times.

"Welcome to the NHL, kid," Plager said. "He tested every rookie. He straightened them out and got plenty of room."

In a 1968 *Sports Illustrated* article, Detroit defenseman Kent Douglas said the only hope of stopping Howe was to "crowd him," getting in his way before he could get up to speed.

"But nobody wants to crowd Gordie," Douglas said. "Nobody wants to get near him." Everyone worried about what he might do to them.

"My first game in the NHL was against the Red Wings," Oakland Seals player Bryan Watson told *Sports Illustrated*. "I was with the Canadiens then, and they threw me out to kill a penalty. I went into the corner with Howe, knocked him down from behind, and skated away with the puck. I hadn't gone very far before I heard heavy strides coming up behind me, and then I felt a stick slipping under my arm. Then there's the blade—not an inch from my nose. It's Howe, and he says, 'Check out, junior.' I got so scared I fell down."

22 Marcel Dionne Exodus Had Catastrophic Consequences

After the Detroit Red Wings franchise crumbled around owner Bruce Norris in the 1970s, it was not difficult to determine the epicenter of the team's collapse.

"The biggest mistake the Red Wings made in the 1970s was letting Marcel Dionne go," said former Detroit goalie Jim Rutherford, who was Dionne's teammate.

At the time of Dionne's departure in 1975, he was portrayed by the Red Wings as a selfish, disloyal young superstar who walked out on his team. However, an analysis of the facts today would undoubtedly conclude that the Red Wings failed to recognize that Dionne was simply using the leverage he had to gain the contract he believed he deserved.

Jim "Catfish" Hunter had become baseball's first official free agent nine months before, and the New York Yankees had made him the sport's highest-paid player. It was clear free agency was going to change Major League Baseball. The Red Wings should have foreseen that changes would also be coming to the NHL marketplace.

"It was an era when players were just starting to stand up for themselves," Dionne said. "I was one of the early ones to do that. It was all about the management."

Former Red Wings great Mickey Redmond recalled that Dionne asked him for advice, and he recommended that Dionne take the Kings' offer because it was too good to pass up.

"He was a good friend, a great teammate, and a heck of a hockey player," Redmond said. "But it was the best thing for him, as it turned out, and it might have changed the industry."

Dionne was merely ahead of his time when he decided to listen to offers after his Detroit contract expired.

"To allow a franchise player like Marcel Dionne to get into a contract dispute and leave the team for the Los Angeles Kings is almost unforgiveable," Rutherford said.

Dionne had scored 366 points in his first four seasons, and no NHL player had ever had such a productive start. Playing for the struggling Red Wings in 1974–75, Dionne had scored 47 goals and added 74 assists for 121 points. He was involved in 46.7 percent of the team's goals. This was not a Red Wings team deep in talent.

"You paid to see Dionne," Rutherford said. "He was so highly skilled that he brought people out of their seats."

More important, Dionne put fans into the seats, a fact that the Red Wings didn't seem to respect.

In 1974–75, Dionne set an NHL record of 10 short-handed goals.

"I believe when he set the record we were playing two men short," Rutherford said. "He even said to someone on the bench, 'I want to get out there and kill this penalty and get the next goal.' When he put his mind to something, he was a phenomenal player."

It was the rebellious 1970s, and Dionne was unhappy that the team wasn't successful and that team management always seemed disorganized. Dionne played for three different coaches in four seasons.

The Red Wings named Dionne captain and gave him Sid Abel's No. 12, with the hope that would inspire him to stay. However, they never convinced him to sign for what they were offering. Teammates believed Dionne would have stayed if they had given him a record-setting deal and made an effort to strengthen the team.

Dionne was represented by agent Alan Eagleson. When he opened up the bidding process to NHL teams, the Buffalo Sabres, Toronto Maple Leafs, Kings, and St. Louis Blues were all interested. As bidding escalated, it came down to the Kings competing against the Maple Leafs. The Leafs offered a five-year deal worth $1.25 million and the Kings offered $1.5 million.

In those days, the league rules still dictated that a team signing another team's free agent had to provide compensation. The Kings offered winger Dan Maloney and defenseman Terry Harper, but the Red Wings preferred what the Maple Leafs could give them. The problem for Dionne was that the Maple Leafs wouldn't match the Kings' offer.

Again, Dionne knew he had leverage. Eagleson notified the Red Wings that they should accept the Kings' offer or Dionne was going to sign with the Edmonton Oilers of the World Hockey Association. If that happened, the Red Wings would receive no compensation.

The Red Wings had no choice except to take the Kings' offer. They couldn't let Dionne go to a rival league.

Maloney and Harper were solid players, but they were not superstars. The situation was a disaster for the Red Wings. They missed the playoffs seven of the next eight seasons.

"The team lost their building block, and they probably didn't recover until they drafted Steve Yzerman," Rutherford said.

Dionne always had regrets about the way the situation unfolded. "My biggest disappointment is that my career with the Red Wings didn't work out," he said. "My decision to leave was strictly business, but in retrospect, I'm convinced that I should have remained in Detroit and finished my career there."

Why Seven Is Greater Than 23

While there were some tense moments, for the second season in a row the Red Wings rallied to qualify for a spot in the 2013–14 Stanley Cup playoffs, the 23rd season in a row that Detroit had been a playoff participant.

That's the longest active streak in major professional sports, and it brought about a debate over its significance within the walls of the Wings' dressing room.

"It's huge," Detroit center Pavel Datsyuk said. "Nobody wanted to break it, 23 straight."

A run that started in 1990–91 and has seen the Wings win four Stanley Cups and skate in six Cup Finals series over its span has set a standard for future Detroit players to aspire to.

"The streak means a lot to all of us," Detroit goalie Jimmy Howard said. "It just says how high the bar was set before us. It's good for us to have high expectations and lofty goals."

Detroit general manager Ken Holland views the streak as a testament to the solid structure within the team's organization.

"We've been in the playoffs 23 consecutive years," Holland said. "Prior to [2011–12] we had 100 points 12 years in a row. We're one of two teams to qualify for the playoffs every year in the [NHL] salary-cap world [which began in 2005–06]. You've got to believe in your philosophy."

Still, as impressive as the run continues to be, not every Detroit player is awestruck.

"I don't think we care that much about the streak," Detroit captain Henrik Zetterberg claimed. "We want to play in the postseason. It doesn't matter if we had been there 22 times or 21 times or three times in a row, we want to play playoff hockey."

Zetterberg may have a point. After all, as impressive a number as 23 might be, it's still far from the NHL standard of excellence when it comes to continued presence in the tournament for Lord Stanley's mug.

That honor belongs to the Boston Bruins, who made a league-record 29 straight playoff appearances from 1968 to 1996. The Chicago Blackhawks appeared in 28 straight playoffs from 1970 to 1997, and the St. Louis Blues recorded 25 consecutive playoff performances between 1980 and 2004. The Montreal Canadiens were in the playoffs 24 years in succession from 1971 to 1994.

That puts the Wings fifth overall on the all-time list, well up the track. However, there's another streak in Detroit's possession that is truly a benchmark—not only in hockey, but in all of sports.

From 1948–49 through 1954–55, the Wings finished first overall in the NHL every season, seven in a row. By comparison, Detroit has posted six first-overall finishes during their 23-year run of playoff success.

"To win seven league championships in a row, nobody's ever going to defeat that record in hockey," former Detroit captain Ted

Lindsay said. "Nobody will ever win it seven years in a row. Not with 30 teams."

Like the current playoff mark, Detroit's seventh straight first-place finish almost came to an unceremonious end. Trailing Montreal by six points in early March 1955, the Wings ran the table, winning their last nine games and sweeping a season-ending home-and-home series with the Habs to finish atop the standings by two points.

"We had the [Richard] riot in Montreal [when Detroit beat Montreal by forfeit after Canadiens fans rioted to protest the suspension of Montreal star Maurice Richard], and then we had to play the last game against them in our rink, and we couldn't lose," Detroit defenseman Red Kelly remembered. "We had to win both games, and we did."

It wasn't merely the NHL mark that the Wings were pursuing. "The [New York] Yankees had won [a North American sports record] six [regular-season titles], and we knew that," Kelly said. "We were trying to win that seventh one."

They did what no other team did before or since, and that's why, while it might be new math, in this case, seven is a greater number than 23.

24 Chelios Is the Greatest American-Born Player

Trying to decide the best of anything is like trying to solve an equation with no right answer.

Is Meryl Streep a better actress than Bette Davis was? Were the Beatles a better stage band than the Rolling Stones or U2? Was Abraham Lincoln a better president than George Washington?

Answers always come down to personal preference. That being said, it's not difficult to make a case for the idea that former Red Wings defenseman Chris Chelios is the greatest American player of all time.

"It's either Chelios or Mike Modano," said Jeremy Roenick, another great American player.

You certainly have to throw defenseman Brian Leetch, Michigan native center Pat LaFontaine, and goalkeeper Frank Brimsek into the conversation.

But the argument for Chelios being the top American-born player comes down to the reality that Chelios could do more for a team than any of the other players. If you were starting a team from scratch and had your choice of any of these players in their prime, wouldn't you want the player who had more layers to his game?

Modano, LaFontaine, and Leetch were all dynamic offensive players, but none had the leadership presence or warrior-like attitude that Chelios possessed. Think of Mel Gibson in *Braveheart*, and you have the proper image of how Chelios played hockey.

Chelios was usually the best-conditioned athlete on his team, a player capable of playing more than half of the game. He was usually the most ruthless player on the ice, and he was the ultimate team player. All he cared about was winning, and on top of everything else, he was a relentless one-on-one defensive player and a highly skilled offensive catalyst. This is a player who once scored 20 goals as a defenseman. He was a three-time Norris Trophy winner.

During his career, Chelios owned a plus-minus of plus-350. This is someone who could run a team's power play and be almost as important to the team's goals-against total as the goaltender.

The final point in favor of Chelios is that he was a born leader. Doug Weight used to joke that when Chelios was born, he came out of the womb with sergeant stripes on his little arm.

For years, Chelios was called "the Godfather" of American hockey, and it was an apt nickname.

In the 1990s the NHL was rich with top American players, and Chelios was the clear leader of that group. Even superstars such as Modano, Roenick, and Keith Tkachuk looked up to Chelios. He was the superglue that held the team together. He helped USA win the 1996 World Cup and he was captain of the 2002 Olympic silver medal team.

Chelios was known for taking care of his teammates, whether they were veterans or rookies. If you needed something, Chelios knew where to find it. If you had a problem, Chelios was the fixer.

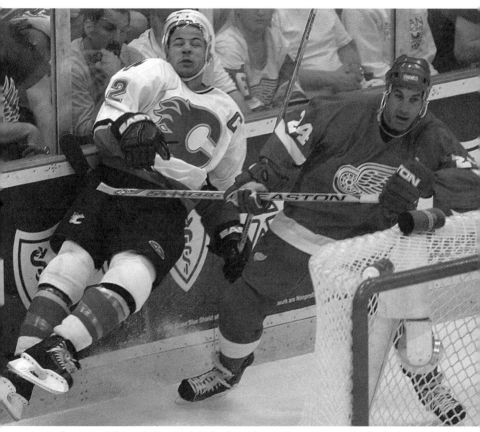

Defenseman Chris Chelios (right) checks Calgary Flame Jarome Iginla during the second period of an NHL Western Conference quarterfinal playoff game in Detroit on April 21, 2007. Many people associate Chelios with the Blackhawks and forget he played just as long for the Red Wings as he did for the Hawks.

He also protected his teammates on the ice. He once totaled 282 penalty minutes in a single season, and he was good for 125 to 200 minutes per season throughout the 1980s and 1990s.

If you wronged Chelios or one of his teammates, you had to pay a price. "You'd end up chewing on Cheli's stick," Roenick said.

No one enjoyed playing against him. "He was nasty," said Dallas Stars general manager Jim Nill, who played against Chelios. "He stood up to everyone and backed down from no one."

His durability was legendary. He was 48 when he played his last NHL game. He finished his career with an American record of 1,651 NHL regular-season games played, plus another 266 playoff games. He only missed the playoffs once in an NHL career that lasted from 1984 to 2010. That's unquestionably not a coincidence.

It was like Chelios discovered the fountain of youth during his playing days. What really happened was Chelios simply worked harder than everyone else.

The Chelios training ritual included riding a stationary bicycle for 45 minutes in a sauna. He called it an "aerobic wash."

"That's just crazy," said Red Wings forward Dan Cleary. "I tried it, and it just burned my nostrils."

Red Wings Scoring Leaders by Country of Birth

Country	Player	G	A	P
Canada	Gordie Howe	786	1,023	1,809
USA	Reed Larson	188	382	570
Sweden	Nicklas Lidstrom	264	878	1,142
Russia	Sergei Fedorov	400	554	954
Finland	Valtteri Filppula	100	151	251
Czech Republic	Vaclav Nedomansky	108	139	247
Germany	Willie Huber	68	140	208
Yugoslavia	Ivan Boldirev	67	95	162
Northern Ireland	Jim McFadden	64	78	142
Scotland	Adam Brown	58	43	101

*Minimum 100 points scored

To train for an NHL season, Chelios would work out with a kayak and a mountain bike in California. He essentially played his entire career at just less than 190 pounds, although he did experiment briefly at playing 15 pounds heavier. He didn't like how he felt and immediately lost the weight. Now in his fifties, Chelios looks like he could still play. He works out religiously.

Nill credits Chelios' work ethic for his longevity and recalled when the defenseman suffered a significant knee injury several years ago that could have signaled the beginning of the end. It wasn't even close to the end.

"The team was on the road, and the arena was dark," Nill said. "I came in and heard something, and it was Chelios skating down the ice. It wasn't long after his surgery. He wasn't allowed to turn, so he'd lift himself on the boards to turn around. He was by himself. No one was there to see it."

Chelios has always had an intangible quality to him that is hard to describe. When the late Herb Brooks was named coach of the 2002 Olympic team, he wondered whether it might be time to move beyond the Chelios era.

He decided to sit down with Chelios before he made any final decision about whether he should be on the roster. He said later when he was done talking to Chelios, he knew he had to be his captain. He said having Chelios as a captain was like having another assistant coach.

Now retired, some people see Chelios more as a Chicago Blackhawk than a Red Wing; he actually played as many seasons in Detroit as he did in Chicago.

The Red Wings have every right to claim that they were the team that had the greatest American-born player in NHL history.

25 The Truth About McCarty's Fight with Lemieux

Kris Draper never asked Darren McCarty to take care of Colorado Avalanche villain Claude Lemieux. In fact, Draper and McCarty never had a true conversation about McCarty's intentions.

McCarty said he only brought up the idea of revenge one time, and that was when he drove Draper home from the hospital after Draper had his jaw wired shut to repair damage suffered at the hands of Lemieux.

"I just said I would take care of it," McCarty recalled.

McCarty said the wired-up Draper didn't say anything, mostly because his ability to communicate was limited to unintelligible mumbles.

Based on McCarty's book, *My Last Fight*, here are facts about McCarty's night of revenge against Lemieux on March 26, 1997, that you may have forgotten or never knew:

1. It didn't have to be that night. McCarty had made up his mind that he didn't want to do anything that would hurt his team just to settle a grudge. Detroit defenseman Aaron Ward rode to the game with Draper and McCarty that night, and he said there was no mention of Lemieux. "Brendan Shanahan had taught me that being a good teammate meant knowing the right time to settle a score," McCarty said.

2. Colorado's Peter Forsberg started it. "If Lemieux wants to be angry at anyone for what happened, he should be mad at Forsberg because it might not have started had he not decided to tangle with Igor Larionov," McCarty said. "As soon as that skirmish broke out, I was looking for Lemieux."

3. In the famous photograph of McCarty and Lemieux, McCarty's fist shows a major stress indentation line. He has never been able to clench his fist with enough force to reproduce that indentation.

4. Lemieux did see McCarty coming. "I can tell you I looked at him directly in the eyes before I hit him," McCarty said.

5. Lemieux has told McCarty that McCarty's first punch that night was the hardest he has ever been hit.

6. McCarty said he brought more anger and fury to that fight than any fight he ever had. McCarty boasted more than 200 fights in his professional hockey career. "I've never wanted to hurt anyone as much as I wanted to hurt Lemieux," McCarty said.

7. McCarty only received a double minor for that attack on Lemieux. "It really wasn't a fight in the truest sense of the word," McCarty said. "Lemieux didn't deserve a penalty, because he didn't fight back."

8. Lemieux and McCarty never talked about the incident together until they appeared on TSN's *Off the Record* with host Michael Landsberg in 2010. Lemieux was complimentary of McCarty's role on the Red Wings. When Landsberg asked McCarty whether he would want Lemieux as a teammate, he said no.

9. In 2011 Lemieux and McCarty were offered $10,000 each to sign autographs together at a Michigan trading card show. They agreed. They were supposed to sign from 2:00 PM until 4:00 PM, but both stayed until 8:00 PM to accommodate the large, overflowing crowd. Lemieux gave his entire fee to charity. As he walked into the building, McCarty said some fans urged him to pound Lemieux again. "I didn't like the on-ice Lemieux, but I did like the off-ice Lemieux," McCarty said.

10. At least once per year, McCarty takes out the video of the Bloody Wednesday game and watches. He thinks sometimes fans forget that he scored 39 seconds into overtime to give Detroit a 6–5 victory in that game.

26 Detroit's First Goal Was Scored by the Human Hockey Stick

Firsts were all the rage for Hal "Slim" Halderson.

He scored his first goal in his first game as a pro with the Victoria Aristocrats of the Pacific Coast Hockey Association, and it proved to be the game-winner in a 4–1 verdict over the Seattle Metropolitans, as well as being a trendsetter.

Actually, the trend was set a couple of years earlier. Hockey was first included in the Olympics as part of the 1920 Games in Antwerp, Belgium, and the Allan Cup–champion Winnipeg Falcons were chosen to represent Canada.

In Canada's opening game against Czechoslovakia, a 15–0 victory, it was Halderson who opened the scoring, becoming the first Canadian ever to score in Olympic competition. After watching Canada and seeing how hard Halderson could shoot the puck, Swedish goaltender Seth Howander sought out extra padding to fortify his protective gear prior to their match with the Canadians.

Canada swept to the gold medal, going 3–0 and outscoring the opposition 29–1. Halderson's 9–2–11 numbers were good for second in team scoring.

That résumé of success helped him earn a pro deal with Victoria in 1921, and in 1925 he was part of that club's Stanley Cup championship, the last one earned by a team from outside the NHL.

The Victoria club had by then changed its name to the Cougars, and in 1925 underwent another change when the franchise was sold to the new owners of Detroit's NHL franchise for the sum of $100,000.

When Halderson first came to the West Coast as a 22-year-old, he stood 6'3" and weighed 165 pounds. Though he'd bulked up to 190 pounds by 1923, his unique stature earned him several

Famous First Goals in Detroit History

First Goal in Franchise History:
Harold "Slim" Halderson, November 20, 1926, Detroit Cougars 1 at Pittsburgh Pirates 4

First Game-Winning Goal:
Frank Fredrickson, November 24, 1926, Detroit Cougars 1 at Chicago Blackhawks 0

First Goal at Border Cities Arena:
Clem Loughlin, November 27, 1926, New York Americans 2 at Detroit Cougars 4

First Goal at Olympia Stadium:
Johnny Sheppard, November 22, 1927, Ottawa Senators 2 at Detroit Cougars 1

First Playoff Goal:
George Hay, March 19, 1929, Toronto Maple Leafs 3 at Detroit Cougars 1

First Goal as Detroit Falcons:
Ebbie Goodfellow, November 13, 1930, New York Rangers 0 at Detroit Falcons 1

First Goal as Detroit Red Wings:
Frank Carson, November 10, 1932, Chicago Black Hawks 1 at Detroit Red Wings 3

First Goal at Joe Louis Arena:
Dennis Sobchuk, December 27, 1979, St. Louis Blues 3 at Detroit Red Wings 2

nicknames, ranging from "Slim," as he was most commonly known, to "String Bean," "the Big Fellow," "the Elongated One," and perhaps the best of them all, "the Human Hockey Stick."

Halderson was the Zdeno Chara of his era—often accused of illegal hits due to his size and his long stick. Halderson was reported to be a wizard with the puck and a brilliant combination player, a stellar defenseman, shrewd and competent and equipped with great hockey sense. A clever all-around player with exceptional stick-handling skills, he was a very good playmaker. Halderson was deceptively fast, and many were fooled by his size. His loose-limbed skating style looked awkward, but he gained speed in a few strides and was difficult to stop.

Prior to coming to Detroit, beyond his Allan and Stanley Cup titles and Olympic gold medal, Halderson was also a Stanley Cup finalist in 1926 and a PCHA All-Star selection in 1921–22 and 1922–23.

Arriving in Detroit, Halderson continued his impressive run of firsts. He played for the Cougars in the first game in franchise history, a 2–0 loss to the Boston Bruins on November 18, 1926, and two nights later, at Pittsburgh's Duquesne Gardens, netted the first goal in franchise history as Detroit lost 4–1 to the Pittsburgh Pirates.

Things weren't going well for the Cougars, and on January 7, 1927, looking to beef up their attack, the club sent Halderson to the Toronto St. Patricks for winger Pete Bellefeuille. The St. Pats were in desperate need of defensive help after Bert Corbeau was injured, leaving only Bill Brydge and Bert McCaffrey to patrol the blue line.

Halderson was sent to the minor leagues the following season but enjoyed a long playing career in both the Can-Am League and American Hockey Association before retiring in 1937. He was a three-time AHA All-Star choice, in 1929–30, 1935–36, and 1936–37. In 1932 Halderson was named to an All-Star Canadian Olympic team selected by the *Winnipeg Tribune*.

In his entire hockey career, including playoff games, he appeared in 749 of 764 scheduled games over a 20-year period, a 98 percent participation rate, an incredible number for a defenseman.

With 656 professional games played by his retirement, Halderson had skated in more games of pro hockey than anyone to that point.

Noble Was the Last of the First

When teams were looking to get something started, they often turned to Reg Noble for leadership.

Early into the 1924–25 NHL season, the fledgling Montreal Maroons paid $8,000 to acquire Noble's services, giving them a veteran presence on their expansion roster.

Noble won two Stanley Cups as a high-scoring center in Toronto and rated among the best in the NHL at that position. While never a speed merchant as a skater, Noble's stamina and durability made him a star. He made the switch to defense with the Maroons after losing a step and won another Stanley Cup with them in 1925–26.

When Jack Adams was appointed manager of the Detroit Cougars in 1927, one of his first roster moves was to reach out and acquire Noble, paying $7,500 to the Maroons for him. Adams immediately named Noble his captain. In 1927–28 Noble was the only defender on the Detroit roster with more than a year of NHL experience.

No one had to tell Adams about the value Noble brought to the ice. In 1917–18, the inaugural NHL season, Adams was a rookie with the Cup-winning Toronto Arenas, who were led in scoring by captain Noble's 30–10–40 totals. He topped the NHL in assists that season and was third overall in the scoring race, becoming the first-ever captain of an NHL Stanley Cup championship squad.

"He was one of the greats of the game," Adams told the *Toronto Star*.

A farmer in the off-season, the stout, hard-as-nails Noble, who carried 190 pounds on his 5'8" frame, provided a punishing physical presence along the Detroit blue line and once touched off a near riot in Montreal when one of his thunderous body checks left Canadiens star Howie Morenz unconscious on the ice. In his first season with Detroit, another hard Noble check left New York Rangers defenseman Leo Bourgeault on the injured list for 10 days with facial fractures.

Noble's ruggedness was never more evident than during the 1925–26 season. Noble suffered a fractured skull when clipped in the lower forehead by the stick of Ottawa's Hooley Smith in a collision. Noble not only finished the game, he missed just four games after team physician Dr. Frank Scully diagnosed the fracture.

Opposing players seldom messed with Noble, because the Detroit defender carried what was considered the heaviest stick in the NHL. If he hacked you with it, you were more likely to break than Noble's lumber. At the end of the 1928–29 season, he and Ching Johnson of the New York Rangers were named to the defense positions on an unofficial NHL All-Star team selected by writers who covered the league.

As well as being a stabilizing influence to the Detroit rear guard, Noble was also adept at dishing out helpers with the disk via that heavy stick. In 1929–30 he moved past Rangers center Frank Boucher to become the NHL's all-time leader in assists with 93.

"He was a fine stickhandler and a fast, hard skater who played excellent positional hockey," former teammate Corbett Denneny told the *Globe and Mail*.

Triple Play
Detroit Players Who Skated with the Cougars, Falcons, and Red Wings

Player	Position	Seasons
Larry Aurie	Right Wing	1927–28 to 1938–39
Ebbie Goodfellow	Defense/Center	1928–29 to 1942–43
George Hay	Left Wing	1927–28 to 1930–31; 1932–33
Herbie Lewis	Left Wing	1928–29 to 1938–39
Reg Noble	Defense	1927–28 to 1932–33

Noble accepted a pay cut in his Detroit contract but balked at a provision that would allow the team to hold a portion of his salary until the end of the season to ensure he'd maintain his fitness.

The stipulation might have held some merit. Noble was twice suspended while with Toronto for breaking training rules, and he was a fellow known to be fond of his bourbon. Noble was also a guy who could keep things lighthearted. When a power outage halted a Toronto-Ottawa game in 1924, Noble, teammate Harry Cameron, and Ottawa's Frank Nighbor grabbed a pair of dice, came back to the ice surface, and kept the fans entertained by playing craps against the boards near center ice.

It appeared as if Noble's NHL playing days were done when Adams placed him on waivers prior to the start of the 1931–32 season. Realizing they still needed him, Noble was quickly recalled from waivers two days later and ended up performing strongly along the Detroit blue line that season. At the end of the season, Noble was voted MVP of the Detroit club, receiving a handsome trophy and diamond stickpin, but things took a much different path the following campaign.

When the Chicago Black Hawks dropped defenseman Georges Boucher at the end of the 1931–32 season, it left Noble as the last original NHLer still skating in the league, but a three-week holdout in a contract dispute kept Noble on the sideline. He was suspended by NHL president Frank Calder, and by the time Noble did agree to terms with the Wings, the regular season was under way and his conditioning was lacking.

"He will get into action when he is in condition to play and he will have to fight for his job on this club," Adams warned his old friend while talking to the *Montreal Gazette*.

Regardless, Noble was awarded what those in attendance estimated as the loudest ovation ever afforded a Detroit player at Olympia Stadium when he took the ice for his season debut on November 22, 1932, in a 4–2 victory over the Canadiens.

The 36-year-old, a 16-year veteran of the NHL wars, seemed a step behind the pace. Claiming Noble was 20 pounds overweight—and being five games into the season and still without a point—the Wings released the veteran.

He was picked up by the Maroons and played 20 games for them in what would be the farewell NHL campaign for the last of the original NHLers.

Named to the NHL referee staff in 1934, Noble was inducted into the Hockey Hall of Fame in 1962 and is among the few players to have worn Detroit colors as a Cougar, Falcon, and Red Wing.

28 Larson Owned the Scariest Shot in Red Wings History

When Reed Larson runs into former NHL opponents at golf tournaments or charity events, their first words are usually about war wounds received blocking one of Larson's cannon blasts.

"Former players always come up to me and tell me my shot broke their ankle or bones in their foot or their hand," Larson said. "Someone told me that I broke his shin pad and gave him stitches."

Larson made the jump straight from the University of Minnesota to the Red Wings in 1976–77, and penalty killers and other defenseman started ducking immediately.

"When he wound up, it was like the sea parted out there," said defenseman Mark Howe.

Larson was only six feet tall and 198 pounds, but he hammered the puck like he had the strength of Atlas.

"He probably had the hardest slap shot in the league," said his former Red Wings teammate Jim Rutherford.

Larson remembered that right after Joe Louis Arena was opened in 1979–80, police officers came in and determined the speed of players' shots with handheld radar guns. It was the only time he ever had his shot assessed.

"Obviously the accuracy then wasn't what it is today," Larson said. "But I remember that John Ogrodnick had some shots between 115 and 130 miles per hour and I had some over 130."

Larson had played against some of the top competitors in the NHL's early hardest-shot competitions and said, "I thought I could shoot with them, players like Al Iafrate, who was clocked at over 100 miles per hour."

When Larson was playing, it was the on-ice officials who were most concerned with his shot.

"They would come up to me in the warm-up and say, 'Whatever you do, don't hit me.'"

Larson was reasonably accurate with his shot, evidenced by the fact that he was a defenseman who netted 17 or more goals for nine consecutive seasons with the Red Wings. He scored 27 goals in 1980–81.

"As you mention Larson, the first thing you think about is that unbelievable shot," said Jacques Demers, who coached against Larson. "It was quick, and it was a heavy shot."

In one game against the Quebec Nordiques, Larson's shot deflected off traffic in front and hit goaltender Clint Malarchuk square in the mask. It fractured his orbital bone.

"I've hurt people in the crowd when deflections would go into the stands, and it would scare me," Larson said. "I hate talking about it, but I've broken some bones."

Once, Dennis Hextall was standing in front of the net, and Larson's blast from the point tore the skate blade off his boot. The puck caromed into the net, and Hextall was credited with a goal. "But he had to limp off the ice," Larson said.

Another time at Philadelphia's Spectrum, Larson's shot broke a Plexiglas pane in a bizarre manner. The puck struck a side brace and nothing seemed wrong at first.

"There was a little chip, and then, almost like a chain reaction, the entire pane disintegrated in five seconds. It cut a fan in the first row," Larson recalled.

The oddity of the story is that Larson was in Philadelphia the following season and broke the same pane of glass.

"What are the odds?" Larson said. "I got a letter, and it said, 'I know you don't like us fans, but you have to stop doing this because I can't take it anymore.' It was pretty funny."

Larson never lifted weights. He water-skied, participated in gymnastics, and wrestled. He thinks all of that contributed to him having well-balanced muscles. "[Shooting hard] is stick design, repetition, practice, technique, timing, and strength in certain muscles," Larson said.

29 Sawchuk and Crozier: Detroit's Tortured Souls

"All goalies are going to heaven," Roger Crozier once explained, "because we've already been through hell."

Perhaps no goalies in NHL history endured more hellish existences than Crozier and the man who preceded him between the pipes for the Red Wings, Terry Sawchuk.

Determining who was the more tortured soul is a difficult question to decipher.

Consider Sawchuk's punishing legacy. Life as a goaltender exacted a tremendous toll upon Sawchuk's body. He took more than 400 stitches to the face and head, lost three teeth, broke his nose twice, dislocated his left shoulder, suffered a pinched nerve in his right shoulder, had two discs removed from his back, suffered three broken fingers and a broken right hand, and needed 175 stitches in his left hand to repair three severed tendons.

He also had a broken instep in his left foot, seven broken ribs, and a broken right elbow that never healed properly, necessitating three surgeries and the removal over the years of 60 bone chips.

"I spend my summers in the hospital," joked Sawchuk, who once checked himself out of the hospital to play a Stanley Cup game.

"If I had been bothered by his physical problems, I'd have thrown a rope over a beam and kicked the chair out from underneath a long time ago," remarked former Detroit defenseman Marcel Pronovost, Sawchuk's closest friend.

Crozier's journey was no less painful. Pancreatitis afflicted him following the 1965–66 season. He spent three weeks in the hospital and lost 20 pounds. The illness would see him hospitalized 30 times during his career.

"It can recur if I overindulge in anything, especially fatty foods," Crozier said.

Stomach ailments also laid him up during the 1969–70 season, and in 1971 he underwent surgery to remove his gallbladder.

A month into the 1967–68 season, Crozier abruptly announced his retirement from the game.

"Roger said he had lost his confidence," Detroit coach Sid Abel explained to UPI. "He might have been near a nervous breakdown, and rather than get to that stage, he decided to hang it up."

Sawchuk also walked away from the game midseason while playing for Boston in 1956–57. Battling a bout of mononucleosis, he was hospitalized, and once he returned to action, he wasn't the same player. Bruins GM Lynn Patrick questioned Sawchuk's intestinal fortitude.

"They didn't believe he was sick," Pronovost said.

Sawchuk offered up in great detail exactly how the mononucleosis was affecting his body. "It's like the red and white corpuscles choose up sides and play hockey in your veins," he said.

The insecurity of the position—there were just six spots for NHL goalies—led both men to play through as much pain as they could endure, getting repaired when time permitted.

"You can't forget how tough it was for those guys," suggested Hall of Fame netminder Patrick Roy, the coach of the Colorado Avalanche.

Both returned to action—Crozier with the Wings four months later and Sawchuk after a trade brought him back to Detroit in the summer of 1957, another parallel between these two troubled goalies.

Both came to Detroit after being named Rookie of the Year in the American Hockey League.

"He's a sure pop to be a National League goalie within a couple of years," Hall of Fame former NHL forward Bill Cook said after seeing an 18-year-old Sawchuk play as a rookie pro.

Sawchuk replaced Stanley Cup winner Harry Lumley in the Wings' net. Crozier replaced Stanley Cup winner Sawchuk in the Wings' net.

Each man accomplished things never before seen from a Detroit goaltender.

Now in Goal

Four Hall of Famers played goal for both Detroit and Toronto. Harry "Hap" Holmes, Detroit's No. 1 goalie for the franchise's first two seasons from 1926 to 1928, was also Toronto's goalie when the team won the NHL's first Stanley Cup in 1917–18. Harry Lumley backstopped Detroit to the 1949–50 Stanley Cup and won the Vezina Trophy with the Leafs in 1953–54. Terry Sawchuk earned three Stanley Cups as a Red Wing (1951–52, 1953–54, and 1954–55) and one with Toronto (1966–67). He's also the only goalie to win the Vezina with both Detroit and Toronto.

The fourth? Well, that's the hard one, because it was right-winger Charlie Conacher, who filled as an emergency goalie for both teams.

The five-time NHL goal-scoring leader and two-time league scoring champion took his first turn in net on December 20, 1932, against the New York Rangers, making six saves in a two-minute turn in net for Leafs goalie Lorne Chabot, who was serving a high-sticking penalty. Goaltenders were required to serve their own penalties in those days. Later that same season, on March 16, 1933, when Chabot again ran afoul of the law, engaging in fisticuffs with Detroit's Ebbie Goodfellow, Conacher stepped into the breech.

Exactly two years later, on March 16, 1935, Toronto goalie George Hainsworth suffered a cut over his left eye against the Montreal Canadiens. Conacher, who scored three goals in Toronto's 5–3 win, guarded the net for three minutes while Hainsworth was stitched up.

Acquired by Detroit prior to the 1938–39 season, late in a 7–3 loss to the New York Rangers, Detroit goalie Tiny Thompson was cut open when struck over the left eye by a shot from Rangers forward Neil Colville. Conacher took over in net for the game's final three minutes.

In total, Conacher played 10 minutes as an NHL puck-stopper and never surrendered a goal.

During his first five full NHL seasons, Sawchuk garnered 56 shutouts, 195 wins, and a 1.94 goals-against average. Sawchuk led the NHL in wins each of those five seasons and is the only goalie in NHL history to post a GAA of less than 2.00 in each of his first five campaigns.

In 1951–52, he had four shutouts, an 0.62 GAA, and a .977 save percentage as Detroit won the Cup in the minimum eight games.

"A lot of people think he was the greatest goalkeeper who ever played the game," Hall of Fame netminder Glenn Hall said. "I include myself in that group."

In 1964, after Sawchuk had carried Detroit to consecutive Stanley Cup Finals appearances, he was let go to Toronto, and Abel handed the reins to the unproven Crozier.

"I'm not worried about his goaltending," Abel said. "I know he can do the job."

As a rookie, Crozier led Detroit to a first-place finish, leading the NHL with 40 wins and becoming the last netminder in NHL history to appear in all of his team's games. In 1965–66, he backstopped Detroit to the Stanley Cup Finals and earned the Conn Smythe Trophy as playoff MVP in a losing cause as the Wings fell to the Montreal Canadiens in six games.

"Roger is a serious guy," Detroit assistant GM Baz Bastien, himself a former NHL goalie, explained to the *Pittsburgh Post-Gazette*. "Even during practice, when the other guys are having fun, Roger was dead serious. He never kidded around."

Due to his illness, Crozier lived in almost constant pain throughout his playing days, and that made many wonder why he continued to stop pucks for a living.

"That's a darn good question," he once told the Associated Press. "But I might as well be doing this. If you're going to be doing any kind of job with responsibility, there's going to be pressure."

Likewise, Sawchuk lived his life in discomfort due to his many ailments, but continued to excel. He backstopped Toronto to the Stanley Cup in 1967, and the first-year Los Angeles Kings grabbed him in the NHL expansion draft that spring.

"I'm counting the time till I can quit," Sawchuk complained.

The following season, he was reacquired by the Wings for a third time and reunited with Crozier for the first time since the 1963–64 season. "I think he can help us," Detroit coach Bill Gadsby said of Sawchuk.

Within a year, both were gone—Sawchuk to the New York Rangers and Crozier to his own first-year expansion club, the Buffalo Sabres.

"If Roger plays well, we may not look too bad," Buffalo coach/ GM Punch Imlach told the AP. "Most of our guys haven't been around too long and he can hold them together."

Sawchuk would never see Crozier play for Buffalo. In the spring of 1970, after the Rangers were eliminated from the playoffs by Boston, Sawchuk was seriously hurt in a scuffle with teammate Ron Stewart, and died from complications that developed from his internal injuries.

"The pain has been so bad that I haven't really cared about pulling through," Sawchuk said shortly before his May 31, 1970, death.

Crozier retired from the game in 1977 and also died young. Cancer claimed his life in 1996, at the age of 53.

Two of Detroit's greatest goalies were also two of the franchise's most tortured souls. But as tough as it was for Crozier, it's hard to imagine any NHLer suffered more during their playing days than Sawchuk.

30 Osgood Deserves a Place in the Hall of Fame

Chris Osgood has long been ensnared in the catch-22 of the NHL goaltending profession. When Osgood was piling up wins, it was said he couldn't be considered great until he won in the postseason.

Then when Osgood won in the postseason, his critics said he won because he was playing on an exceptional team.

"I don't think he ever got the respect he deserved for what he did," said former Red Wings player Darren McCarty.

Osgood is ranked 10th all-time in goalie wins with 401, and he was a member of three Stanley Cup teams (1997, 1998, and 2008). He was the starting goalie on two of those championship teams. He is eighth all-time in NHL history with 74 playoff wins.

"People can say what they want," said NHL Network analyst Craig Button, a former Calgary Flames general manager. "In 1997–98 the Red Wings had lost [Vladimir] Konstantinov, and Sergei Fedorov was holding out; Chris Osgood needed to be good, and he was."

Button said Osgood was "outstanding" when he posted a .930 save percentage to help the Red Wings win the Stanley Cup in 2008.

The Red Wings, with Osgood playing brilliantly, also made it to Game 7 of the Stanley Cup Finals in 2009. The conventional wisdom is that Osgood would have won the Conn Smythe Trophy had they won that Game 7 against the Pittsburgh Penguins. Instead, they lost 2–1, and now people wonder whether Osgood will gain entry to the Hall of Fame.

"There are people who argue Ken Dryden's credentials for the Hall of Fame because they say anyone could win for the Montreal Canadiens in that era," Button said. "I'm baffled when people say,

'Well, Osgood played on a good team.' Well, part of having a good team is having good goaltending. Osgood did more than his part."

Osgood had 15 playoff shutouts and owned a .916 postseason save percentage. His lifetime 2.09 playoff goals-against average is almost half a goal lower than his regular-season GAA. The Red Wings were willing to deal Mike Vernon to San Jose after the 1996–97 season because they believed in Osgood.

"I think Mike Vernon and Chris Osgood both are Hall of Fame players," Button said.

Goalie Chris Osgood—repeatedly snubbed for inclusion in the HOF—stops Pittsburgh Penguin Jordan Staal during Game 6 of the Stanley Cup Finals in Pittsburgh on June 9, 2009.

Vernon and Osgood were the goalies on the last back-to-back Stanley Cup championships. Osgood won 57 percent of his playoff games. By comparison, Patrick Roy won 61 percent. Marty Brodeur has won 55 percent of his postseason appearances.

"If I had to play just one game, I would want [Dominik] Hasek," McCarty said. "But if I had to play in front of one guy for a playoff series, I'm going with Ozzy. He's in my Hall of Fame."

Detroit general manager Ken Holland believes Osgood is Hall of Fame worthy.

"The league has been around for almost 100 years, and he is one of 10 to get 400 wins," Holland said. "If it were easy to get 400 wins, he would be one of 40 or 50."

Osgood's strength has always been his ability to let go of what happened yesterday. He never dwelled on his poor performances. He was pulled after giving up four goals in his NHL debut for Detroit in Maple Leaf Gardens.

"I know Scotty [Bowman] came up and said, 'Don't worry, kid, there are going to be plenty more games,'" Osgood recalled. "I wasn't disappointed. I thought it was the coolest thing, starting out in Maple Leaf Gardens. I wasn't nervous…I came [away] thinking, *I can play in this league.*"

Osgood played 14 seasons in Detroit, most of them in the non–salary cap era when the Red Wings had the budget to sign top free agents.

"If we thought there was someone who could do a better job than him," Holland said, "we would have gone out and got someone who could do a better job than him."

31 A Shot He Didn't Want to Stop

Decades after he played his last game, Alec Connell's name remains prominent among NHL goaltending records. He backstopped both the Ottawa Senators (1926–27) and Montreal Maroons (1934–35) to Stanley Cup titles. He still holds NHL marks for consecutive shutouts (six) and the longest shutout streak (460 minutes and 49 seconds). Connell tended goal for Ottawa in the NHL's first scoreless tie, a 0–0 deadlock with the Hamilton Tigers on December 17, 1924, and on November 13, 1934, was beaten by Ralph "Scotty" Bowman for the first penalty-shot goal in NHL history.

While there's no doubt that Connell wanted desperately to block that attempt by Bowman, there were some other shots about to be aimed his way in the dark alleys of New York City the night of March 6, 1932, and Connell held no desire to get in the way of any of them.

With the Great Depression taking its toll on the world, Ottawa, in desperate financial straits, took a year's leave of absence from the NHL. The Senators' players were divided up among the remaining nine NHL clubs, with Detroit receiving Connell, defenseman Alex Smith, and forwards Art Gagne, Danny Cox, and Hec Kilrea.

Connell was a solid performer in Detroit, posting six shutouts and a 2.12 goals-against average, but when the Falcons came to Madison Square Garden the night of March 6, 1932, Detroit was in a futile bid for a playoff spot and in desperate need of points.

Detroit was tied 2–2 with the New York Americans in the third period, when Americans defenseman Mervyn "Red" Dutton rang a shot off the goal post and the red light behind Connell's net immediately illuminated.

It was also the era of prohibition, and the Americans were owned by Big Bill Dwyer, the most prominent bootlegger in the New York area, whose associates included a who's who of the cast of the HBO series *Boardwalk Empire*—Owney Madden, Dutch Schultz, Lucky Luciano, Meyer Lansky, Arnold Rothstein, and Frank Costello—some of America's most feared mobsters. Many of Dwyer's henchmen worked as minor officials at Americans home games, which Connell was about to find out the hard way.

As soon as the goal light lit up, so did Connell's fury. He stormed from the net, and a brouhaha commenced. Amid the melee, referee George Mallinson quietly allowed to Connell that he'd seen the puck ring off the pipe and he would be disallowing the goal.

The goal judge began jawing at Connell through the chicken wire, pressing his face right up against the fence to ensure that Connell heard him, and the Detroit goaltender responded by slamming the wire fence back into the fellow's face, cutting him open and spilling blood.

The game concluded in a 2–2 overtime draw, and as Connell exited the MSG ice surface, he was surprised to see two long lines of police—some 75 uniformed officers and another half dozen detectives—forming a corridor from the ice surface to the Falcons' dressing room.

"I did not know they were guarding me from gangsters until I got in the dressing room," Connell explained to *Ottawa Journal* writer Bill Walshe in 1946.

Upon taking his seat in the room to doff his goalie garb, Connell was immediately flanked by a pair of New York police detectives with guns drawn.

"What's the big idea?" Connell asked the detectives. "Why," he was told, "the goal judge you hit is one of the toughest in the underworld, and you are to be bumped off."

An army of officers provided Connell a police escort to the hotel where the Detroit team was staying. He was advised to lock his door and not answer it until they arrived to see him safely to the train station the next morning. But an old friend was in town to visit Connell, and they decided to go out for a meal.

"We stepped out of the hotel and almost smack into a big fellow who loosened his coat and started to follow us," Connell related. "The first open door was a crowded drug store, and we slipped in, in an attempt to hide.

"I heard a voice call 'Connell,' but I didn't answer, even when it was repeated several times. Then I felt a tug on my coat and a rough voice asked, 'Are you Connell of the Detroit [Falcons]?'"

Connell played coy. "What do you mean?" he asked the fellow. Connell continued, "He repeated the question, but I told him I did not know who he was talking about. After a close look, he rushed away to again take up his position in front of the hotel.

"I slipped into the hotel by another entrance and was sure worried when I left next morning to catch a train. In fact, I was worried every time I returned to New York."

Regardless, the traits that made Connell a world-class netminder—his quick reflexes and calmness under pressure—saved this puck-stopper from blocking a fatal shot.

Years later, Connell's fears were somewhat allayed when a New York reporter informed him that the goal judge/gangster who had his name on a bullet had been done in by a similar fate, meeting an untimely end when he found himself on the wrong end of a life-ending blast.

32 James Norris Was the Mike Ilitch of the 1930s

Today, the Detroit Red Wings travel by private jet and eat catered meals. In the late 1920s, Detroit's NHL team traveled by day coach, and players were given cheese sandwiches, oranges, and candy bars on the road.

After the Detroit Cougars joined the NHL as an expansion team in 1926–27, they were under constant threat of bankruptcy.

Montreal Canadiens great Howie Morenz was the NHL's best player in that era, and Cougars general manager Jack Adams joked that if he were available "for $1.98 we couldn't afford to buy him."

The team was $80,000 in debt after its first season, when all 22 home games had to be played in Windsor. Owners hoped their financial outlook would be improved when the club moved into the newly built Olympia Stadium.

An instant love affair between Detroiters and the Cougars didn't happen right away for a variety of reasons:

- Hockey was still considered a Canadian sport and a novelty in the United States. It didn't help that the Cougars had launched their franchise in Windsor, further convincing Detroiters that it was a Canadian team.

- The Cougars were a sad-sack team on the ice. In their first four seasons, the Cougars made the playoffs only once, in 1928–29, and were quickly dispatched by the Toronto Maple Leafs.

- With the stock market crashing on October 29, 1929, automobile sales plummeted, and disposable income dwindled in Detroit. People simply didn't have money to spend on entertainment.

Canadian Adams should be given credit for keeping the NHL alive in the early years in Detroit. The Hall of Fame player was only 32 when he took over as general manager and coach of the Cougars. In those years, Adams was known to walk in front of Olympia Stadium trying to coax people into buying tickets to see the games.

Since the country was in the Depression, fans would barter with the Cougars for tickets. According to a newspaper report, a farmer once drove up and traded produce to see the Cougars play.

Adams did grow frustrated. He couldn't understand when Detroiters would boo his team, even during the rare times they were winning.

He admitted publicly that the team barely had enough money to buy sticks for his players. HistoricDetroit.org quotes Adams as saying, at one point, "Last week, a gang of kids over near the stadium stole some of our sticks, and if the police hadn't recovered them, we'd be kicking the puck with our skates."

Owners changed the team's name from the Cougars to the Falcons with the hope that it would improve the team's image. It didn't help; the Falcons were 16–21–7 in 1930–31. The team entered bankruptcy. Adams used his own money to meet payroll.

The franchise's savior was Canadian businessman James Norris, who purchased the Falcons on September 2, 1932, for $100,000, or as he called it, "loose change."

A month later, Norris changed the team's name to the Red Wings. He had once belonged to the Montreal Amateur Athletic Association sporting club, whose teams were known as the Winged Wheelers. The Winged Wheelers had won the Stanley Cup in 1893.

"Our emblem will be a winged wheel," Norris announced in Detroit in 1932. "That's appropriate for Detroit. And we'll call the team the Wings—the Red Wings."

The man loved his team, and that passion fueled unflinching financial support. The *Ottawa Journal* reported that when his team was playing, Norris wanted a call every few minutes to get an update.

"When the Red Wings were winning, everybody wanted to answer the telephone to give him the news," the *Journal* reported. "But when they were losing, even his relatives and best friends knew he was going to take it hard and so nobody wanted to answer the telephone."

Norris owned an estate in Lake Forest, Illinois, and had a regulation-size outdoor rink built on his property. He hired servants who could skate to assure he had more participants for his family hockey games.

Thanks to Norris' financial support, Adams was able to transform the Red Wings into an NHL powerhouse team. They reached the Stanley Cup Finals for the first time in 1934, losing to the Chicago Black Hawks. Then they captured back-to-back titles in 1936 and 1937.

"The hockey virus was in Mr. Norris' blood," said Toronto Maple Leafs general manager Conn Smythe.

33 Kris Draper: The Best Dollar the Wings Ever Spent

So what's a dollar buy these days? A pound of butter? Dream on. A loaf of bread? Maybe, if it's on sale. How about a checking-line center?

On June 30, 1993, the Detroit Red Wings purchased the contract of Kris Draper from the Winnipeg Jets for one dollar. Among the vast array of multimillion-dollar talent that populated the Wings' dressing room, he was the team's bargain-basement banger. Their dollar-store special.

Ten-Four

The 10 Players Who've Won Four Stanley Cups in a Red Wings Uniform

1. Kris Draper (1996–97, 1997–98, 2001–02, 2007–08)
2. Tomas Holmstrom (1996–97, 1997–98, 2001–02, 2007–08)
3. Gordie Howe (1949–50, 1951–52, 1953–54, 1954–55)
4. Red Kelly (1949–50, 1951–52, 1953–54, 1954–55)
5. Nicklas Lidstrom (1996–97, 1997–98, 2001–02, 2007–08)
6. Ted Lindsay (1949–50, 1951–52, 1953–54, 1954–55)
7. Kirk Maltby (1996–97, 1997–98, 2001–02, 2007–08)
8. Darren McCarty (1996–97, 1997–98, 2001–02, 2007–08)
9. Marty Pavelich (1949–50, 1951–52, 1953–54, 1954–55)
10. Marcel Pronovost (1949–50, 1951–52, 1953–54, 1954–55)

It was the wisest buck the Wings ever parted with.

You spend more on your morning cup of coffee or that pack of gum you grab at the corner store than the Wings gave the Jets to acquire Draper's services.

"I think it was even a Canadian dollar," Draper said.

In those days, that wasn't worth much.

Apparently, Mike Smith, the Jets' general manager at the time, felt the same way about Draper.

"I saw in baseball once that somebody got traded for 10 bats," said former Red Wings winger Darren McCarty, one of Draper's best friends. "That's way more than a dollar. A dollar, that's pretty much giving a guy away. You give a guy away who wins four Stanley Cups. And you wonder why some people don't have jobs."

Anchored solidly as the center on Detroit's famous Grind Line, Draper played 17 seasons in a Red Wings uniform, becoming one of six players in franchise history to play more than 1,000 games for the team.

Besides his four Stanley Cup wins with the team, Draper skated in six Cup Finals series, and his 222 playoff games put him in the NHL's all-time top 10.

Kris Draper: a dollar well spent. Draper demonstrates his stickhandling in game action against the Columbus Blue Jackets on February 13, 2009.

He was part of a half dozen Presidents' Trophy–winning teams. In 2003–04 Draper won the Selke Trophy as the NHL's best defensive forward. He played for Canada in the World Cup of Hockey (2004), Winter Olympics (2006), and world championship (2000, 2001, 2003, and 2005).

That's a lot of bang for a buck.

"I never dreamt I'd get a player for the price of a smoothie at McDonald's," Red Wings owner Mike Ilitch said.

Selected 62nd overall by the Jets in the 1989 NHL entry draft, Draper originally struggled to find his niche. "I felt I was getting buried in Winnipeg," Draper said. "My first camp with Winnipeg, I came in and played really well. They told me they liked what I showed them, but they didn't think they were going to have a very good club and they didn't want me exposed to that kind of environment, so they sent me back [to the Canadian National team].

"The next fall I came to camp and was one of the first guys sent to the minors. It was a really unusual feeling, to go from being considered a top prospect to being one of the first guys sent down a year later."

Draper went to Jets management following the 1992–93 season and suggested that if they didn't have any plans for him, he'd appreciate a trade, a request that was accommodated when he was sent to Detroit.

Originally, he felt equally buried in Adirondack, Detroit's American Hockey League farm club. In the last year of his contract, Draper was weighing possible post-hockey options.

"He was wondering what he was going to do," remembered former Wings goalie Kevin Hodson, who roomed with Draper that season.

Shortly thereafter, on January 24, 1994, Draper was called up to Detroit, where he remained until he retired from the game following the 2010–11 season.

"I consider myself one of the luckiest athletes of all time to be able to play with this organization for 17 years," Draper said. "To be able to play over 1,000 games with the Red Wings is probably what I'm most proud of. It was great."

Draper's combination of elite skating ability, tenacity, and dedication to fitness allowed him to excel in the role of pest, driving the other team's key offensive players to distraction.

"If you can skate and you work, you can wear people down," former teammate Dan Cleary said of Draper. "The one thing about him is he was so competitive. He had a hate on for everybody he played against."

At the rink, Draper was a big kid. There is no other way to describe the passion he brought to work every day.

"He still skated like a kid. He had all that experience in the league and yet still had the enthusiasm of a 20-year-old," remembered Wings coach Mike Babcock. "He was a really important guy in our room, and that's why he was there so long."

When it was game time, he was determined to lead the way. When it was play time, Draper was equally determined to lead the fun.

Out between the boards during a game, Draper ensured you were aware he was there.

"He just did everything right," Babcock said. "He was allowed to hold everyone accountable because he did it right."

McCarty, who arrived in Detroit the same season as Draper, puts it into simpler terms. "Drapes, he was the heartbeat," McCarty said. "He was the pulse in here. We knew his value."

The best dollar the team ever spent.

34 Kilrea Was a Hec of a Soldier

As an NHLer, Hec Kilrea was a strong two-way player who could always be counted on to give his best.

His first experience in Detroit came on loan from the Ottawa Senators to the Detroit Falcons during the 1931–32 season. The right-winger suffered a career-threatening eye injury that season in a game against the New York Americans, but later returned to action.

Coming to the Red Wings in 1935 and staying into the 1939–40 season, Kilrea, whose brothers Wally and Ken and nephew Brian also played for Detroit, won three Stanley Cups, including back-to-back triumphs with the Wings in 1935–36 and 1936–37.

He set up Mud Bruneteau for the goal that won hockey's longest game in 1936 and the following spring scored in triple-overtime to put the Wings back in the Cup Finals. But Kilrea's most heroic performance came on the battlefields of Germany.

On December 12, 1945, on the outskirts of the German village of Bennwihr, Kilrea engaged in action during which he drove off a tank.

"Staff Sgt. Kilrea spotted an enemy Mark VI tank, 100 yards away, advancing slowly down the street supported by foot troops heavily armed with machine guns, rifles, and machine pistols," noted the US Army in its official report of the event. "Kilrea immediately grabbed an M-1 rifle and fired upon the advancing troops from an opening between the wall and the house.

"His fire caused the enemy foot troops to take cover in positions along the road and in the doorways of houses. The tank came to a halt eight yards from Kilrea. Despite the personal danger involved, he took a bazooka and, after loading it, ran out alone into the open street.

"Standing up, in full view of the enemy, he fired his weapon, although the small arms protection given the tank made it extremely dangerous. Enemy small arms fire was being directed on him and down the road.

"His first round hit the tank. He then ran into the yard, loaded his weapon and again went into the street. Hitting the tank again, he forced it to withdraw behind a nearby building. He repeated the loading procedure a third time and, again exposing himself to point-blank fire, held his weapon at a slight angle and fired over the corner of the building.

"Although enemy fire still was on him, he repeated this a fourth time, firing over the building corner. He returned to the yard to reload four more times. On the eighth time, his bazooka was put out of commission by a rifle bullet. However, his action forced the tank and troops to withdraw, thereby eliminating a serious threat to the entire company."

The following day Kilrea, utilizing a borrowed bazooka, crawled within 50 feet of another enemy tank in order to destroy it.

"Although he had no position from enemy observation, Kilrea from a kneeling position fired three well-aimed rounds at the tank, hitting it each time to knock it out. Kilrea's calm and deliberate action not only saved the company from serious threat, but inspired those who witnessed his actions," the official US Army report of the event stated.

For his heroism, Staff Sgt. Kilrea, 35 at the time and a member of the US Army's Company K of the 143rd Infantry Regiment, was awarded the Distinguished Service Cross, the second-highest army battle award.

The Ontario-born Kilrea, a naturalized US citizen, saw action on the Anzio beachhead, helped to liberate Rome, and fought in France. He was also awarded the Purple Heart, the Combat Infantryman's Badge, and three battle stars.

Detroit's First Scotty Bowman

When Scotty Bowman first arrived in Detroit, it was a big deal.

No, silly, not *that* Scotty Bowman.

On February 11, 1935, defenseman Ralph "Scotty" Bowman and left-winger Syd Howe were acquired by the Wings from the St. Louis Eagles for a princely sum of defenseman Teddy Graham and $50,000; it was the largest cash transaction in NHL history.

A Doctor in the House

Hockey players are known for losing teeth, but Detroit defenseman Stan Brown was known for repairing molars. Dr. Brown was a dentist who had a practice for years in Windsor, Ontario, and was sometimes called upon to attend to the dental needs of his teammates.

Here's how the Associated Press reported Brown's first NHL goal against George Hainsworth of the Montreal Canadiens: "Brown secured the puck behind the blue line, drilled his way through the Canadien team, extracted George Hainsworth from the net, then slapped a rubber filling into it."

For the cash-strapped Eagles, the deal was a godsend. "It was too attractive to pass up," Eagles managing director Clare Brunton told the Associated Press. "We had an opportunity to make a profitable trade and we accepted it."

It terms of titles, the trade would prove far more profitable for the Red Wings. Detroit coach/GM Jack Adams saw the deal as the beginning of a rebuild that would turn the Wings into Stanley Cup contenders for the 1935–36 season, and he'd be proven correct in that assessment.

While Howe was the flashier of the two newcomers, rated sixth in NHL scoring at the time of the trade, Bowman would also prove to be a vital cog in Detroit's back-to-back Stanley Cup wins of 1935–36 and 1936–37.

A punishing hitter and defensive dynamo, the burly Bowman paired with Ebbie Goodfellow to give the Wings two solid blue-line pairings, the other being the duo of captain Doug Young and Bucko McDonald. In St. Louis, Bowman worked in the top pairing with Irvine Frew, skating nearly 50 minutes a night of ice time.

Bowman also was equipped with a decent offensive touch, and in fact, on November 13, 1934, scored the first penalty-shot goal in NHL history, driving a hard shot past Alec Connell. Bowman netted a pair of goals in Detroit's drive to the first Stanley Cup in franchise history in the spring of 1936, including the series-deciding goal in the semifinal against the Montreal Maroons, going hard to the net to bury Larry Aurie's rebound past Maroons goalie Lorne Chabot from the edge of the goal crease.

Occasionally referred to as the second Eddie Shore, the stout 190-pounder admired the legendary Shore as a youngster, and like Shore, Bowman could rush with the puck and mix it up with the best. "I get a bigger thrill out of landing a hefty body check than in denting the twine," Bowman told the *Ottawa Journal.*

His hard work often made him a target of boobirds in enemy rinks and also left a mark on Bowman, who was known as one of the most stitched men in hockey. It took 23 of them to sew him up during the 1935–36 season.

The occasional confusion between this Scotty Bowman and the man who shared his nickname, William Scott Bowman, coach of the Wings from 1993 to 2002 and a winner of three Stanley Cups in Detroit, left the latter in stitches.

"I got a letter once asking me about scoring the first penalty-shot goal in NHL history, saying it must have been quite a feat," the latter Scotty Bowman once related. "I wrote him back and said, 'It certainly was, considering I was barely a year old at the time.'"

36 Maple Leaf Gardens, a Special Place for Wings Fans

It was the site of the first game in NBA history. It was the only North American venue to play host to the Beatles on all three of the Fab Four's North American tours. And it's the only rink where both the Stanley Cup and Memorial Cup were won in the same season.

Sure, it's where the Toronto Maple Leafs were at home from 1931 to 1999, but Maple Leaf Gardens was frequently a cozy place for the Red Wings as well.

The Wings won their first Stanley Cup on that ice surface in Game 4 of the 1936 Stanley Cup Finals on April 11, 1936.

It was third-line right-winger Pete Kelly who netted the first Stanley Cup–winning goal in Red Wings history, and Kelly's huge marker was also his first playoff goal as an NHLer.

The Wings were leading Toronto 2–1 as the game neared the midway point of the third period. Kelly, as was usually the case, was seated at the end of the Detroit bench, watching the action, awaiting one of his rare shifts, when he noticed a tired Larry Aurie lagging slowly toward the bench, waving for a replacement.

"[Detroit coach] Jack Adams was looking the other way, so I jumped on the ice before he saw me," Kelly explained in a 2001 interview. "The puck came right to me, and I moved across the Toronto blue line with [teammate] Herbie Lewis. I think [Toronto goalie George] Hainsworth figured I was going to pass it, because I noticed he was leaning away from his post, so I snapped a shot for the short side, and it went in.

"It was lucky I scored, because Adams was sure going to be mad when I got back to the bench."

Toronto got a late tally, but Detroit's 3–2 win made the Wings the holders of Lord Stanley's mug for the first time and turned Kelly into a Stanley Cup hero.

It was one of two big scores for Kelly that year. On June 13 in Charlottetown, Prince Edward Island, he married the former Pearl Marguerite Hobbs.

It was the first of five times that a Detroit-Toronto Stanley Cup Finals series was decided on Maple Leaf Gardens ice, but the only time the game would go in the Wings' favor. Overall, Detroit played 55 playoff games at Maple Leaf Gardens, more than any other visiting arena. The Wings and Leafs have clashed in 23 series

Maple Leafs Forever After

Detroit blasted the Toronto St. Patricks 5–1 in a game played February 16, 1927, at Windsor's Border Cities Arena. The next day, Conn Smythe, the new owner of the Toronto franchise, announced that the team would be renamed the Maple Leafs.

over the years, making Toronto Detroit's most frequent postseason opponent.

It was during a 1956 semifinals series between the Leafs and Wings that an anonymous caller to a Toronto newspaper claimed he'd shoot Detroit stars Gordie Howe and Ted Lindsay when they took the ice as the series switched to Maple Leaf Gardens for Game 3 on March 24, 1956. But Howe and Lindsay were the only ones who did any shooting, combining for three goals in Detroit's 5–4 triumph.

After the game, Lindsay turned his stick around like a rifle and pointed it at the Toronto crowd, circling the rink while making machine-gun noises. "I guess you could say I had the last laugh," Lindsay said.

Some other big things happened in Wings history on Maple Leaf Gardens ice. On March 27, 1973, Mickey Redmond beat Leafs goalie Ron Low twice in a span of 18 seconds to become Detroit's first-ever 50-goal scorer in an 8–1 Red Wings victory.

Before the game, Jean Murney, a neighbor of Redmond's in Peterborough, Ontario, dropped off some taffy suckers for good luck. "Sure, I ate mine," Redmond said of the only sucker bet to ever pay off in sports history.

There were also some bleak moments for the Wings on MLG ice. On February 2, 1977, the Wings lived a Groundhog Day they'll never want to repeat, losing 9–1 to the Leafs as Toronto defenseman Ian Turnbull netted an NHL-record five goals. But the worst of all came January 2, 1971, when the Wings suffered a record defeat, a 13–0 shutout loss to Toronto.

"It would have been worse if we hadn't blocked the kick after Toronto's second touchdown," an unnamed Red Wings player cracked to *Sports Illustrated*.

The good news is that you can still take in a game at the Gardens. Recognized as a National Historic Site of Canada in 2007, the building was renovated in 2009. The lower level is a grocery store, but the upper level remains a rink with seating capacity for 2,539. Renamed the Mattamy Athletic Centre, it is home to the Ryerson Rams of Ontario University Athletics.

37 Johnny Gallagher's Worst Head Case Scenario

When he first arrived upon the NHL scene, Johnny Gallagher was the cause of great headaches, but those would prove trivial compared to the headache he suffered during the 1933 Stanley Cup Playoffs.

The Toronto Maple Leafs announced that they'd signed the promising amateur defenseman on July 30, 1930, and immediately, the Montreal Maroons filed a protest. Gallagher, it seemed, had signed a pact with the Maroons while he was still playing with the Montreal Amateur Athletic Association, the team that won the Allan Cup title as senior champions of Canada in 1929–30. The Maroons insisted that the contract stipulated that Gallagher would turn pro for the 1930–31 NHL campaign.

At the NHL meetings on September 27, 1930, NHL president Frank Calder heard both cases, then awarded Gallagher's NHL rights to the Maroons.

Gallagher never found his footing with the Maroons, and in 1932 his contract was sold to the Red Wings. In the spring of 1933, he was performing on the Detroit defense when the Wings faced the Maroons in the opening round of the Stanley Cup Playoffs.

As the Red Wings eliminated the Maroons with a 3–2 victory on March 28, 1933, at Olympia Stadium, it was reported that Gallagher netted the game-winning goal.

What wasn't noted in any of the game reports was that Gallagher had struck his head when he fell into the boards, nor was he ever checked out by team medical personnel for any sort of head injury.

In fact, he continued to play into the next round against the New York Rangers, and a couple of weeks after the Wings were eliminated from the playoffs, Gallagher drove from Windsor to Toronto to watch the opening game of the Stanley Cup Finals series between the Rangers and Leafs.

It was there, in his room at Toronto's Royal York Hotel, that Gallagher appears to have suffered from the effects of a severe case of post-concussion syndrome, which led to his incarceration in a psychiatric hospital.

JOHNNY GALLAGHER CRITICALLY ILL, screamed the headline in the April 10, 1933, edition of the *Montreal Gazette*.

"Suffering from loss of memory, the result of injuries received several weeks ago in a National Hockey League game at Olympia, Johnny Gallagher was taken to Whitby [Ontario] Hospital Sunday afternoon for observation," reported the *Border Cities Star*.

The article continued, "Complaining of illness and pains in his head after his arrival in Toronto, Gallagher did not attend the game. His condition became worse, and late Saturday, Dr. C.P. Fenwick, house physician for the Royal York Hotel, was called in. A nurse kept watch over him throughout the night.

"With no signs of improvement Sunday, Dr. W. Wray Barraclough, a [neurology] specialist, was summoned to the hotel and it was decided to remove Gallagher to Whitby Hospital for observation."

The description of Gallagher's condition, and the behavior he displayed, mirrored the symptoms of post-concussion syndrome, which include headache, dizziness, fatigue, irritability, anxiety, insomnia, and loss of concentration and memory. Extreme cases can include irrational acts, changes in mood, and a suspicious, argumentative, and stubborn nature.

"Gallagher seemed to be suffering from mental disorders Saturday night and Sunday," the *Border Cities Star* reported. "He recognized friends readily and conversed with members of the Leafs and Rangers team at the hotel, but frequently lapsed into incoherent conversation.

"Twice he wandered from his room. Unobserved by friends, he left the hotel and returned minus his topcoat and wristwatch. Apparently, he had given them away to persons he had encountered on the street."

Things grew even more bizarre once the decision was made to transport Gallagher to the psychiatric ward for further tests.

"He was placed in the charge of a nurse and started out by automobile [for Whitby], but while on the way he jumped from the speeding car and then caught another travelling in the opposite direction while it was going 40 miles an hour," reported the *Gazette*.

Police were called in to locate Gallagher and found him a short while later.

"He did not become violent at any time, but it was necessary to commission two policemen to accompany him in the auto to Whitby," the *Border Cities Star* noted.

Gallagher was eventually transferred to the psychiatric ward in Penetanguishene, Ontario, where the more difficult cases of mental illness were treated. His absence was described in newspaper reports as a nervous breakdown caused by the strain and stress of the season and head injuries.

Gallagher arrived at training camp with the Wings in the fall of 1933, but after a few sessions, it became clear that all was not well. Complaining of severe head pain, Gallagher discontinued workouts, and X-rays revealed pressure on the brain.

He underwent what was described as "a major brain operation" on October 30, 1933, at Detroit's Harper Hospital, performed by noted neurosurgeon Dr. Frederic Schreiber, who cut an opening through Gallagher's skull to relieve the pressure on his brain.

Border Cities Star sports columnist Vern DeGeer visited Gallagher in the hospital a few days after his surgery and noticed a complete turnaround in Gallagher's behavior.

"Johnny was more like his genial self than he had been at any time since last spring," DeGeer wrote.

The Wings were confident that they'd soon have their man again in the lineup.

"Johnny should be back with us within five or six weeks at the latest," Detroit coach/GM Jack Adams told the *Border Cities Star*, but Gallagher's troubles were far from over.

He sat out all of the 1933–34 season recuperating from surgery, then when he sought to return to Detroit for the following campaign, even though a board of 12 medical examiners gave him a clean bill of health, Gallagher was informed by United States Immigration authorities that due to his stay in a psychiatric hospital, he would not be permitted to enter the country for a calendar year.

Unable to play in the US, Adams worked out a deal to loan Gallagher to the Windsor Bulldogs of the International League for the 1934–35 season, where he was able to play in all home games and in games at London and in Fort Erie, Ontario, which was home base for the Buffalo Bisons.

In the fall of 1935 Gallagher appeared before a board of United States Immigration medical examiners and officials and was cleared to enter the United States a few days later.

Gallagher spent the entire 1935–36 campaign with Detroit's International League farm club, the Detroit Olympics, then was traded to the New York Americans prior to the 1936–37 season. But he was reacquired by the Wings when the club suffered a rash of injuries along the blue line, and he helped Detroit retain the Stanley Cup title that the club had first won the previous spring.

Gallagher's playing days ended in 1939, and he returned to live in his birthplace of Kenora, Ontario, where he died on September 16, 1981, at the age of 72.

38 Normie Smith: The First Wing to Tell Jack Adams Where to Go

When Normie Smith first arrived in Detroit, he was set on pulling out all the stops to ensure he'd make the stops on the ice.

When Smith was asked to depart from Detroit, he determined that he would not play anywhere else.

It was a battle that he eventually won, a rarity in the fiefdom of pro hockey of the so-called Original Six era.

When the Red Wings acquired Smith from the St. Louis Eagles prior to the 1934–35 season, it was to be the netminder's third NHL stop. He'd launched his career with the Montreal Maroons in 1931–32.

Smith wanted to be certain that he remained on top of his game, so when he was away from the rink in his Windsor, Ontario, home, he didn't rest on his laurels. Instead, Smith would flip the living room sofa on its side, don his gear, position himself in front of his makeshift net, and have his wife fire pucks at him.

Regardless, there was unrest over whether the inexperienced Smith was the answer between the pipes for a team that was a legitimate Stanley Cup contender. Smith heard the jeers of Detroit fans at Olympia Stadium, and behind the scenes Detroit coach and general manager Jack Adams worked the phones seeking a replacement.

Adams, who suggested that high-end NHL netminders were worth more to a hockey team than 20-game-winning pitchers were to baseball clubs, offered the Montreal Canadiens $20,000 for goalie Wilf Cude, who had backstopped Detroit to the 1934 Stanley Cup Finals, but the Habs declined his overtures.

Come playoff time, the Wings were happy they'd kept Smith. He posted consecutive shutouts in his first two Stanley Cup games and backstopped the Wings to their first Stanley Cup title, winning the Vezina Trophy as the NHL's top goalie.

"Now that he has the confidence, Normie Smith will become one of the greatest goalminders of hockey," Adams told the *Ottawa Journal*, insisting he'd been wrong to pursue Cude so vociferously.

The Wings won another Cup in 1936–37, although Smith missed much of the playoffs due to an elbow injury.

Once he had stature in the game, Smith also looked to improve his status. In an era when players basically accepted contract terms from teams with little fuss, Adams learned that Smith was a hard man to deal with. When 1937 contract negotiations between Smith and Adams reached an impasse, Adams sought to lighten the mood, reaching into his desk drawer and pulling out a footlong piece of lead pipe.

"How do you like my new invention?" Adams asked Smith, according to the Canadian Press. "It's a new goal post that is covered with a thin rubberoid. Players won't fracture their skulls so easily if they crash into it."

Adams handed the pipe to his goalie. "That's swell," Smith said, quickly raising the pipe above Adams' head and gripping it with both hands like a baseball bat. "Now will you give me what I ask?"

That was the end of the debate. Smith got his raise.

The Wings, though, were about to sink. They missed the play-offs in 1937–38, and when Smith lost his first four starts of the

1938–39 season and then missed a train to New York for a game against the Rangers, Adams first indefinitely suspended his goalie and fined him $150, and then assigned him to the minor league Pittsburgh Hornets of the International-American Hockey League.

Smith suited up for one IAHL game—a 5–0 loss to the Hershey Bears—and then announced that he was done.

"One night in Pittsburgh was enough for me," Smith explained to the Associated Press, insisting that Adams had shown him a telegram from Wings owner James Norris saying that he'd only have to play the one game before returning to the NHL ranks. He told the AP, "I won't play minor-league hockey. I am either good enough to play for the Red Wings or not at all.

"I told Adams at the start of the season that when I had to play minor-league hockey, I was through. And I am. Detroit is my home and my living is there, and I intend to stay."

Adams contacted Boston GM Art Ross and shipped Smith's rights to the Bruins along with $10,000 for four-time Vezina winner Cecil "Tiny" Thompson. Boston assigned Smith to Providence of the IAHL, but Smith wasn't about to play minor-pro hockey for the Bruins, either, and retired from hockey.

The main reason why Smith could tell Adams where to go— and, in essence, where he wouldn't go—was because he'd landed himself a plum job in Detroit with the Ford Motor Company.

Harry Bennett was a wiry little man who always wore a big bow tie. He was also Henry Ford's most trusted lieutenant. Bennett was a huge sports fan and liked to surround himself with athletes. Baseball's Wally Pipp and Eddie Cicotte and football's Jim Thorpe were other Bennett hires.

Smith was hired to work as Bennett's assistant, and when the Wings sought to send him packing, he opted to pack it in and go to work for Ford full-time.

It wasn't long until the Wings sought to get Smith back.

With so many players unavailable to NHL teams due to the war effort, in 1943 Adams sought to deploy Smith as a practice goalie. After only a couple of workouts, Adams realized that Smith had lost none of his game and was clearly Detroit's best goalie, so Adams approached Smith about coming out of retirement and rejoining the Red Wings.

At work in a war factory, Smith would only be available for home games, but soon, it appeared that he wouldn't be available at all.

Ross quickly reminded Adams of two things—his old opinion of what a top NHL goalie is worth and that the Bruins owned Smith's rights.

"How much do you think Smith is worth?" Ross asked Adams.

"I'd give, rather I'd ask, $10,000 for him," Adams replied.

Realizing he'd snared Adams in his own trap, Ross rapidly countered his adversary. "You were right the first time, for you'd have to give," Ross said. "We happen to own Smith."

Thinking at first that Ross was joking, Adams smiled, then he recalled their 1938 trade. "You're right," he sighed. "You do."

"I had forgotten all about the deal when I engaged Smith this season, for I hadn't seen him on any club's reserve list," Adams told the Associated Press.

Then, it was Ross who was smiling. "Well, stop worrying, Jack," Ross said. "The Boston Bruins take great pleasure in presenting Smith to your club as a New Year's gift. I realize that he would never play for any other club."

Smith suited up five games during the 1943–44 season and one more in 1944–45 before leaving the game for good, knowing a sensation that no other Red Wings player had savored up to that point.

He got Adams' goat.

39 Winging It to the Stanley Cup

Stanley Cup heroes come in all shapes and sizes: Goalies who stand on their head. Muckers who pop in a rare goal at exactly the right time. Veterans who deliver the goods when called upon. And rookies who seemingly come out of nowhere to shine under the spotlight's glare.

In NHL history, 26 players hold the rarest of honors—earning a Stanley Cup title before they'd ever played a regular-season NHL game.

"For me it was a surreal thing," recalled current Red Wings forward Drew Miller, who won a Stanley Cup with Anaheim in 2007. His first NHL action came in Game 5 of Anaheim's opening-round series clincher against the Minnesota Wild.

"I just couldn't believe it. I knew I wanted to get to the NHL, but I never thought in my first season, after playing the whole year in the minors, that they would call me up in the playoffs at such an important time of the season."

While Miller didn't do it as a Red Wing, five other players have known the unique feeling of earning a Stanley Cup this way while wearing a Detroit uniform, an NHL record.

This amazing achievement was first accomplished by two goaltenders during Detroit's run to its second straight Stanley Cup engraving in the spring of 1937.

In Game 3 of the Wings' semifinals series with the Montreal Canadiens, Detroit goalie Normie Smith injured his right elbow in the second period, suffering a torn ligament and nerve damage when teammate Herbie Lewis fell on him. With Smith unable to continue, spare netminder Jimmy Franks hurriedly donned his gear in the Detroit dressing room.

Signed as a pro prior to the season, Franks played part of his rookie campaign with Detroit's farm club in Pittsburgh but hadn't played in quite some time when he was called into action in the midst of the Stanley Cup Playoffs.

Seven years earlier, when Franks was a juvenile netminder in his hometown of Melville, Saskatchewan, the senior goalie in town was Wilf Cude, who just happened to be guarding the Canadiens' net at the other end of the ice. As Franks suited up, a messenger delivered him a handwritten note. It was from Cude, wishing Franks all the best of luck on his NHL debut. When they skated out to resume the contest, Franks and Cude waved to each other from their respective nets.

Detroit was down 1–0 at the time Franks entered the game. The Wings tied it early in the third period, but two Montreal goals in the final 10 minutes earned the Habs a 3–1 win.

At the end of the game, Cude skated the length of ice to shake Franks' hand and congratulate him on how well he played, a factor agreed upon by the Detroit brass.

"It was just his lack of experience, not anything wrong with his mechanical skill, that made the difference," Wings owner James Norris told the *Montreal Gazette* of Franks, who would never play another Stanley Cup game.

Detroit coach Jack Adams opted to recall the more experienced Earl Robertson from Pittsburgh for Game 4, sending Franks down to fill his spot. Robertson was also new to NHL competition and lost his debut 3–1. Facing elimination in Game 5, the Wings went back to Smith and were 2–1 winners on Hec Kilrea's goal in triple-overtime, advancing to face the New York Rangers in the Stanley Cup Finals.

But when Smith was unable to continue after one period of the series opener, Robertson took over, and things looked bleak as the Rangers rolled to a 5–1 triumph. He bounced back to win Game 2 by a 4–2 count and then allowed just one goal over the next three games, posting back-to-back shutouts in the last two games of the set as the Wings won the Cup in the maximum five games.

"Robbie, you're wonderful," Adams said as he wrapped his pinch-hitting goalie in a bear hug.

"I could die happy today," Robertson told the *Windsor Star* afterward.

His teammates predicted a long NHL career for their new puck-stopper. "They just can't keep you in the minors now," forward Marty Barry said. "You were great, kid—sensational."

Even the vanquished Rangers acknowledged that Robertson was the difference maker. "Robbie was unbeatable," New York forward Butch Keeling said.

Robertson would stay in the NHL, but elsewhere. He was dealt by Detroit to the New York Americans.

Thirteen years later, the Wings and Rangers again battled in the Cup, and a trio of Detroiters made their NHL debuts in this Stanley Cup run.

When Detroit star Gordie Howe suffered life-threatening head injuries in the playoff opener against Toronto, the Wings recalled forward Gord Haidy from Indianapolis of the AHL. Haidy dressed for Game 4 of this semifinals series, a 2–1 Detroit double-overtime win, and was used sparingly during the first two periods on a line with George Gee and Steve Black before being welded to the bench for the third period and overtime.

Someone who marched to the beat of a different drummer, Haidy wasn't afraid to tell Adams what he thought of some of his ideas, and wasn't averse to walking away from a contract offer he didn't find to be enough, as former Detroit coach Jimmy Skinner once explained to the *Windsor Star*.

"I was going through the lobby one night when I happened to spot Gord and suddenly remembered that he hadn't signed his contract yet," Skinner recalled. "I had some other business to attend to first, so I told him to come up to my room in about an hour. He promised he would. He never showed up.

"The next day at practice, I asked him what had happened and he said he had forgotten all about the appointment. Imagine a pro athlete forgetting such a thing as a chance to talk about money.

"Just for fun I decided to see how long he would let it go. Believe it or not, he never did come around, and I finally handed him his contract to sign just before the Indianapolis team, to which we had assigned him, left Detroit to open the season."

The Wings also recalled forward Doug McKay during the playoffs, and he made his NHL debut in Game 3 of the final set against the Rangers, two nights after picking up an assist in a 3–2 victory as Indianapolis beat Cleveland to win the Calder Cup title. McKay's NHL career was shorter than Haidy's—he played just one brief shift in the third period and, like Haidy, never appeared in another NHL game.

Haidy and McKay did accomplish another unique feat, winning the Stanley Cup and Calder Cup in the same season. And McKay and Chris Hayes of the 1971–72 Boston Bruins remain the only players to skate their lone NHL game in the Stanley Cup Finals for a Cup-winning team.

The third member of the Detroit debut group that spring enjoyed a vastly more successful NHL career.

Defenseman Marcel Pronovost, still a teenager and a rookie with Detroit's USHL farm club in Omaha, was recalled when the Knights concluded their playoffs and immediately inserted into the Wings' lineup for Game 5 of the semifinals series against Toronto.

Pronovost wouldn't come out the rest of the way and immediately turned heads with his poise and skill level.

"The 19-year-old Pronovost, another Omaha recruit, will be working regularly on defense," wrote Paul Chandler in the *Detroit News* as the two teams headed to Game 7. "Pronovost was a dazzling discovery in the two games. He seems to be the most promising defenseman to appear in the National Hockey League in years."

Pronovost stayed in Detroit through 1965, winning four Stanley Cups, and added a fifth in 1967 when traded to the Leafs. He won three more as a scout with the New Jersey Devils and was inducted into the Hockey Hall of Fame in 1978.

The key to his success was that Pronovost felt instantly that he belonged in the NHL the moment he arrived in Detroit.

"A lot of people ask me if I was surprised to be called up from two leagues below the NHL to skate in the Stanley Cup Playoffs without a game of NHL experience, but to tell the truth, I wasn't shocked at all," Pronovost said. "I was a confident kid. When I signed my C-form contract with Detroit in 1947, I figured, 'I'm there.'

"Indianapolis, they were in the playoffs in the AHL, so it made sense that the big club would call."

40 The Brawl of the Century

The headline in the March 29, 1940, edition of the *Windsor Daily Star* said it all: GREATEST BRAWL IN HISTORY CLIMAXES WINGS' ELIMINATION.

It was Game 2 of the best-of-three Stanley Cup semifinals series between the Red Wings and Toronto Maple Leafs, and of the many showdowns in the storied rivalry between these two Original Six franchises, reporter Doug Vaughan reported that this was "a chapter of unreasoning hysteria, written with flailing fists and punctuated with blood, black eyes, busted noggins, and bruised bones."

The tone of the evening was set early, when Toronto defenseman Rudolph "Bingo" Kampman crushed Detroit right-winger Cecil Dillon hard into the boards, twisting Dillon's knee and finishing his night. In the second period, Toronto defenseman Reginald "Red" Horner and Detroit rear guard Alex Motter doffed the mitts and tangled, Horner's fists leaving Motter with significant swelling over his left eye. They continued their fight in the penalty box, and local police were called in to break up the combatants.

Later in the frame, Red Wings forward Don Grosso planted his stick under the chin of Toronto rookie Hank Goldup and lifted Goldup over the boards and into the laps of some surprised rinkside fans. Goldup struck his head on the cement floor as he fell. Spectators helped the groggy Toronto player to get back to his feet, and he had to be assisted from the ice.

Early in the third period, Detroit defenseman Jimmy Orlando was assessed a major penalty after he cut open Horner behind the ear with a high stick. But the mayhem truly started in the last minute of play, shortly after Syd Howe scored for the Wings to narrow Toronto's lead to 3–1.

The melee was ignited when Detroit's Sid Abel and Toronto's Gus Marker engaged in a wrestling match near the Leafs' blue line. Within an instant, every player on the ice dropped their gloves and engaged an opponent in fisticuffs. Remaining players from both teams streamed over the boards to join the donnybrook.

"It was here a fight, there a fight, everywhere a fight," Vaughan wrote.

Detroit tough guy Orlando and Toronto captain Syl Apps took center stage, standing toe to toe and trading blows for a full five minutes. Orlando wasn't done, though. After pummeling Apps, he sought out Horner, the NHL's heavyweight champion, who'd left the penalty box to join the fray. They scrapped once, separated, then later in the fray found each other again and tangoed a second time.

Everyone on the ice fought, including both netminders. Detroit's Cecil "Tiny" Thompson put a severe pummeling on Toronto forward Pete Langelle, while Toronto's Walter "Turk" Broda was involved in three separate fistic encounters, tangling with Detroit's Ebbie Goodfellow, Ken Kilrea, and "Black" Jack Stewart.

Ten minutes into the brawl, things subsided, but it turned out that the players were merely catching their breath. Finding new dance partners, they got back to punching, and only sheer exhaustion finally brought a halt to the scraps. The last two to be engaged were Orlando and Horner, who continued to trade blows a full minute after everyone else had ceased fire.

With peace finally restored, referee Ted Graham assessed majors and misconducts to Marker and Abel, a major to Orlando, and a misconduct to Horner for leaving the penalty box to fight. Every player who left the bench to join the altercation was fined $25 by the NHL.

While seated in the penalty box, Horner was slugged in the back of the head by an overzealous fan. Fist cocked, he turned to return the favor, but the eight-time NHL penalty-minute leader chose the gentlemanly route and pulled his punch when he realized his assailant was a woman.

Another fan who swung at Detroit coach Jack Adams as the Wings headed to their dressing room at the conclusion of the game wasn't as lucky. Adams decked him.

Toronto moved on to the Stanley Cup Finals but lost the best-of-seven set to the New York Rangers in six games.

41 Luke Glendening Is Hockey's Mr. Outside

For the longest time, Luke Glendening seemed to be on the outside looking in when it came to the NHL dream, so perhaps it's only appropriate, then, that he should be the man who's played more outdoor games than any player in hockey history.

Five times the Red Wings center has skated in outdoor games in three different leagues, even playing in a pair of them that were separated by three days.

Glendening's outdoor odyssey began February 6, 2010, when he played for the Michigan Wolverines before 55,032 in the Camp Randall Hockey Classic at Camp Randall Stadium against the Wisconsin Badgers and future Detroit teammate Brendan Smith, dropping a 3–2 decision.

Later that year, on December 11, Glendening and the Wolverines played host to the Michigan State Spartans in the Big Chill at the Big House, setting a world-record attendance of 104,173, and the Wolverines blanked their archrivals 5–0.

"I remember walking out there for the first time, and it was just unbelievable," Glendening said. "I had seen football games there, and one of the Michigan hockey conditioning tests is running the stadium, so I had run the stadium before, and I'd been in it a lot.

"To get in there and just see the place packed was unbelievable. There is no other way to describe it."

A little over a year later, on January 15, 2012, Glendening made it a hat trick of outdoor contests at the NCAA level when he and the Wolverines traveled to Cleveland's Progressive Field to face Ohio State in the Frozen Diamond Faceoff, as Michigan downed the Buckeyes 4–1 before a gathering of 25,864.

Luke Glendening's Outdoor Odyssey

With Michigan (NCAA):
February 6, 2010, at Camp Randall Stadium vs. Wisconsin (lost 3–2)
December 11, 2010, at Michigan Stadium vs. Michigan State
   (won 5–0)
January 15, 2012, at Progressive Field vs. Ohio State (won 4–1)

With Grand Rapids (AHL):
December 30, 2013, at Comerica Park vs. Toronto Marlies
   (lost 4–3 in shootout)

With Detroit Red Wings (NHL):
January 1, 2014, at Michigan Stadium vs. Toronto Maple Leafs
   (lost 3–2 in shootout)

All this from a guy who had to battle to earn a spot on the Wolverines roster.

"He came to Michigan as a walk-on, a recruited walk-on with no promise that he'd ever play," recalled Michigan coach and former Red Wings center Red Berenson. "He just wanted a chance with the team.

"He hadn't been drafted, hadn't been highly recruited, but he made a mark every day in practice. He ended up being our captain his junior and senior years. He never led the team in scoring, but he was our leader on and off the ice."

A native of Grand Rapids, Michigan, Glendening signed an American Hockey League contract with the hometown Griffins for the 2012–13 season and after one season there earned a one-year, two-way pact with the Wings in the summer of 2013.

Glendening made his NHL debut with the Wings during the 2013–14 season but was sent down to Grand Rapids just prior to the Griffins' December 30, 2013, outdoor game at Comerica Park against the Toronto Marlies, part of the Hockeytown Winter Festival.

"I wasn't sure he was going to be able to play in the [January 1, 2014, Winter Classic] for us," Detroit coach Mike Babcock said. "I thought it was unfair if he didn't play [in either outdoor game]."

Glendening turned in his best individual performance of his outdoor career, scoring twice, but the Marlies won 4–3 in a shootout before a crowd of 20,337 at the home of the Detroit Tigers.

"It was special. It was in Detroit," Glendening recalled. "I've been coming to Tigers games with my family and friends my whole life, so to get to play there was fun.

"Obviously we were frustrated by the outcome, but to soak in the whole experience was special. I was looking around a lot and just trying to soak it all in."

On the ride home from the game, Glendening got some startling news. Deciding he needed another center for the Winter Classic at Michigan Stadium against the Toronto Maple Leafs, Babcock recalled Glendening for the game.

"I was driving home with my mom and got a call from [Grand Rapids coach Jeff] Blashill that I needed to be [in Ann Arbor] by 11:00 [AM the next day for practice]," Glendening remembered. "I was so excited."

Though his team wasn't hailed as a victor—Toronto were 3–2 winners in a shootout—Glendening was just thrilled to be back where he'd attended college and was the only player on the ice who wasn't skating in his first game at the Big House.

"It was great to be back on the ice," Glendening said. "To be back in Ann Arbor is fun for me. It was a little overwhelming, but I just tried to take it all in and enjoy it.

"The fact that I went [t]here and played a game [t]here, at the Big House before, all of that culminated together and made it extra special. I had planned on watching that one on TV, excited to see how it turned out. When I had the opportunity to be a part of it, I was excited.

"I had a great time playing in the game with Grand Rapids. That was a special moment, special game, but obviously it was a little disheartening to think I was not going to be able to play in [the Winter Classic].

"Once I had the opportunity, it was pretty cool."

Berenson wasn't surprised to see his old student skating on hockey's biggest stage.

"Now he's showing that he can play pro hockey, and now he's in the NHL," Berenson said. "He's a good example for young kids that aren't getting all the attention and aren't draftable and aren't this and aren't that, but they really want a chance."

As Glendening has proven time and again, being on the outside isn't always a bad thing.

42 Three Up, Three Down, Times Two

Only one NHL team has ever won three games in a row in a Stanley Cup Finals series and not won the Cup, and it was the Red Wings. In fact, they've done it twice.

The Toronto Maple Leafs were known as the bridesmaids of the NHL. They'd been to the Stanley Cup Finals seven times in 10 years but owned just one title in that span.

The Leafs were favored to take the Wings in the 1942 Cup Finals, but the form charts went out of whack as Detroit opened the set with 3–2, 4–2, and 5–2 victories. "They're unbeatable," Toronto goalie Turk Broda told the Canadian Press of the Wings. "They're too hot. They can't seem to do anything wrong."

Naturally, the Wings were a confident bunch. "If we keep right on the way we're going—well, we ought to wind it up soon," Detroit coach and GM Jack Adams said.

Looking to shake his team out of its doldrums, Toronto coach Hap Day dramatically altered his lineup for Game 4. He dropped veteran defenseman Bucko McDonald and forwards Hank Goldup and Gordie Drillon—the 1937–38 NHL scoring champion—in favor of Ernie Dickens, Gaye Stewart, and Don Metz.

The shakeup worked when the Leafs posted a 4–3 victory to stave off elimination, and things really began to go off the rails for the Wings late in the contest. In the last minute of play, Detroit forward Eddie Wares was assessed a misconduct and $50 fine by referee Mel Harwood after he refused to get set for a faceoff. When Wares wouldn't leave the ice, a minor penalty was added to his infractions, and Don Grosso was designated to serve the penalty. But as he headed to the penalty box, Grosso dropped his gloves and stick and left them on the ice, so Harwood fined him $25.

Grosso accused Harwood of using abusive and foul language toward him. "I just asked him to throw the puck down, and he started calling me names," Grosso told the Canadian Press.

Meanwhile, Wares wouldn't go to the penalty box because he insisted that Harwood explain the infraction for which he was penalized. "When I asked what I had done, Harwood refused to say, and I refused to leave the ice," Wares explained.

As the game ended, Wares and Grosso engaged in a shouting match with Harwood near the penalty box. Meanwhile, Adams charged across the ice and began trading punches with the referee.

The next day, Adams was suspended for the remainder of the series by NHL president Frank Calder, who did allow the Detroit coach to be in the dressing room between periods and in the seats, but he could not be on the bench. The fines to Wares and Grosso were both increased to $100, and Wares grew cryptic about where the series was headed.

"You know what's going to happen?" Wares assessed. "It's going to go seven games."

When Toronto whipped Detroit 9–3 in Game 5 and then Broda blanked them 3–0 in Game 6, Wares proved a prophet.

In Game 7 at Maple Leaf Gardens, Syd Howe gave Detroit the lead in the second period. The Wings were just 12:13 away from lifting Lord Stanley's mug when Jimmy Orlando was penalized for tripping Toronto captain Syl Apps. Just as Orlando stepped back on the ice, Sweeney Schriner tied it, and two minutes later, Pete Langelle scored the eventual Cup winner for the Leafs in a 3–1 victory.

Toronto outshot Detroit 16–7 in the final frame of the series.

"It was while I was off that the Leafs really turned it on," Orlando told the Canadian Press. "Someone had to lose, and we just happened to be the unlucky ones."

Detroit captain Sid Abel tipped his cap in tribute to Toronto, feeling the depth of the Maple Leafs ultimately wore down the Wings. "The Leafs had three strong lines on the ice all the time, which wasn't always the case with us."

"They had a little better club," agreed Ebbie Goodfellow, who coached Detroit the last three games during the enforced absence of Adams.

Leafs coach Hap Day was exhausted at the end of the set. "We did it the hard way," Day said. "There will never be another experience like this."

Well, no, but three springs later, the same two teams came close to a repeat performance, in reverse roles.

Detroit were the favorites in the 1945 Cup Finals, but it was Toronto, behind the sensational netminding of rookie Frank McCool, that rolled to a 3–0 series lead on 1–0, 2–0, and 1–0 victories. It was the first time in a Cup Final set that a goalie had posted three consecutive shutouts.

"It looks like the puck is never going to go in again for us," Adams lamented to the Canadian Press. "I guess we'll have to take the series the hard way."

Detroit forward Mud Bruneteau, part of the vanquished Wings in 1942, felt that they were up to the challenge.

"They can't be that good," Bruneteau said of the Leafs. "We have to win four straight and we can do it."

They nearly did.

After a 5–3 win in Game 4, it was the turn of rookie Detroit goalie Harry Lumley—at 18 the youngest goalie to play in a Cup Finals series in NHL history—to get the whitewash brush out. Lumley posted 2–0 and 1–0 shutouts, and the two teams were headed to a decisive Game 7 at Olympia Stadium.

Mel Hill gave the Leafs the lead, but Murray Armstrong tied it at 8:16 of the third period. Almost four minutes later, Detroit's Syd Howe went to the sin bin for high-sticking Toronto's Gus Bodnar. He'd barely settled into the penalty box when Babe Pratt fed a pass to Nick Metz, who fired a low shot at Lumley. The Detroit goalie got a pad on it, but before he could corral the rebound, Pratt lurched in to bat home the rebound for the Cup winner in a 2–1 Toronto victory.

The Wings became the first team in NHL history to lose Game 7 of the Stanley Cup Finals on home ice. And they remain the only franchise to win three successive games in a Stanley Cup Finals series and not lift the Cup.

43 Darren Helm Is Usain Bolt on Ice

Chicago Blackhawks captain Jonathan Toews has been chasing Red Wings center Darren Helm around the ice since both were 10-year-old kids playing youth hockey in the Winnipeg suburbs, and he admits all that pursuit is beginning to wear on him.

Darren Helm—perhaps the fastest man on ice—skates against the Dallas Stars in Detroit on November 7, 2013.

"He could always fly," Toews said. "We can't lose track of him, because he's got a great jump and he can beat you. He can make a difference."

The old saying that speed kills was never more appropriate than in Helm's case. He utilizes his wheels mainly in a penalty-killing and checking role but is able to create numerous scoring chances thanks to his blazing blades.

"He's the fastest skater in the NHL," Toews said early in Helm's career. Detroit scout and former Helm teammate Kris

Draper is willing to amp up the praise even further, comparing Helm to the quickest man on the planet.

"I would put him in the class with the fastest man in the world, Usain Bolt," Draper said, referring to the man who captured the gold medals in the 100 and 200 meters at both the 2008 and 2012 Summer Olympic Games.

Draper was known for his breakaway pace when he played more than 1,000 games in a Detroit uniform, but willingly hands the crown as hockey's fastest man to Helm.

"He's faster than me," Draper said. "I'm okay with that. In a race, I might be able to slide in and get a silver or bronze.

"The kid just flat-out flies. His first couple of strides, he just explodes. He's very agile, too. He's just a pure, power skater. The way he finishes checks is so impressive. He gets there fast, and he gets there with so much speed, he can really lay on the body."

Helm joked that his speed is the result of being a younger brother growing up in St. Andrews, Manitoba.

"Being a young kid, my older brother would say, 'Go get something, and I'll time you,'" Helm recalled. "I would always bite on that real hard and be racing up and down the stairs for my brothers."

Playing junior with the Medicine Hat Tigers of the Western Hockey League, Helm recognized that his skating ability was definitely capable of separating him from others, both literally on the ice and figuratively in the eyes of pro scouts, but it wasn't until he was first called up by the Red Wings during the 2007–08 season that he came to understand that he possessed world-class speed.

"Probably my first year [in the NHL] was when I started to realize that," Helm said. "Guys were always joking around in the dressing room here, seeing that I got a few chances with my speed and breakaways from chasing down loose pucks. I knew that was going to play a big role in my career."

"I was always working hard at that in junior. I would be training all summer, working with a trainer, working constantly on my speed and the power in my legs. I've always brought speed and energy. I saw that as an asset of mine. I've been working on it a long time," Helm continued.

Joe McDonnell, a Wings scout when Helm was selected 132nd overall in the 2005 NHL entry draft, agreed that it was Helm's blazing speed that caught their eye. "He skated like the wind, competed really hard, made plays as a 17-year-old at a high level," McDonnell remembered. "He is so strong from the waist down, so strong on his skates, and this was what we liked about him."

Helm remembers well the battles with Toews and appreciates that one of the game's most talented players puts him atop the speed demon list.

"We had some good battles here and there," Helm said. "He's a very good player in this league. I have a lot of respect for him, and for him to say that means a lot."

44 A Reluctant Flash Was the First Blue-Liner to Pop 20

The moment that Bill "Flash" Hollett became a Detroit Red Wing wasn't a day of celebration for the veteran defenseman. Soon, though, he had 20 good reasons to remember his time in Detroit.

At first, Hollett insisted that he would never don the Winged Wheel. Dealt to the Red Wings January 5, 1944, by the Boston Bruins, his NHL home for the previous nine years, Hollett was adamant that he wouldn't go to Detroit.

"I don't mind saying I am deeply hurt," Hollett told the Canadian Press after the trade was announced. "As long as I am able to play hockey I want to play in Boston. I have been here nine years and it is like home to me. I'm going home and will not play for Detroit."

Hollett was even more insistent that the Red Wings weren't going to be a part of his future in an interview with the *Boston Herald*. "I'm grabbing the 4:50 for Toronto and what happens from then on is in the laps of the gods," Hollett said. "No, I'm not taking my skates. I'll leave them here. My wife has been after me to quit hockey for three years now, and maybe I'll quit and get a job up home. I've got a nice fruit farm at Clarkson, about 17 miles outside of Toronto. I'm disappointed over it and I want a couple of days' rest to think it over.

"You know I love to play hockey here. Yeah, I know about the money angle, but money isn't everything. I know that being shifted from one city to another is part of a hockey player's career, but that doesn't lessen my disappointment."

Hollett headed back home to Clarkson, and Detroit coach and GM Jack Adams was left dumbfounded by the actions of his newly acquired player.

"What does he think Detroit is—Siberia?" Adams asked. "What's the matter with him? We like him in Detroit. He's a great hockey player and he'll like Detroit as soon as he spends a little time there.

"If it's money that's bothering him, we will take care of that, too. If he's worrying about playoff money and a bonus, he shouldn't count us out. We're going to be in.

"We're the Stanley Cup champions and the Bruins have beaten us only once this year. What's he upset about?"

Pat Egan, a rugged body-checker and puck-mover who was favorably compared to legendary former Bruins defenseman Eddie Shore, was the player Detroit shipped to Boston for Hollett, and he couldn't have been more delighted. He'd grown weary of playing for Adams, who'd put a tight rein on Egan's rushing of the puck, and sought more freedom to play his game, something that the Bruins offered him.

"I can't get there fast enough," Egan said.

After a little time to cool down, Hollett also softened his hard stance, reaching out to Adams, calling him on the phone. After their conversation, Adams felt confident that he'd get his man.

"I talked to Hollett," Adams told the Associated Press. "He says he has some grievances with the Boston club in connection with the deal, but I think maybe we can fix things up. Anyway, he made the call and I'm quite sure he's interested in staying in the National Hockey League."

Boston GM Art Ross, who a year earlier turned down a $25,000 offer from the New York Rangers for Hollett, also did his best to calm the waters, praising Hollett for his years in Boston, which saw the Bruins win Stanley Cups in 1938–39 and 1940–41. Hollett scored the Stanley Cup–clinching goal in 1939 and was selected to the NHL Second All-Star team in 1942–43 after setting the NHL record for points in a season by a defenseman (44) and tying the league standard he'd set the previous season for goals by a blue-liner (19).

"Flash Hollett has played with the Bruins for nine seasons," Ross told the *Ottawa Journal*. "He has been well-liked by the Boston fans. He has been a valuable man for us and we hope he continues to be just as valuable and outstanding in Detroit."

The day after he spoke with Adams, Hollett had a change of heart and reported to Detroit with a chip on his shoulder and a target replacing the *B* on the front of the Boston sweater.

Though he was a Red Wing, Hollett would never forgive Ross for sending him away from the home he loved so much, and he'd gain his vengeance on the ice.

One of the NHL's greatest rushing defensemen, Hollett was also considered among the NHL's most versatile players, capable of playing every position but goal. Equipped with blazing speed,

Detroit Defensemen Who Scored 20 Goals in a Season

Season	Defenseman	Goals
1944–45	Bill "Flash" Hollett	20
1979–80	Reed Larson	22
1980–81	Reed Larson	27
1981–82	Reed Larson	21
1982–83	Reed Larson	22
1983–84	Reed Larson	23
1999–00	Nicklas Lidstrom	20

it was that quickness afoot that led to Hollett's nickname. Others referred to Hollett as "the Smiling Defenseman" due to his seemingly ever-present grin.

His shot rated with the hardest in hockey, though it took Hollett, who broke into the NHL with the Ottawa Senators in 1933–34, a few seasons to harness his power.

"The Flash has always packed a terrific shot, even if he took some time to control it," noted the *Ottawa Journal*. "When he was a rookie getting a bit of experience with the old Senators in the NHL, he could rifle a puck as hard as anyone in the circuit, but he had an unfortunate habit of locating the rush end with some of his efforts."

By the time he arrived in Detroit, Hollett had polished all facets of his game to an elite level.

He was a solid performer for the Wings in 1943–44, collecting six goals and 18 points in 27 games, but blossomed into a record-setter the following season.

Named Detroit's captain for the 1944–45 season, the campaign opened with a game against his old club the Bruins, and Hollett started his route to history by putting a puck past Bruins goalie Harvey Bennett. A month later, Bennett was victimized for a pair of Hollett tallies, and 13 games into the year, Hollett already had collected eight goals.

A five-point night December 21 in an 11–3 rout of the Rangers included three goals, as Hollett became the first defenseman in franchise history to record a hat-trick, among five multi-goal games Hollett posted during the 1944–45 season.

Another two-goal performance against the Bruins, and Bennett allowed Hollett to tie his own league mark with 19 goals, but this time, he didn't stop there. Less than a minute into the second period of Detroit's 4–3 March 17, 1945, victory over Toronto at Maple Leaf Gardens, Hollett took a feed from Murray Armstrong and beat Frank McCool to become the first NHL defenseman to record a 20-goal season.

His old club proved to be his favorite victim, as Hollett, who vowed he would make Ross regret trading him, scored nine times against Boston.

Adams gloated to the *Montreal Gazette* about how lopsided the deal turned out in his favor. "Hollett's beaten Boston for us a half-dozen times almost by himself, but Egan hasn't been able to do anything right against us," Adams said. "The last time they played us Pat tried to give it to Hollett, but Flash saw him coming. Flash made a little deke and got out of the way and Pat hit one of his guys, young [Bill] Cupolo, and nearly knocked him through the rink. The kid was finished for the night."

Named to the NHL First All-Star team, Hollett also finished fourth in Hart Trophy voting as the Wings reached the Stanley Cup Finals before falling in seven games to Toronto. But though Flash shone brightly in the 1944–45 season, his star quickly flamed out in 1945–46.

Knee and groin injuries limited him to 38 games and 4–9–13 numbers. In June Adams dealt Hollett to the Rangers, but Hollett balked at the deal, went home, and this time retired for good.

His goals record held for much longer, however. No NHL rear guard reached the 20-goal plateau again until 1968–69, when Boston sensation Bobby Orr scored 21 times.

45 Joe Turner Made the Ultimate Sacrifice

The Red Wings believed that Joe Turner possessed a bright future.

A top prospect in their farm system, Turner led the Ontario Hockey Association in goals-against average with Stratford in 1937–38 and the following season with Guelph he was tops in shutouts. Advancing to senior hockey, he led the Michigan Ontario Hockey League in wins, shutouts, and GAA in 1939–40. Adjectives such as *brilliant* and *sensational* often accompanied published reports of his work between the pipes.

It was while playing in the MOHL, which played games at the Olympia, that Turner was spotted by Detroit GM Jack Adams, who was impressed by his lightning-quick reflexes. As an American Hockey League rookie with Indianapolis in 1941–42, Turner earned All-Star status while posting a league-leading 34 wins and backstopping the Capitols to the Calder Cup title. In December of that season, New York Rangers GM Lester Patrick sought to acquire Turner from the Wings, but Adams flatly refused to part with his budding prospect. Indianapolis fans came to refer to Turner as "No-No" because of his stinginess in net.

"He was the whole team in Indianapolis," former teammate Les Douglas remembered to the *National Post* in 1998. "We could attack all we wanted. We knew Joe was back there for us."

Late in that season, Turner earned his first look with the big club. When Johnny Mowers injured his leg in a practice mishap, Turner was called up for a February 5, 1942, date at Olympia Stadium against the Toronto Maple Leafs and played solidly in a 3–3 overtime tie, stopping former NHL scoring champion Gordie Drillon on a breakaway in the late stages of the game to preserve the tie.

He returned to finish the season with Indianapolis, and then in the summer, Turner signed up for a different squad. He enlisted in the United States Army.

"Jack Adams thought the world of him," Sid Abel, Detroit captain at the time, once recalled to the *National Post.* "As a player, I took it for granted that he would be our netminder.

"Then, the next thing we knew, he was gone to the Army. And then he was really gone."

Though he hailed from Windsor, Ontario, Turner met his wife, Mae, in Indianapolis and his father James worked as an electrician in Detroit, so it wasn't a surprise that he enlisted in the US military.

Turner rose to the rank of second lieutenant by the time he finally shipped out for combat duty in the winter of 1945. His unit was sent to the Hürtgen Forest along the Belgium-Germany border. A forerunner to the more famous Battle of the Bulge, it was in the Hürtgen Forest—known as "the Death Factory" by those lucky enough to survive the ordeal—where the US Army fought

His Biggest Save

Clarence "Dolly" Dolson, Detroit's goalie from 1928 to 1931, was reluctant to discuss his World War I combat duty. But when some members of his old unit visited him in Detroit, they revealed Dolson's heroism on the battlefields of France while fighting with the Canadian Army.

Eagle-eyed Dolson spotted a German grenade flying into their trench, and the goaltender in him took over. He blocked the shot, scooped up the rebound with the butt of his rifle, and cleared it back toward the enemy a split second before it exploded.

Luckily for Dolson and those in his unit, it was against the rules of hockey back then for a netminder to smother the puck.

Dolson was awarded the Distinguished Conduct Medal, the second-highest award for gallantry in action available to members of the Canadian military.

its longest battle in history, a three-month siege that cost American military forces an estimated 33,000 killed or incapacitated. Among that group was Turner.

Turner did basic training at Camp Buckner in North Carolina and was assigned to Company K, 311th Regiment, 78th Infantry Division, known as the Lightning Division. In the early hours of December 13, 1944, the 311th Infantry Regiment positioned itself to stage diversionary tactics. Lt. Turner's assault team received orders to move through the dense forest and attack a German machine-gun enclosure along the heavily fortified enemy lines.

The mission was to cause confusion among the enemy and distract attention away from the more intense attack being launched in the south. Immediately, Turner's unit was met with a hail of machine-gun fire and rained upon by mortars.

Turner was wounded in the initial assault, but when he heard the pleas of an injured comrade, he and another soldier set out to rescue him. They never returned.

Originally reported missing in action, on January 12, 1945, Turner was classified as killed in action, reportedly felled by German machine-gun fire. At first buried in an unmarked grave in Belgium, in 1950 his remains were returned home and interred in Windsor's Victoria Memorial Cemetery. Turner was 25 at the time of his death.

Turner's tour of duty was exactly like his NHL career. Both lasted one day.

After the war, the Red Wings helped organize the International Hockey League to replace the MOHL, which had disbanded when so many of its players enlisted, and the new league's championship trophy, the Turner Cup, was named to honor Joe Turner's memory.

The IHL folded in 2001, and the Turner Cup took up permanent residence in the Hockey Hall of Fame. But in 2010 the Central Hockey League named one of its conferences in Turner's memory and also created a new award, the Turner Trophy, to be presented annually to the conference champion.

"Joe Turner's heroic life is a symbol that all athletes should revere and appreciate," CHL commissioner Duane Lewis explained in announcing the recognition for Turner.

Turner and Dudley "Red" Garrett, a New York Rangers defenseman, were the only NHL players to lose their lives in combat during World War II. The AHL named its Rookie of the Year award in Garrett's memory.

46 Adams Was Not Always the NHL's Darth Vader

History has already judged the late Detroit Red Wings general manager Jack Adams to have been a managerial bully.

He ruled the Red Wings through intimidation and scare tactics. Many former players remember Adams walking around with Greyhound bus tickets poking out of his lapel pocket to remind players that they were always in danger of being sent to the minor leagues.

Adams played hardball in salary negotiations, often making players feel like they were indentured servants more than employees.

The general impression of Adams was that he was a tyrant who oppressed players and didn't pay them a fair wage.

"Trying to talk contract with Jack Adams was like going to hell," former Red Wings defenseman Benny Woit said.

Adams could get every player signed in a single afternoon, each negotiation lasting no more than 10 minutes or so. Players would file, one by one, into his office, and he would have three contracts drawn up for each player. One contract said the player would play for the NHL team, one contract said the player would play for a minor league team in Indianapolis, and the final contract was for a minor league team in Omaha.

The late Johnny Wilson once told of asking Adams for $14,000 per season in the 1950s and Adams showing him that he had a contract for $12,500 to play in Detroit, another contract at $9,500 to play in Indianapolis, and third contract to go to Omaha for $7,500.

"Where do you want to play?" Adams asked.

Wilson got Adams' point. "Give me the pen, and I'll sign right now for Detroit," Wilson said.

But the truth is that Adams' hockey savvy and business acumen helped the Red Wings navigate through difficult financial troubles in the 1930s. He came to the organization as the coach and general manager in 1927–28. Detroit was not Hockeytown in those days, and Adams spent considerable time figuring out how to coax fans into the building. Sometimes, he used his own money to pay players and team bills.

He would undoubtedly argue that he had to hold down player costs to make the team a viable business entity. Did the end justify the means? Players would argue no, although there were players through the years who believed Adams treated them fairly.

It's impossible to criticize Adams' knowledge of the game. As a player, he won the Stanley Cup with the Toronto Arenas in 1918 and Ottawa Senators in 1927.

As a coach, Adams guided the Detroit Red Wings to Stanley Cup titles in 1936, 1937, and 1943. Under his command as GM, the Red Wings won the Stanley Cup in 1950, 1952, 1954, and 1955.

Adams' stewardship yielded a steady stream of talented players, including Terry Sawchuk, Glenn Hall, Roger Crozier, Red Kelly, Ted Lindsay, Gordie Howe, and Alex Delvecchio, among others.

Before former Red Wings coach Jimmy Skinner died in 2007, he defended Adams' record in a lengthy interview. "I don't know how people can say that Jack was bad for the game," Skinner said.

But Skinner didn't dispute that Adams was a tough coach. "A lot of players and coaches were afraid of Jack Adams because he was a disciplined man," Skinner said. "He was a perfectionist, even at practice. He didn't like guys fooling around. A lot of guys resented that."

Clearly, sportswriters enjoyed regaling their readers with tales of Adams terrorizing players with his gruff, tough-love style. But Skinner said his acts of kindness were never reported.

"When Teddy [Lindsay] couldn't get rid of a cold in his chest, Jack handed Teddy some tickets to go to Florida for seven to 10 days," Skinner recalled. "And we were in the middle of a playoff fight."

When Mud Bruneteau's dad became ill midseason, Adams told the player to go home until his father was out of danger. That was not commonplace in that era.

"I can tell you that a lot of people wanted to be traded to the Red Wings," Skinner said. "If we traded them, they wanted to get traded back. When we traded Red Kelly, he had tears in his eyes."

Skinner said Adams' reputation for treating players unfairly in negotiations was simply a reflection that Adams believed he had to be loyal to the owner who was paying his salary.

"Jack didn't cut salaries," Skinner said. "He backed his people 100 percent. To Jack it was all about respect. He respected the players who played hard and he respected the people he worked for. If Jack got respect from a player, he did everything he could for the player."

In the end, Adams had more loyalty to ownership than they had for him. After spending more than three decades with the organization, Adams was fired abruptly in 1962. He died six years later.

"People behind the scenes put a knife into Jack," Skinner said. "When Jack got fired, he had tears in his eyes. Jack was very hurt. He put his whole life into that hockey club."

47 Gordie Was Not the First Howe to Star for the Red Wings

When rookie Gordie Howe played his first NHL game in 1946–47, Red Wings Coach Jack Adams truly had no idea who he had playing for him.

Howe has often told the story about Adams bellowing, "Syd. Syd, get in there" and then becoming furious when nobody moved.

Adams then looked directly at Howe, and said: "Get in there, Syd."

"But I'm not Syd," Howe said. "I'm Gordie."

"I don't give a damn," Adams supposedly said. "Get in there anyway."

It probably was excusable for Adams to confuse the first names because Syd Howe had been on Adams' bench for the 12 previous seasons, and Syd Howe had been Detroit's best player for most of those seasons. He helped Detroit win Stanley Cups in 1936, 1937, and 1943. Howe was on the ice when teammate Mud Bruneteau scored in the sixth overtime period to end the longest game in NHL history in 1936. Howe had also scored 25 seconds into overtime to win a playoff game in 1940.

When Gordie arrived in Detroit, it was common for people to ask him if he were related to Syd. He was not related to Syd, who was from Ottawa, Ontario.

It was natural to believe Gordie was related because Syd Howe had been an elite player as well. He never won a scoring title. Yet when he retired from the NHL in the summer of 1946, he was the NHL's all-time leading scorer.

The Red Wings paid $50,000 and gave up Teddy Graham to the financially troubled St. Louis Eagles for Syd Howe and another player named Ralph "Scotty" Bowman (Not THE Scotty Bowman)

Brother Combinations Who Were Detroit Teammates
Frank and Johnny Sheppard (1927-28)
Desse and Earl Roche (1934-35)
Hec and Wally Kilrea (1935-38)
Hec and Ken Kilrea (1939-40)
Ed and Mud Bruneteau (1940-41; 1943-46)
Carl and Dalton Smith (1943-44)
Johnny and Larry Wilson (1949-50; 1951-53)
Frank and Peter Mahovlich (1968-69)
Bryan and Dennis Hextall (1975-76)

in 1935. It turned out to be a sound investment because Howe developed into one of the NHL's most consistent offensive threats.

The *Ottawa Journal* once quoted the late Red Wings executive Jim Norris as saying Howe "saved the franchise and got the crowds coming."

When Howe died in 1976, the *Journal* wrote: "He was fast and clever and possessed of a great shot, and while some of the modern players still haven't learned to keep the shots low, Syd Howe had mastered that skill when he was just a boy on Ottawa's outdoor rinks."

Syd Howe was a versatile left wing who could also play center, right wing or defense.

His best NHL season had come in 1943–44 when he scored 32 goals and registered 28 assists for 60 points in 46 games.

Syd Howe is most remembered for setting the modern-day record of six goals scored in a game, set on February 3, 1944, in a 12-2 win against the New York Rangers. The woeful Rangers only won six of 50 games that season.

Howe scored a pair of goals in each period, in front of a crowd of 12,293 that included 900 safety patrol boys from area schools.

"They were going in the net tonight," Howe told the *Detroit News.* "I don't remember any goal in particular. The boys were feeding me nicely."

He told reporters that he wouldn't be participating in any revelry after the game. He needed to get home to get some sleep because he worked during the day as a machinist on a Ford assembly line.

"I'm due at work at 7:10 AM," Howe said.

When Howe retired, the team gave him a grand piano in a pregame ceremony at center ice. Syd Howe sat down and played it.

48 Detroit's Black Jack Didn't Like His Nickname

Following the 1942–43 season, defenseman Jack Stewart was voted the most popular player on the Stanley Cup–champion Detroit Red Wings.

"The greatest defenseman in the game today," Detroit GM Jack Adams told the *Ottawa Journal* in 1943.

Had the balloting been conducted league-wide, it's more likely that Stewart would have finished well up the track.

Hockey's biggest hitter in the 1940s wasn't exactly a big hit elsewhere.

Considered the king of NHL body checkers in his prime, when Stewart hit you, you stayed hit. In his first season with the Wings, Stewart lit into an unsuspecting Chicago Black Hawks player as he attempted to cross the Detroit blue line and dropped the fellow with such authority that he struck his head on the ice and was out cold.

Stretchered away, when the player came to, his first words were, "Who hit me with the blackjack?" With that, Black Jack Stewart was how the rugged Detroit defender was known forevermore.

On the ice, no one in an enemy uniform was Stewart's friend. Opponents recalled how Stewart's teeth would form a huge grin as he was about to lay them out with one of his patented hip checks. He once hit Toronto defenseman Gus Mortson so hard that Mortson's left leg shattered three inches above the ankle.

"There weren't too many who got by him," former Detroit defenseman Clare Martin said.

Some of Stewart's most memorable battles came against long-time Boston Bruins star Milt Schmidt.

"That thing started in the late 1930s and didn't end until 1954," Schmidt told the *Boston Herald* of his feud with Stewart. "There was no high-sticking or butt-ending in it, just two railroad cars colliding, or dog-eat-dog.

"It got so bad that [Boston GM] Art Ross threatened to bench me against Detroit. I once asked [Detroit forward] Joe Carveth what Stewart was mad about, and Joe said Stewart claimed I had hurt him, but I never remembered that."

In the *Boston Daily Record*, Schmidt remembered a discussion with Jimmy Peters Sr., when the latter was dealt from the Wings to Boston.

"Why are you and Stewart always at each other?" Peters asked Schmidt. "I know Jack pretty well. He's a nice guy."

"Oh yeah," Schmidt answered. "Wait and see what happens now when you're playing against him."

In their first meeting, Peters tried to go wide past Stewart, who caught Peters with a solid hip check and sent him spiraling into the air. Upon landing, Peters crawled his way back to the Boston bench.

"Milt," Peters said to Schmidt in a barely audible tone. "Now I know what you mean."

As rugged as he was to the opposition, Stewart also earned their respect, because he played the game tough but fair. He didn't use his stick on players and wasn't known to dish out cheap shots. That's why he didn't care for his nickname, because Stewart felt it made him out to be a dirty player.

"He was tough, as tough as anyone's ever been, but he was also one of the most likable fellows you'd ever want to meet," former teammate Sid Abel told the *Windsor Star* upon Stewart's 1983 death.

"Others called him Black Jack, but we on the team used to call him Silent Jack. He was a man of action, not words," Abel said.

Stewart was the E.F. Hutton of his era. He didn't say much, but when he spoke, people listened. He could intimidate anyone, including his own teammates.

Detroit was facing elimination against the New York Rangers in the 1950 Stanley Cup Finals when the soft-spoken Stewart felt it was time to hammer home a point.

"What I remember when we were down 3–2 was that we had a big meeting in Toledo, where we stayed during the playoffs," Detroit defenseman Marcel Pronovost recalled.

"Abel was [Stewart's] roommate. Bones Raleigh was playing for New York, and he was Sid's check. Jack said, 'Don Raleigh is making a fool out of you.'

"I remember Sid said, 'I was afraid to go to bed that night.'"

Abel scored two goals in Detroit's 5–4 Game 6 victory, and the Wings won 4–3 in Game 7 on Pete Babando's double-overtime goal.

Stewart insisted it was nothing personal, just business. Much like his feud with Schmidt.

"Schmidt was the most dangerous player in the league at that time, so I had to pay special attention to him," he told the *Springfield Union*. "He was one of the real good hockey players, and that line [of Schmidt, Woody Dumart, and Bobby Bauer] was the best I ever played against.

"As long as I could keep him bothered, he wasn't scoring goals. It was more of a benefit to us to have Milt worrying about me than playing the puck."

Stewart took more than 230 stitches to his face during his career, getting 33 of them in one gash from a stick during a game

Famous Red Wings Nicknames
The Mule—Johan Franzen
Mr. Hockey—Gordie Howe
The Count—Don Grosso
Scarface—Ted Lindsay
The Professor—Igor Larionov
Ol' Bootnose—Sid Abel
Papa Bear—Slava Fetisov
The Perfect Human—Nicklas Lidstrom
The Grim Reaper—Stu Grimson
Tombstone—Harvey Rockburn
The Big M—Frank Mahovlich
The Little M—Peter Mahovlich
Beast—Brad McCrimmon
Fido—Cliff Purpur
Dutch—Earl Reibel
Motor City Smitty—Brad Smith
Stumpy—Steve Thomas
Wild Thing—Howie Young
Monster—Jonas Gustavsson

against Toronto. Blood oozing through his bandages and smearing onto his sweater, Stewart returned to action and finished the game after being stitched up.

Longtime Boston Garden physician Dr. Tom Kelley rated Stewart as one of the toughest players who ever came through his infirmary—and with good reason.

"Stewart came into the first aid room before a game," Kelley recalled to the *Boston Traveler*. "He had two huge boils on his elbow and a fever because of the infection. I told him I would have to lance the boils right then and there and that he would have to go right back to the hotel and go to bed."

Stewart's answer caught Kelley off guard.

"He said, 'Listen, Doc, I just came in here to get the things dressed…and will you hurry up so I can get on the ice.'"

After hockey, Stewart became a respected harness-racing judge, and he proved to be as equally tough and fair with horse people as he'd been with hockey players.

"In hockey I used to take penalties," Stewart explained to the *Springfield Union* in 1966. "Now I hand them out."

49 Turk Broda: The One Who Got Away

After the Detroit Red Wings opened the 1936 Stanley Cup Finals with a 3–1 victory over the Toronto Maple Leafs, Detroit coach/ GM Jack Adams sought to get a further dig in at Toronto owner Conn Smythe as he celebrated the triumph in the Detroit dressing room.

"This is the guy that Toronto gave away," Adams told the gathered newsmen, throwing his arm around the shoulders of defenseman Bucko McDonald. Adams was smiling devilishly, but Smythe would have the last laugh, and for many years to come.

Years earlier, Smythe and Adams had shared a train ride, when Smythe let it slip that the Leafs were about to acquire McDonald. Adams acted quickly and scooped up the defenseman before Toronto could strike.

When Detroit lit up the Leafs 9–4 in Game 2 of the series, it became painfully evident that 40-year-old Leafs goalie George Hainsworth was nearing the end of his Hall of Fame career. Word got out that Smythe was in the market for a replacement, and hockey people pointed him toward Earl Robertson of the Windsor Bulldogs, about to start the International League final against Detroit's farm club, the Olympics. Four coaches in the league— London's George Hay, Rochester's Carson Cooper, Cleveland's

Bucko's Gold Mine

Yukon gold miners would have been jealous of the precious metal that populated the mouth of Detroit defenseman Wilfred "Bucko" McDonald. He owned a set of false teeth that possessed enough gold to fill a bank.

"[Detroit coach Jack] Adams thought I was slowing up," McDonald explained to *Montreal Gazette* writer Dink Carroll in 1944. "He asked me to go get my teeth examined. The dentist X-rayed them and said I'd have to have some of them pulled. He pulled them, and then I had to get a bridge.

"When he found out I wasn't paying for the bridge, he said he'd make me a good one. He did, too. It cost $250.

"When Adams got the bill, he was choking. He called me in right away. He was sitting there with the bill in his hand and he says, 'What did you get instead of teeth—diamonds?'

"Come to think of it, I guess me and Adams finished about even."

Hap Holmes, and Syracuse's Eddie Powers—advised Smythe that Robertson was far and away the best netminder in the league.

Smythe stayed in town while his Leafs returned home for Game 3 of the Cup Finals. In the afternoon, he talked terms with Windsor officials to get a handle on what it might cost him to purchase Robertson's contract. Then he set out to watch the Detroit-Windsor opener, but Robertson was as off-form as Hainsworth, fishing nearly as many pucks from his net during an 8–1 Detroit rout.

At the other end of the ice, the Olympics' goalie, a pudgy 22-year-old first-year pro by the name of Walter "Turk" Broda, garnered Smythe's attention. A month later, when NHL moguls gathered at Detroit's Book Cadillac Hotel for meetings, Smythe paid the Wings $8,000, a record payment for a minor league goalie, to garner Broda's rights.

It was a surprise to all, considering Broda was cut by the New York Rangers in 1933, with Rangers GM Lester Patrick declaring that he was not an NHL prospect.

A year later, Detroit scout Gene Houghton convinced Adams to sign Broda to a contract, and he spent the 1934–35 season working as a practice goalie for the Wings. Assigned to the Olympics the next season, Broda turned heads in a preseason series between the Olympics and the parent club, stoning the Wings as their farmhands won twice and tied the third contest.

A gambler at heart, Smythe was confident he'd found a keeper in Broda.

"I think the boy is a high-class goaltender," Smythe told the *Windsor Star*. "I wouldn't have paid $8,000 for him if I hadn't.

"I'll admit I was after Earl Robertson when I checked over a Windsor-Olympics playoff game at Olympia, but Broda caught my eye. I'm satisfied he's major-league stuff."

As a youngster, when Broda tried out for the team at David Livingstone Public School in his hometown of Brandon, Manitoba, the plump child was deemed too slow afoot to make it as a forward or a defenseman, and was relegated to the goaltender spot by default. It was there that he also acquired his nickname, originally known as "Turkey Egg" due to his freckle-faced complexion, and later shortened to "Turk."

The Wings were convinced that they were more than set in goal and could do without Broda. Normie Smith had just backstopped them to the Stanley Cup and won the Vezina Trophy in the process. For insurance, Adams signed Melville, Saskatchewan, amateur Jimmy Franks the same day he dealt Broda and likely figured he'd pulled a fast one when he scooped up Robertson from Windsor for the bargain price of $1,500. The sentiment was no doubt reinforced when Robertson pinch-hit for the injured Smith and backstopped Detroit to the 1937 Stanley Cup.

Meanwhile, Broda won an early season battle with Hainsworth for the Toronto netminding job, and Hainsworth was released early into the 1936–37 season. "Broda will have the job as long as he can hold it," Smythe proclaimed.

He held it for a very long time, and in the process broke the hearts of Red Wings fans time and again.

Broda first got the better of Detroit in the 1940–41 season, when he nosed out Red Wings goalie Johnny Mowers, the sixth goalie Detroit had tried since giving up on Broda, for the Vezina Trophy, becoming the first Toronto netminder to earn the award as the NHL's best goalie. The Leafs were on hand in Boston to watch Detroit's farewell game against the Bruins, and because Bill Cowley potted the goal that gave Broda the trophy, Turk showed up on Cowley's door the next morning with a box of cigars.

The next spring, Broda barred the door as Toronto rallied from a 3–0 series deficit to down Detroit 4–3 in the best-of-seven Stanley Cup Finals, the first time that had happened in NHL history.

With Broda between the pipes, Toronto swept the Wings in back-to-back Stanley Cup Finals series in the springs of 1948 and 1949, helping the Leafs' netminder establish his reputation as the best clutch puck stopper in hockey.

"He's terrific, simply terrific," Smythe said of Broda. "And what I like about him is that he is generally that way when the chips [are] on the line.

"In Turk Broda we've got the greatest money goaltender in hockey."

A goalie who could have very easily been blocking pucks for the Wings, instead of blocking their path to glory.

50 Mr. Hockey Survived Two Near-Death Experiences

Gordie Howe always had an aura of indestructibility. Howe stood 6'0", but goalie Glenn Hall said Howe always seemed 6'8".

To those who played against him, Howe was the real-life version of a comic book superhero. Opponents were certain bullets would bounce off Howe, a reputation that was bolstered by the truth that he cheated death twice during the prime of his career.

The first near miss happened after Howe had returned to Saskatchewan after his 1946–47 rookie NHL season. Howe was 19, and he and his younger brother, Vic, were tooling about the prairie in Howe's newly acquired assembly-line-fresh Dodge.

The Howe boys were hunting, looking for partridges or prairie chickens, when Gordie spied a hawk sitting defiantly on a fence post along the side of the road.

Gordie was driving, and according to Vic, he told his younger brother to see if he could pick off the hawk. Vic grabbed a 12-gauge shotgun, forced a shell into the chamber, swiveled the gun outside the window, and fired.

The bird took flight, and Vic pulled the gun inside the car. But he heard Gordie yell, "Shoot again. I think you hit him."

In telling the story more than a half century after the event, Vic admitted that he is not sure exactly how the mishap occurred. All he has is a theory about what occurred as he popped another shell in the chamber.

"I must have had my finger still on the trigger," Vic said, "because the ol' shotgun went off, and it blew a hole in the roof of the car about three inches above the rear door."

Vic estimates the shotgun blast was about 10 to 12 inches behind Gordie's head.

"I'm not sure what Gordie said, because the shot made so much noise I couldn't hear for five minutes," Vic said. "But it scared the hell out of us."

Vic was also present on March 28, 1950, when Gordie almost lost his life because of a brain injury suffered after he had a collision with Toronto Maple Leafs forward Teeder Kennedy during their opening-round playoff game at Olympia Stadium.

Descriptions of what happened between Kennedy and Howe depended upon which jersey you were wearing.

The debate over what happened raged long enough that *Sports Illustrated* wrote a story about it in 1967, 17 years after the event happened.

Summing up the climate going into the series, *Sports Illustrated* writer Stan Fischler wrote, "An atmosphere of imminent open warfare hung over Detroit's Olympia Stadium before that first game."

Gordie Howe is carried off the ice on a stretcher after suffering a severe head injury against the Toronto Maple Leafs in the 1950 playoffs.

What isn't in dispute is that Toronto had a 4–0 lead in the third period when Kennedy was carrying the puck through the middle of the ice with "Black Jack" Stewart chasing him from behind and Howe coming at him from the side.

One of the eyewitnesses that night was Vic Howe. In 1950 he was playing for the Windsor (Ontario) Spitfires, and he had come across the border to watch the game.

"Near as I could tell Kennedy had come from behind the Toronto net and started up through center, and Gord was coming from his right to cut him off," Vic recalled. "Kennedy was swinging over toward the left boards."

Vic's memory places Toronto's Howie Meeker on the right wing.

"Just before Gord got there, I know what Kennedy was thinking," Vic said. "Jack Stewart was coming at him from one direction, and Howe was coming at him from another direction. *Get rid of the puck.* So he threw the backhand pass across the ice to Meeker. When he did, the stick came up."

According to Vic, Kennedy's stick caught Howe just below the eye, opening a deep gash.

"If it would have been a half inch higher, he would have lost the eye," said Vic.

Mr. Hockey Was Mr. All-Star

Gordie Howe played in a record 23 NHL All-Star Games. He still holds All-Star Game marks for power-play goals (six) and penalty minutes (25).

In the 1965 game at the Montreal Forum, Howe achieved an All-Star moment that no other Red Wings player has accomplished—he was named MVP of the game.

Howe scored twice—once on a power play and once shorthanded—and set up two other goals as the All-Stars dumped the Montreal Canadiens 5–2.

Howe also went down hard on the ice. Vic remembered that Stewart ended up on top of Howe and Kennedy.

Seeing Gordie being carried off the ice, Vic hustled down to the Red Wings' dressing room to make sure his brother was not seriously injured. Vic recalled that trainer Lefty Wilson was leaving the first aid room, and he assured Vic that Gordie was cut, shaken up, but otherwise was fine.

Vic returned to his seat to watch the rest of the game. When he returned to the dressing room after the game, he could tell immediately by Wilson's expression that Gordie's condition had deteriorated.

"You had better wait around, because they have called an ambulance," Wilson said.

Gordie was unconscious and still wearing his equipment when he was loaded into the ambulance. Vic sat with him during the ride to Harper Hospital.

Vic recalled that two X-ray technicians couldn't align Howe's bulky body properly for the machine. Vic was called in to assist. When Gordie was being moved, he woke up and asked where he was. He also said his stomach hurt, and then he slipped back into unconsciousness.

Later that night surgeons drilled a hole in Gordie's skull to relieve pressure on his brain.

Gordie's mother and other family members were flown in the next day, because it was evident that Howe's injuries were life-threatening.

Vic recalled that his mother always worried about Gordie being hurt playing hockey, and that incident didn't ease her worries.

The fallout from that game was severe. The Detroit players accused Kennedy of "spearing" Howe deliberately.

"I saw Howe lying on the ice with his face covered with blood," Kennedy told *Sports Illustrated* years later. "I couldn't help thinking what a great player he was and how I hoped he wasn't badly hurt.

Then Detroit players started saying I did it with my stick. I knew I hadn't and, as I've always regarded [Detroit] coach Tommy Ivan as a sensible, level-headed man, I went over to the Detroit bench and told him I was sorry Howe was hurt, but that I wasn't responsible."

A report from referee George Gravel exonerated Kennedy, as did league president Clarence Campbell.

"Kennedy," Campbell said, "as a right-handed player, had the butt part of his stick tight to the fence as he was going up the ice. He was being checked from his right. The injuries to Howe were on the right side of the head. Kennedy had stopped to avoid the check, and went in front of him."

That didn't halt the debate. The Red Wings were threatening to sue because Maple Leafs general manager Conn Smythe supposedly had said that the Howe injury had been payback for Detroit player Stewart breaking Gus Mortson's leg.

Mayhem ensued in Game 2. The Red Wings went after Kennedy aggressively and won the game. Afterward, Detroit players said they won for Gordie.

Campbell threatened major fines if both teams didn't calm down. The extracurricular violence stopped, but the Red Wings still played under the banner of "winning for Gordie."

They won in Game 7 in overtime against Toronto and then beat the New York Rangers in overtime of Game 7 in the Stanley Cup Finals.

Howe had recovered enough to attend Game 7 against the Rangers. After the Red Wings won the game, the crowd of 13,095 at Olympia chanted, "We want Gordie. We want Gordie."

As Howe stepped carefully onto the ice, Ted Lindsay playfully grabbed Howe's hat and hurled it into the crowd.

Only Howe could get a sustained standing ovation with his mere presence.

51 They Were the Best Red Wings Team Ever

Two teams separated by half a century, yet forever linked together.

Besides their dominance of the NHL and their respective Stanley Cup titles, there are so many other parallels between the 1951–52 Red Wings and the 2001–02 Red Wings.

Each team was led by a veteran captain on his last legs—Sid Abel in 1951–52 and Steve Yzerman in 2001–02. Both were backstopped by goaltenders who were as unbeatable as they were unusual—Terry Sawchuk (1951–52) and Dominik Hasek (2001–02).

For irascibility, the 1951–52 Wings had Ted Lindsay and the 2001–02 Wings had Chris Chelios. Both teams carried power forwards who could score and fight and were capable of physically dominating games—Gordie Howe (1951–52) and Brendan Shanahan (2001–02).

The 1951–52 Wings included two Hart Trophy winners (Howe, Abel). The 2001–02 Wings included three Hart Trophy winners (Brett Hull, Sergei Fedorov, and Hasek). The 2001–02 Wings suited up two Norris Trophy winners (Chelios and Nicklas Lidstrom). The 1951–52 Wings listed Red Kelly, who would be the first defenseman to win the Norris, in their lineup.

Two players on the 1951–52 Wings (Alex Delvecchio and Red Kelly) won the Lady Byng Trophy. Two players on the 2001–02 (Brett Hull and Pavel Datsyuk) would win Lady Byngs.

Howe would be the first player in NHL history to net 600 career goals. The 2001–02 Wings carried three 600-goal scorers—Yzerman, Hull, and Luc Robitaille. Like Howe, Hull would eventually top the 700-goal plateau.

"They were so offensively stacked," Dallas Stars winger Erik Cole remembered of the 2001–02 Wings.

Detroit's 2001–02 roster included 13 players with Stanley Cup rings. Detroit's 1951–52 roster featured 11 Stanley Cup winners.

The 1951–52 Wings were deep in grinders—Metro Prystai, Tony Leswick, Glen Skov, and Marty Pavelich. The 2001–02 Wings were deep in grinders—Kris Draper, Kirk Maltby, and Darren McCarty.

The 2001–02 Wings were coached by a curmudgeonly disciplinarian (Scotty Bowman), who'd been part of eight Stanley Cup winners. The 1951–52 Wings were managed by a curmudgeonly disciplinarian (Jack Adams) who'd been part of six Stanley Cup winners.

Seven players from the 1951–52 Wings are enshrined in the Hockey Hall of Fame. Thus far, seven members of the 2001–02 Wings are Hall of Fame inductees.

Comparing these two great teams is easy. Deciphering which one was the better team is difficult.

We'll give the nod—but just barely, mind you—to the 1951–52 Wings, because they accomplished something no team in the history of the Stanley Cup had ever done before—sweeping through two best-of-seven series to capture Lord Stanley's mug.

"That team could have kept playing all summer long and would have never stopped winning," Pavelich said.

During the regular season, the Wings lost back-to-back games just once.

"I used to feel sorry for the teams we played the night after we'd lost, because we'd just kick the hell out of them," Pavelich said.

Individually, Howe won the Art Ross and Hart Trophies and Sawchuk captured the Vezina Trophy. Sawchuk, Kelly, Lindsay, and Howe were all named to the NHL first All-Star team.

"We had great skaters," Lindsay said. "We had great puck handlers.

"A lot of people think we were all old fogies back in those days who couldn't skate. We had guys who could skate with anybody today."

When the members of that team reminisce, it's not the greatness that they recall as much as it is the great times they enjoyed together.

"I think it was just camaraderie," Delvecchio said. "We all got along with each other."

Team activities were planned, including a weekly bowling league.

"We all liked being together," Howe said. "We were all taught the same things. Lines were created and left together. You would room as pairs. Conversations took place."

Some of those conversations were game-related, but never were they accusatory in nature.

"We did a lot of train travel, and after the games, you always met and had a discussion of what went on and who was causing problems," Delvecchio said. "It just helped you in your next game.

"If you had a bad game, they didn't bring it up at all. They just let it slide. You knew if you had to try better next game."

The Wings had won the Cup in 1949–50, and 10 players remained from that club, but they were just reaching the apex of a dynasty that would capture two more titles in 1953–54 and 1954–55.

The 2001–02 Wings were more like a collection of hired gunslingers. There was still a nucleus from Detroit's back-to-back Cup winners in 1996–97 and 1997–98 remaining, including Yzerman, Fedorov, Igor Larionov, Shanahan, Lidstrom, Tomas Holmstrom, Maltby, Draper, McCarty, and Mathieu Dandenault, but realizing that their Stanley Cup window of opportunity was closing, Detroit GM Ken Holland moved to acquire Robitaille, Hull, and Hasek in the off-season to strengthen their chances.

"You look around here and it's like being at the All-Star Game," Robitaille said when he scanned the Wings' dressing room at the start of that season.

Others accused the Wings of buying the Stanley Cup, but the Detroit players just scoffed at such talk.

"I guarantee you other players were wishing their GM had done it," Hull said.

Both the 1951–52 and 2001–02 Wings finished first overall in the NHL regular-season standings, but the 2001–02 team wasn't nearly as dominant, enduring a 1–5–1 skid in December and a winless April (0–5–2). Lidstrom captured the Norris, the only individual award earned that regular season by a Detroit player. Lidstrom and Chelios were named to the NHL first All-Star team.

In the playoffs, the Wings were nearly Hall of Fame busts. They fell behind 2–0 in the opening round to Vancouver before capturing the set in six games, and faced elimination against Colorado in the Western Conference Finals, trailing the series 3–2 before rallying to win the last two games.

In the end, both teams got the job done, but when you add up all the numbers and break down all the accomplishments, the 1951–52 Wings were better, making them the best Detroit team of all time.

52 Ericsson Is Living Proof That It's Better Late Than Never

It's a good thing that Jonathan Ericsson is a patient man.

"I think I've always been a late bloomer when it comes to everything," explained the Red Wings defenseman, the final player chosen in the 2002 NHL entry draft at 291st overall, but someone who has played seven seasons in the NHL with the Wings and who won a silver medal with Sweden in the 2014 Winter Olympics in Sochi, Russia.

"When I got drafted, this was a long shot for me," Ericsson admitted. "Just being able to maybe one day play for the Red Wings, that's one thing, but to be able to play here for I don't know how many years it's going to be now, it's an amazing feeling. Being a part of this top-ranked organization for my whole career is great."

And yes, Ericsson is well aware of the title awarded to the last player chosen in the NFL draft.

"Mr. Irrelevant," he said. "I think they called me that lots of times."

They didn't hold a parade and a weeklong festival in his honor as they do for the last pick of the NFL Draft each year in the California town of Newport Beach, but Ericsson is still somewhat pleased that he was the NHL's last choice in his draft year.

"I'm actually glad," Ericsson said. "I'd rather be the last pick than the fifth-to-last pick. I'm making some kind of history.

"I know there won't be any later picks than me now [because the NHL draft was shortened from nine to seven rounds in 2005], and I don't think there has been a later pick than me that's playing in the NHL, so that's pretty special. I'll take that."

Ericsson is the first to acknowledge that it's been a battle for him to first garner a place as a regular in the NHL, and then a spot as a top-four defenseman.

"I think working out and being determined in what you want to do is a key factor," he said. "I haven't always been the most talented guy."

Ericsson's determination was one of the reasons that the Wings were willing to wait for him to develop, though his 6'5", 220-pound frame also helped them to be patient.

"It's taken him time," Detroit coach Mike Babcock said. "He was the last pick in the draft, he spent a long time in the minors for us, and then he was our fifth *D* for a long time here."

Ericsson arrived in Detroit first for eight games during the 2007–08 season but watched from the sideline as the Wings won the Stanley Cup. He played 19 regular-season games in 2008–09, but by the time Detroit was making a run to the Cup Finals series again that spring, Ericsson was taking a regular turn in the Wings' third defense pairing.

"I think back to the playoffs of '09 when we called him up from the minors," Detroit GM Ken Holland remembered. "We got injuries to [Brian] Rafalski and someone else was hurt, and we had to call him up. We ended up going to the Finals and playing Pittsburgh [before losing in seven games].

"I remember against Anaheim Mike Babcock put him out, and he played a lot, I think with [Nicklas] Lidstrom against [Corey] Perry and [Ryan] Getzlaf. He did a real nice job and we got through that series [in seven games]. Probably at that point in time, playing against that caliber of players in that type of playoffs, big games, that was when we thought we had a guy who could be a real good defenseman."

Still, a number of seasons would pass before he'd garner significant ice time on a regular basis.

"When you have Rafi and Nick [Lidstrom], Kronner [Niklas Kronwall] and Stewie [Brad Stuart], it was a hard thing to become more than the fifth *D*," Babcock said. "He evolved, and now he plays in our top pair [with Kronwall]."

Holland witnessed the same evolution with Ericsson.

"For the longest time he was behind Kronwall, Lidstrom, Stuart, Rafalski, so he's paid his dues, he's waited his time, and the last two years he's taken full advantage of the opportunity," Holland said.

Certainly, taking raw material like Ericsson and molding him into a full-time NHLer is not a project without its pitfalls and setbacks.

"It's not like Big E didn't have his moments here where he struggled," Babcock said. "That's most of these guys' careers. It's hard. There's only so many stars, and even those guys have up and down times. It's no different than all of us. Sport mirrors life. You've got to choose your attitude every day, bring it every day. Sometimes it doesn't go good. So what? Get up and go again the next day.

"It's just a process. There's a lot of players, and it takes them some time. Your top five or seven picks in the draft might play right away, but even those guys take a long time. It's a process to be a good player in this league. If you're mentally strong and you're willing to live in the gym, you've got to eat right and train right, you've got to be mentally tough, and in the end maybe you can make it happen for yourself."

Holland credits the infrastructure within the Detroit hockey brain trust for unearthing late-round gems such as Ericsson.

"It's a great pick by our scouts, especially [European scout] Hakan Andersson," Holland said. "He's paid his dues, he's gone to [Detroit's American League farm club in] Grand Rapids. He was a forward earlier in his career—not in pro, but he made the transition from forward to a defenseman. I think when he was 14, 15, 16, he played up front, so it's been a learning process.

"To me he's a unique player. He's 6'5" and he's really mobile. That's a tough combination. There are some defensemen like him in the league, but there's not a lot of 6'5" guys that are mobile. He's homegrown; we've watched him from the draft table through Grand Rapids into a bottom-pair defenseman to a top-pair defenseman, and certainly into a real important guy to our team."

Ericsson is the perfect example of how the Red Wings' system works, a game plan that is to let youngsters go to the minor leagues and grow as a person and a player while they learn the Detroit way of doing things.

"We don't pick very high in the draft, so we have to have patience," Holland said. "We don't draft players that go from the draft table to the National Hockey League. There was a stretch from 1995 to '05 that we traded eight first-round draft picks trying to acquire players to win, so since then we've hung on to most of our picks. We've traded the odd pick since 2005, but we've had to have patience.

"Then when they get here, the formula for us, I guess, is we hold on to some older players longer because again, we don't have those blue-chip kids coming up to our team. We think we have kids who can develop into NHL players, so patience has to be a part of our program. Fortunately in this situation it's worked out good."

Babcock likes being able to look down his bench and tap the big, powerful Ericsson on the shoulder to go over the boards and deal with the other team's best forwards.

"He's a big man, and he can pass the puck," Babcock said. "He's smart, and he obviously likes playing here and we like having him.

"It's good for all of us."

53 Check Out the Wings in Popular Culture

One of the NHL's most popular franchises, the Wings frequently pop up in the world of entertainment. For example:

1. Paul McCartney Has a Red Wings Logo on His Guitar

One of the two surviving Beatles, if you see Sir Paul in concert, get a close-up look at his acoustic guitar. It features a sticker of a Red Wings logo at its base.

McCartney explained how this came to be during a Detroit radio interview prior to a concert at the Palace of Auburn Hills a few years ago. McCartney explained that he affixed the sticker after it was presented to him by a Wings fan when his band Wings played Olympia Stadium in 1976.

It's the same guitar that McCartney played on *The Ed Sullivan Show* when he sang the Beatles' hit "Yesterday." And the guitar itself has Michigan ties. It's a Gibson Epiphone Texan model, first produced at the company's Kalamazoo, Michigan, factory in 1964. McCartney said he purchased the guitar for $175 in 1965.

In 2006 the company produced a limited-edition run of 1,964 replicas of McCartney's famous guitar. "It's exciting to have my old guitar reproduced by Gibson," McCartney said. "It's exact, and what's more, it sounds great."

A word of warning, though. When McCartney played the first show at Pittsburgh's new Consol Energy Center in 2010, he added a Penguins logo to his guitar just above the Wings sticker.

2. Gordie Howe Was in *The Simpsons*

During the third season of the iconic animated series, in 1992, just in time for Valentine's Day, *The Simpsons* aired the Episode "Bart the Lover," in which Bart Simpson, angered over a monthlong detention issued by his teacher, Edna Krabappel, opts to prank her by creating a fictional character to respond to a personal ad placed by Krabappel.

Bart dubs his creation Woodrow Wilson but sends Krabappel a photo of Gordie Howe to represent Woodrow. Realizing the monster he's created, Bart sends a goodbye letter to Krabappel near the end of the show, and just before the credits roll, Mr. Hockey's NHL and WHA stats appear on the screen.

Considered by critics to be among the best all-time Simpsons episodes, Marcia Wallace, who provided the voice to Krabappel, won a prime-time Emmy for her performance.

3. Jason Voorhees Wears a Red Wings Goalie Mask

The *Friday the 13th* horror franchise was into its third film when killer Jason's trademark goalie mask first appeared, and you can thank the Wings for that.

Doing a lighting check and not wanting to have to apply hours of makeup to Richard Brooker, the actor portraying Jason, 3-D effects supervisor Martin Jay Sadoff came up with a plan B. An avid hockey fan, he just happened to have his gear in his car and retrieved a fiberglass goalie mask from his hockey bag. It was a replica of masks worn by Wings goalies Doug Grant, Bill McKenzie, and Terry Richardson in the mid-1970s.

Director Steve Miner loved the mask, and so did audiences. It's become a staple of the film and an ever-present item on the shelves of costume stores each Halloween.

Derek Mears, who played Jason in the most recent *Friday the 13th* film in 2009, believes the mask serves as the ultimate metaphor for the horrors Voorhees faced in his life, having witnessed the decapitation murder of his mother.

"Essentially, the mask serves as his protection from society and as a shield," Mears explained to the *Hockey News*.

4. The Wings Clobbered the Park County Peewees

"Stanley's Cup" was the 2006 season finale of popular cartoon *South Park*. A parody of the 1992 film *The Mighty Ducks*, it's built around South Park character Stan Marsh being forced to do community service as coach of the local peewee hockey team.

The Park County Peewees are invited to play Denver County in a mini-game during the intermission of a Red Wings–Colorado

Avalanche game at the Pepsi Center. But the Denver team fails to show, and Stan's squad is told they won't get to take the ice.

Seeing the disappointment of the children, the Avalanche players offer the kids the chance to play the third period against the Wings, with predictably disastrous results. Tied 2–2 after two periods, the Wings pound the children physically and on the scoreboard, winning 32–2. Certainly the fact that *South Park* creators Matt Stone and Trey Parker are from Colorado played a role in turning the Wings into villains for this episode.

54 The Day the Pros Faced Off With the Cons

It started out as part of a promotional tour and quickly developed into a publicity stunt.

Long before they were selected to play in a pair of NHL Winter Classics, the Red Wings suited up for their first outdoor game in a setting ripped right from the pages of *The Longest Yard*.

The difference being, in this case, the convicts wouldn't be playing football. And they wouldn't be playing against the guards.

The opposition on this day would be the reigning NHL regular-season champions, the Detroit Red Wings.

In late June 1953 Detroit general manager Jack Adams and team captain Ted Lindsay embarked on a promotional tour of Michigan's Upper Peninsula sponsored by Stroh's Brewery, including a stop in, of all places, Marquette Branch Prison—known in prison circles as the Alcatraz of the north.

As they walked through the prison, Lindsay, one of the NHL's toughest customers, remembered asking one of the guards if they should harbor any concerns about their well-being. "If anybody thought of doing anything, they would be dead before he took two steps," Lindsay was told.

When warden Emery Jacques met with Adams, he put forth a suggestion out of the blue—why not bring the entire Red Wings team back during the winter for an exhibition game against the convicts?

As someone who was always seeking out ways to bring attention to the team across the state of Michigan, Adams was immediately enamored with the notion. He told Jacques that if the prison was willing to cover the travel, food, and lodging costs to bring the Red Wings north, the game was on.

The convicts had constructed an outdoor rink in the yard, under the direction of Leonard "Oakie" Brumm, a former Michigan Wolverines hockey player who served as the prison's director of physical activity.

"Marquette is the only penal institution in the nation with either an organized varsity or a boarded regulation hockey rink," boasted Brumm to the Associated Press, adding that he hoped eventually to get the prison team into an organized league, adding, "all their games, of course, will be home games."

"The ice rink turned out to be the conversation piece of United States penology," Brumm, who died in 2006, wrote in his book *We Only Played Home Games*. "Once it was up and operating we had inquiries from all over North America about it.

"We played two varsity games every weekend and I don't know how many intramural games. Not only did convicts play, but we always had a lot of convict spectators who were into the game either because they had bet on it or their friends or 'girlfriends' were involved.

"It was an exceptional facility and was maintained to the highest degree possible under the conditions by a crew of five convicts all night every night and six during the day."

On a Roll

On September 21, 1955, the defending Stanley Cup–champion Red Wings fell 3–1 in a preseason game against the Edmonton Flyers, Detroit's Western Hockey League minor-pro affiliate that was played in Sault Ste. Marie, Ontario. From that point onward, the Wings went unbeaten in 69 consecutive exhibition contests, going 64–0–5 until suffering a 4–1 defeat against their American Hockey League affiliate, the Hershey Bears, on October 8, 1961, at Olympia Stadium.

Besides his hockey rink, during his tenure at Marquette from 1953 to 1957, Brumm was also responsible for developing an 18-hole miniature golf course, shuffleboard courts, and a regulation-sized bocce court. He built a curling rink and formed a football team, which, like the hockey team, also played host to outside squads.

His piéce de résistance, though, was the hockey game against the Wings, the only time an NHL team has ever played in a penitentiary.

The Wings arrived for their date with destiny against the Marquette Prison Pirates on February 2, 1954.

Marquette Branch Prison was populated with the worst of Michigan's felons, some of the most hardened criminals in the state, but Lindsay insists he felt no fear as he took the ice on a rink situated within barbed-wire-lined stone walls and watched over by armed guards trained to shoot to kill.

"I was leading the league in penalty minutes at the time, so I fit right in with the boys," Lindsay joked, before turning serious. "I was never concerned, because I figured that I could take care of myself. But I felt very strongly from having been close to them in the summertime and mingling with them that there was no reason to be worried."

Detroit coach Tommy Ivan put his team through their paces, displaying a series of drills to their captive audience before getting down to the business of playing the game.

As it turned out, the Pirates had about as much of a chance of succeeding against the Wings as they did in front of a parole board.

The Wings easily took control. Detroit led 10–0 before the game was 10 minutes old, and it was 18–0 by the end of the first period.

"It could have been 50–0," said Wings defenseman Marcel Pronovost, who admitted that they took it easy on their prison foes, perhaps out of courtesy, possibly out of concern for their personal safety.

Brumm, who suited up alongside the inmates, wrote of their plight, "The only time we touched the puck was when we pulled it out of our net."

Not wanting to rub it in, the Wings engineered a few trades to even up the sides. Lindsay and goalie Terry Sawchuk switched to the striped uniforms of the convicts to start the second period, and by the midway point of the frame, Detroit superstar Gordie Howe donned a prison uniform as well.

In another gesture of sportsmanship, official reports of the game in the next day's papers listed the Wings as 5–2 winners.

While most of the opposition would never get out from behind those prison walls, the Wings returned to Detroit and wound up winning the Stanley Cup that spring in seven games over the Montreal Canadiens.

Brumm enjoyed a career in hockey after leaving his prison job. He coached the Des Moines Oak Leafs, the Waterloo Blackhawks, and finally the Marquette Iron Rangers over a 15-year period. Among his players with the Iron Rangers were the Carlson brothers—Jack, Steve, and Jeff—the basis for the Hanson brothers characters in the 1977 film *Slap Shot*.

As a coach, Brumm also proved an innovator. In 1970 he signed female goalie Karen Koch to play for Marquette.

A Quiet Riot

It wasn't uncommon for the visiting team to be in for a rough night when they played at the Montreal Forum in the 1950s. But the Red Wings were even more hesitant upon their arrival the night of March 17, 1955.

Just two days earlier, NHL president Clarence Campbell had suspended Rocket Richard for the remainder of the regular season and the Stanley Cup Playoffs after he attacked Boston players and NHL officials during a March 13 game.

The Wings would be the next team to play in Montreal, and considering they were battling the Habs for first place, people anticipated there would be trouble at the game.

"There was a feeling before the game that something could happen," recalled Marcel Pronovost, a Red Wings defenseman from 1950 to 1965.

By the time the game started, an unruly mob of some 6,000 had gathered on the street outside the rink, while the Forum was filled to capacity with 15,000 spectators, including Richard, who watched from a rinkside seat.

Although advised to stay home, Campbell arrived and took his usual seat in the Forum stands, next to Phyllis King, his secretary. Campbell endured eggs and four-letter words tossed in his direction, but with Detroit leading 4–1 after 20 minutes, the trouble began to escalate.

A fan approached Campbell with hand extended, but instead of shaking hands, when Campbell leaned forward, the fellow slapped his face. Among those who came to Campbell's defense was former Detroit defenseman Jimmy Orlando, a past NHL penalty-minute leader and a Montreal resident.

Police immediately intervened, but as they sought to corral Campbell's assailant, the melee was on. A tear-gas bomb was detonated, and fans, some with their faces covered with coats and handkerchiefs, rushed for the exits in a growing panic.

Down below in the visitors' dressing room, the Wings were aware of the commotion above.

"We could hear a lot of noise, so we had a feeling something was going on," Pronovost said. "But we didn't know what."

"I remember looking at my watch and thinking the intermission was running too long," Jimmy Skinner, coach of that Wings team, said in a 1995 interview.

"Just then, the two GMs, Jack Adams and Frank Selke of Montreal, came into the room and told us someone had thrown a bomb into the rink and the game had been forfeited to us. They told us to stay put until somebody came to get us."

Soon, evidence of the trouble crept into the Detroit quarters. "Smoke started seeping into the room under the dressing room door," Pronovost said. "We took some wet towels and jammed them under the door so the smoke couldn't get in."

Not long after, police and arena security staff came to get the Wings, slipping them out the back entrance to a waiting bus. They were taken to their hotel and then to the train station, where they departed for Detroit.

As the crowd spilled out of the rink on to Saint Catherine Street, the mob began smashing windows and looting stores. By the time order had been restored, some $50,000 in damage had been inflicted and 52 people were arrested.

The next day, as they awoke in their own beds back in Detroit, this was news to the Wings players. "We missed the whole thing," Pronovost said. "We didn't know about the riot until the next day."

With Richard suspended, the Wings rallied to finish first overall and went on to win the Stanley Cup from the Richardless Canadiens in a seven-game series.

56 The Cougar Who Fathered a Colt

The Detroit Cougars lineup during the 1929–30 NHL season included a half dozen rookies, and one of them went on to produce big—in another sport.

Roland Joseph Matte, a defenseman who broke into the NHL with the Cougars late that season, was the father of legendary NFLer Tom Matte. The younger Matte, who played 12 years as a running back for the Baltimore Colts and one famous stint as an emergency quarterback in a 1965 playoff game against Vince Lombardi's Green Bay Packers, makes no bones about his choice of sporting entertainment.

"Hockey is my favorite sport," Tom Matte said. "I was on skates from a young age."

Born in 1939, Tom caught the end of his dad's pro career as he played in the minor leagues, but remembers his father's on-ice demeanor well.

"He was the toughest, meanest, dirtiest guy," Tom recalled. "He didn't have any teeth left, but he didn't back down from anybody. He was a tremendous athlete."

Just where those teeth went and how that attitude developed might be garnered from an interview Matte's dad conducted with *Chicago News* writer John Carmichael in 1942. A life in the minors—Matte's lone NHL experience was 12 games for Detroit in 1929–30 and another dozen with the Chicago Black Hawks in 1942–43, when World War II deprived the NHL of many of its players—seemed to harden the fellow.

"Why, they can sure carve you up in those small leagues," Papa Matte explained. "They're butchers, not hockey players. If a guy got going good…he was removed.

The Wolfman Chose Football

Don Dufek lived to hit. He couldn't get enough body contact.

"When I hit a guy hard, I knew he was going to be apprehensive about coming my way later on," explained Dufek, who played the Wolf position—a hybrid between safety and linebacker—for the Michigan Wolverines from 1973 to 1975.

Named to the 1975 Football Writers Association of America All-American team, Dufek also did plenty of hitting on the ice, skating as a hard-checking winger with the Wolverines hockey team, earning four letters and a call from the Wings.

Detroit selected Dufek 99th overall in the 1974 NHL amateur draft, but he didn't see a future for himself at the rink.

"I didn't want a long tour in the minors," said Dufek, whose Michigan teammates included future NHLers such as Pat Hughes, Greg Fox, Kris Manery, and Rob Palmer.

Selected by the expansion Seattle Seahawks in the fifth round of the 1976 NFL Draft, Dufek opted to stay with the gridiron, playing for Seattle until 1984, serving as special teams captain and leading the Seahawks in special teams tackles a franchise-record four times.

Today Dufek, 60, works as a general contractor who builds and remodels homes in Ann Arbor, Michigan, and his son Mike recently added another sport to the Dufek legacy, playing first base for the Wolverines baseball team.

"Some poor guy would have the puck in the corner and three or four of the other side would go after it—and him. When they had him surrounded, they forgot about the puck. They just chopped him down."

The elder Matte made his NHL debut on February 4, 1930, for Detroit against Boston and collected his first point with an assist on a Carson Cooper goal in an 8–1 win over the Pittsburgh Pirates on February 9, 1930.

Tom, who holds dual Canadian-American citizenship, played both football and hockey at Ohio State. Originally, his dad forbade him from playing football.

"My mom secretly signed me up for high school football in ninth grade and brought my dad to the game to surprise him," Tom said. "Wouldn't you know it, I tore up my knee in that game. Was my dad ever mad. He didn't speak to me for three months."

As part of his rehab from the injury, Tom would skate to strengthen the knee.

Later, during his tenure with the Colts, Tom—a two-time Pro Bowler who holds the Super Bowl rushing record for yards per carry of 10.5, set in Super Bowl III—nearly took a turn in pro hockey. Terry Reardon, who was coach of the AHL Baltimore Clippers at the time, would let Matte and fellow Colt Danny Sullivan, who played at Boston College, come out and skate with the team.

"Reardon and my dad were friends," Tom explained. "Baltimore is a football town. Reardon started thinking, *If we got a couple of Colts to play, we'd draw a pretty good crowd.* But Carroll Rosenbloom, the owner of the Colts, got wind of the idea and wouldn't let us play anymore."

While the Mattes formed a hockey-football father-son tandem, the O'Connells were a football-hockey duo. Mike O'Connell, who played defense for the Red Wings from 1986 to 1990, is the son of former NFL quarterback Tommy O'Connell. The elder O'Connell started at quarterback for the Cleveland Browns in the 1957 NFL Championship Game when the Browns lost 59–14 to the Detroit Lions—the most recent NFL crown earned by the Lions.

57 Guyle Fielder Was the Gordie Howe of the Minor Leagues

Imagine the possibilities for productivity had Gordie Howe skated on the right wing with Wayne Gretzky at center. It happened a couple of times in All-Star competition, but never in a real game.

However, for a brief time during the 1957–58 NHL season, the guy who ranks third all-time behind Gretzky and Howe in professional hockey scoring worked as Mr. Hockey's center.

At the June 1957 NHL meetings, Detroit GM Jack Adams swung a deal with the Boston Bruins to purchase the contract of center Guyle Fielder, who tore up the minor-pro Western Hockey League during the 1956–57 season with Seattle, leading the league with 89 assists and 122 points.

At training camp that fall, Adams immediately installed the playmaking Fielder, 26 at the time, as center on his top line with Howe on the right wing and Johnny Wilson on left wing.

"He may be the best center Howe has had since Sid Abel," Adams boldly told the *Montreal Gazette* of Fielder at the launch of the 1957–58 campaign. "He may even lead the league in assists."

Instead, Fielder went scoreless in six games, his only NHL stat a minor penalty in a game against the Toronto Maple Leafs. In early November Fielder was returned to Seattle, and Adams willingly admitted that he'd been mistaken in his assessment of the minor-pro legend.

"He's too slow for the NHL, and he has been in the minors too long," Adams told the *Quebec Chronicle-Telegraph*. Norm Ullman replaced Fielder on the top line.

It was the fourth and final NHL trial for Fielder. After leading the AHL with 61 assists for Detroit's St. Louis farm club and earning the league's Rookie of the Year Award, he'd been called up to the Wings during the 1952–53 playoffs and went scoreless in four games. He was also blanked in two playoff games with the Bruins in 1953–54 and in three regular-season games for the Chicago Black Hawks in 1950–51.

For his part, Fielder told the *Seattle Post-Intelligencer* that he'd requested a reassignment to the minors rather than ride the pine in Detroit in 1957, noting he'd make the same pay ($7,500) whether he was playing in the minors or the NHL.

"I said, 'I came here to play hockey, not sit on the bench,'" Fielder explained.

"He called me and said, 'Get me the hell out of here,'" recalled former Wings defenseman Keith Allen, Seattle's coach in 1957–58.

Fielder expanded more on his Detroit tenure in an interview with writer David Eskenazi in 2011.

"I had a good tryout in Detroit in 1957," Fielder told Eskenazi. "I went all through training camp—I played with Gordie Howe— but we got off to a terrible start. I went to the second line, the third line, and then to the bench. I told Jack [Adams] that I was wasting my time and his time. Anybody can sit on the bench.

"Jack gave me a $500 raise, and I stuck around a few more games. Then I wasn't even dressing. I told Jack, 'Just get me out of here. We're wasting each other's time.'

"I like to think that I could have played in the NHL. I was a little smaller [5'9", 165 pounds], but agile. I just didn't have the patience to stick. I only wanted to play, and to the best of my ability."

Fielder also believes his chances of success would have improved had he not been assigned the task of centering Howe's line.

"It might have been different if I'd been able to play on a line without Howe," Fielder claimed to *Canadian* magazine in 1973. "You see, he [was] the same type of player that I [was]. He liked to have control of the puck, make the plays, set up the others to score when he couldn't score himself.

Spartan Existence

Red Wings 2005 draft pick Justin Abdelkader scored the winning goal for the Michigan State Spartans in their 3–1 2007 NCAA Championship Game victory over Boston College. Both of Michigan State's previous NCAA champions also were led by a Red Wings flavor. Future Wings Kevin Miller, Joe Murphy, and Bob Essensa were all part of the 1986 title team, while Doug Volmar, who made his NHL debut with the Wings in the 1970 playoffs, was the only member of MSU's 1966 championship squad to reach the NHL.

"There wasn't much point in having both of us out there on the same line."

Fielder did acknowledge that, had he stuck it out in the NHL, he probably wouldn't have come close to putting up the numbers that he did as a minor-pro superstar.

"I kind of doubt I could do it on that level, but I would have liked to have had more time to see that style," he said. "It never happened. But I wasn't going to sit around."

Allen believed that given a longer tenure, and had he been allowed to play the offense-first game Fielder preferred, he could have made his mark as an NHLer.

"He was the greatest minor-league player I've ever seen in my life," Allen told *Sports Collectors Digest.* "He could make a play as well as anyone in hockey."

Fielder was an 11-time WHL All-Star and a six-time league MVP. He earned nine league scoring titles and finished his pro career with 1,929 regular-season points, a minor-pro record and third behind Gretzky (2,967) and Howe (2,406) in pro hockey history.

He finished as the WHL's all-time leader in games played (1,425), assists (1,430), and points (1,868).

"It's totally mind-boggling to me he couldn't play in the NHL and not be a great player in the NHL," former Seattle teammate Bill MacFarland told the *Post-Intelligencer.*

For NHL people, it wasn't as difficult to fathom.

"I could have had Fielder, but I didn't want him," New York Rangers GM Muzz Patrick told the *Montreal Gazette* in 1957. "He can make plays like [former NHL scoring champion] Max Bentley, but he'll never be another Bentley because he can't make them often enough.

"There's something lacking. If he played up to his potential all the time, he'd be terrific. But he just doesn't seem to be able to do it."

A fellow who posted a pair of 100-point seasons as a junior and four more as a minor leaguer failed to register a single point in nine NHL regular-season games and six Stanley Cup contests.

"I was born too soon," Fielder said, feeling he'd have made his mark in the NHL if he'd been in his prime during the expansion era.

58 Duke's Swing and a Miss

Gordon "Duke" Keats was a hockey legend whose feats are often overlooked because the majority of his career was played outside of the NHL.

A scoring champion with the Edmonton Eskimos of the Western Canada Hockey League in 1921–22 with 30 goals and 56 points in 25 games, Keats was a savvy stickhandler and deft passer of the puck also armed with a terrific shot. Old-timers in Edmonton suggested he was the greatest player seen in the city until Wayne Gretzky came along. But Keats also had quite the temper, as exhibited in 1925–26, when he led the Western League with 134 penalty minutes in 30 games.

To Keats went the honor of scoring the first goal ever tallied in a game involving Detroit's NHL franchise, though he scored it for the Boston Bruins, the game-winner in a 2–0 decision over the Cougars on November 18, 1926, at Border Cities Arena.

Soon Keats would be scoring goals for Detroit. Traded by Boston to the Cougars in a four-player deal on January 7, 1927, Keats scored the first hat trick by a Detroit player on March 10, 1927, against the Pittsburgh Pirates. Detroit's leading scorer that campaign, Keats took over from Art Duncan as player/coach of the Cougars for the final 11 games of the 1926–27 season.

He was also quite the character. During one Detroit game when Keats wasn't seeing much ice time, he dozed off on the bench. Awoken by the crowd's roar, Keats asked, "Who barged that one?" before lapsing again into slumber.

Early into his second season with Detroit, the dark side of Keats emerged. Assessed a major penalty for rough play in the second period of a scoreless tie at Chicago on November 26, 1927, Keats argued the call with referees Dave Ritchie and Alex Romeril and didn't head immediately to the penalty box. Heckled by a rinkside fan who told him to stop complaining and get off the ice, Keats raced to the boards, took his stick in both hands, and swung it baseball style in his antagonist's direction. The man ducked, and Keats' stick struck the chair next to where Irene Castle, the wife of Black Hawks owner Major Frederic McLaughlin, was seated, then glanced off an usher. He was ejected from the game for his actions.

Castle was a legendary dancer and actress from the silent film era. Teamed with first husband Vernon Castle, they were credited with popularizing ballroom dancing, removing the stigma of vulgarity from close dancing. In 1914 they starred in Irving Berlin's first Broadway musical, *Watch Your Step*.

Vernon Castle died in a 1918 plane crash, and in 1923 Irene Castle married McLaughlin. The two remained married until McLaughlin's death in 1944, and she is credited with designing the first Black Hawks jersey and logo in 1926.

Writing in the *Border Cities Star*, Dick Gibson suggested the whole Keats affair was much ado about nothing. "Weird and wonderful stories of what Duke Keats did to draw a suspension in the game at Chicago last Saturday have appeared in papers all over the world interested in hockey," Gibson noted. "Some of them must have taxed the imagination of even the most fanciful of scribes who write of the pastiming in the Windy City. But the truth is that Keats did nothing more than take a swing at an usher who undertook to supply a name or two to the Detroit forward that wouldn't sound nice in company.

"Mrs. Frederic McLaughlin, the former Irene Castle and present wife of the president of the Chicago Black Hawks, may have been sitting nearby. But neither she nor any other spectator was in any danger, for the rink flunky was standing in an aisle all by himself.

"The story of Irene Castle being endangered is the purest fiction. Between the papers and the Chicago officials, a tempest was created in a tea cup. And Keats, for losing his temper over a nasty remark by an employee who was equally guilty, is made the goat."

Frank Calder, president of the NHL, disagreed with that assessment. On November 28 Keats was fined $100 for misconduct and suspended indefinitely.

Perhaps his track record played a role in the outcome. Keats was what is known in hockey circles as a serial offender. During his days in the WCHL, a major league competitor to the NHL in the 1920s, Keats was frequently fined and suspended. On January 1, 1924, in a game at Edmonton while serving a sentence for an on-ice infraction, Keats scaled the wall at the rear of the penalty box and waded into the midst of some taunting fans to take a swing at someone who was razzing him. He was fined $50 by WCHL president E.L. Richardson for his actions.

Less than two weeks later in a game against the Calgary Tigers, a scuffle between Edmonton's Spunk Sparrow and Calgary's Rusty

Crawford led to both being penalized. When Calgary player/manager Eddie Oatman came to the penalty box to protest the calls to referee Skinner Poulin, Keats raced in and shoved his glove into Oatman's face. Oatman responded with a punch of his own. That's when Crawford grabbed a spare goalie stick that was situated near the penalty box and cracked Keats over the head with it, opening a significant wound on Keats' head. Crawford was handed a one-game suspension for his assault.

Calder eventually reinstated Keats on December 15, 1927, after a three-week sit-down. At the same time, with the Black Hawks in the midst of a 1–7–1 slide, McLaughlin made a pair of deals. First, he acquired forward Ty Arbour in a three-cornered trade with the Toronto Maple Leafs and the Pittsburgh Pirates, and then he made a much more shocking move, shipping defenseman Gord Fraser and $5,000 to the Cougars for Keats.

To say the deal caught hockey people by surprise would be an understatement.

"When Duke arrives at the city of gunmen, it's an even bet that there'll be one usher at the Chicago arena out of a job," wrote Vern DeGeer in the *Saskatoon Phoenix*.

59 Listen to Mickey Redmond, the Voice of the People

Color analyst Mickey Redmond receives his checks from Fox Sports Detroit and yet speaks as if he works for the fans.

"He is truly the voice of the fans. What else can you say?" said longtime Red Wings fan Pat Brown. "He's Red Wings hockey."

Redmond played for the Red Wings for six seasons, earning a place in team history by becoming the franchise's first 50-goal scorer. But what he is now known for are his three decades of colorful, homespun analysis of the Red Wings games on TV.

The Peterborough, Ontario, native has become as Michigan as Vernors, Greenfield Village, and Better Made Potato Chips.

"It's his attitude," said Detroit radio personality Art Regner. "He wears a lumberjack shirt and jeans even if it's 100 degrees out. He's genuine. He's honest, and he has a passion for people."

He's also known for his memorable catchphrases. When a trailing player scores the goal, Redmond's analysis would be that "sometimes the last one at the dinner table gets the pork chop."

Mickey Redmond—inextricably linked with Red Wings hockey, both as a player and most notably as an announcer—makes a pass into the offensive zone against Toronto Maple Leafs alumni during the first period of the inaugural Showdown in Hockeytown alumni game on February 12, 2005.

When he senses that the Red Wings are about to give up an odd-man rush, he warns them on-air. "Look out here," he says.

Many people, including Regner, like his now-famous line, "Folks, this is no place for a nervous person."

It's also fully established that Redmond doesn't like how modern rules have changed the game. "He's not going to like this one," Mickey will opine when he believes a player has been victimized by a weak penalty call.

Bingo Bango. Holy Mackerel. He loves to get the telestrator out and show you how the puck hit someone on the way to the net. He always thanks his video crew for coming up with the video he wants.

At 9:00 on a Saturday at Joe Louis Arena, with the regular crowd shuffling in, the team employees running the entertainment center will play Billy Joel's "Piano Man" on the speakers. On TV, Mickey will sing along for a few seconds.

"He's been around as long as I've known hockey, and returning to Michigan on our winter and spring breaks, it's how we knew we were 'home,'" Brown said. "We'd turn on PASS [later Fox Sports Detroit], and there would be Mick with his color and stories."

Redmond, who broke into the NHL with the Montreal Canadiens, winning Stanley Cups in 1967–68 and 1968–69, and then first got into broadcasting working for *Hockey Night in Canada*, likes to say that it was like getting a Harvard education in both professions.

It's hard to find anyone who doesn't like Mickey. That's how it was when he played in the NHL. He was a colorful, popular player.

"He had the great slap shot," Regner recalled. "He had the moustache, the flowing hair. People could relate to him. He looked like an average Detroiter. He looked like a guy who could be working on the assembly line putting a bumper on the car."

As a player, Redmond was known for working on his craft.

"He was a natural goal scorer, but he would stay out after practice and shoot pucks for a long time," said former Detroit goalie Jimmy Rutherford. "He made his mark as a goal scorer, but he could be an all-around player when he needed to be. He really understood the game."

The *Real* Story of Red Kelly's Trade to the Rangers

Before the Detroit Red Wings announced the major trade with the New York Rangers on February 5, 1960, Gordie Howe announced it to Bill Gadsby as Gadsby was trying to ram him through the boards. "Hey, lighten up," Howe told Gadsby. "You are coming here tomorrow in a trade."

Howe was telling the truth. After the game, it was announced that Rangers had traded Gadsby and Eddie "the Entertainer" Shack to Detroit for Red Kelly and Billy McNeill.

This was one veteran All-Star defenseman being traded for another. Both Gadsby and Kelly were 32. Kelly had one Norris Trophy to his name, and Gadsby had been a Norris runner-up three times.

In 1958–59 Gadsby had registered 46 assists to break Doug Harvey's NHL record of most assists in a season by a defenseman.

The trade created a stir around hockey. It was a fascinating deal because Kelly and Gadsby were both future Hall of Famers. Kelly was smoother and more accomplished offensively. Gadsby was more physical.

Gadsby was thrilled with the deal because he had always wanted to play for Detroit. Plus, the Rangers were a last-place team.

Shack was also an intriguing piece because he was only 22 and he had already proven he could be a major agitator. He also seemed to have some potential to be a 15- or 20-goal scorer.

As soon as the deal was announced, Shack was ecstatic. He had not enjoyed his experience with the Rangers. Shack and Rangers coach Phil Watson had major differences from the beginning and had often butted heads.

Gadsby recalled that one day Watson was making a point in practice and asked Shack if he understood. Shack took his two fingers and pretended like he was putting information into one ear. Then he took two fingers from his other hand and pretended he was pulling it out the other side. Watson sent Shack to the minor leagues over that incident.

Watson had been fired and replaced by Alfie Pike before the Gadsby-Kelly deal was made. But Shack still had a bad taste about New York, and he was itching to tell the media what he thought about playing there. Wily veteran Gadsby advised Shack to take the high road, but he didn't listen.

Shack let his emotions overflow in his interviews with the media. It was a scorched earth–style session with reporters.

Gadsby said he had felt right from the beginning that something was going to go wrong with the deal.

Shack accused him of being a psychic when Pike came to them the next morning to say the deal was off because both McNeill and Kelly had refused to report.

League president Clarence Campbell placed a 48-hour hold on the deal to give the Rangers time to talk Kelly and McNeill into reporting.

Gadsby recalled that McNeill's issue was child care. He had lost his wife to polio, and he was raising his children by himself. He had child care arranged in Detroit, and he had nothing in place in New York.

The rumor was that Kelly didn't want to report because of family reasons. But that wasn't true, Kelly said. "It was because [the Red Wings] were saying we didn't make the playoffs for the first time in 1958–59 because I had a bad year," Kelly said.

Kelly said that the impetus for the trade was an article penned by *Toronto Globe and Mail* writer Trent Frayne.

Frayne had interviewed Kelly in Toronto on the premise that Kelly was playing better in 1959–60 than he had the previous season. He wanted Kelly's opinion on why that was the case.

Kelly originally claimed it was merely the ups and downs of a playing career, and then decided to tell him the truth. Kelly had broken his ankle and had played on it to help the team. "[Adams] came and asked if I could take the cast off, tape it up, and play," Kelly said. "I said I would try."

Kelly admitted that he couldn't turn to the left on his ankle. "I did what I could to play with the injury," he said. "That's what I told him, and he wrote the story. He wrote it for the weekend magazine."

The problem occurred when the *Detroit Free Press* wrote its version of the story under the headline: WAS RED KELLY FORCED TO PLAY WITH A BROKEN FOOT?

"The story didn't come close to matching what the headline said," Kelly said.

But the damage had been done. Kelly's wife was sitting in the stands during the game and heard that her husband had been traded.

Kelly told Detroit general manager Jack Adams he would think about going to New York, and he did think about it. The way he viewed it was the Rangers were in last place, and he wasn't going to be in the playoffs. He decided to call the management of a tool company where he worked in the summer and ask if he could start there "tomorrow."

After Kelly was told he had a job, he called Adams and said he was retiring. Adams was furious.

"That's the story of why I didn't report," Kelly said. "When Detroit blamed me for missing the playoffs, it made me mad. I broke the bone just below my ankle and played on it because players always did that back then. We didn't tell anyone about it because we didn't want anyone taking a swing at it."

Campbell nullified the trade, but Kelly soon was dealt to the Toronto Maple Leafs for Marc Reaume. Reaume played 47 games for the Red Wings, and Kelly played eight more seasons for the Maple Leafs. Moved to center, Kelly had 20 goals and 70 points in his first full season in Toronto. The Reaume-for-Kelly swap has to make the list of worst trades in Red Wings history.

61 Shouldn't We Call It a Brendan Shanahan Hat Trick?

When an NHL player registers a goal, an assist, and a fighting major in the same game, it's called a Gordie Howe Hat Trick.

No one seems sure who called it that first, but it clearly pays homage to the truth that Howe was an offensive star who also had skill as a fighter.

The only oddity of honoring Mr. Hockey with that name is that Howe only recorded two GHHTs during an NHL career that lasted 26 seasons.

His first came on October 11, 1953, at Detroit's Olympia Stadium when he fought Fern Flaman and generated a goal and two assists in a 4–0 triumph against the Toronto Maple Leafs.

Howe's second GHHT also came against the Maple Leafs, when he fought Teeder Kennedy on March 21, 1954. Newspaper articles confirm that Kennedy had started the fight with Howe because Howe had sliced open his ear with a high stick. The article is important because box scores from other newspapers didn't show Howe's penalty as being for fighting.

Howe scored the first goal of that game, and then assisted on Ted Lindsay's goal to complete the Gordie Howe Hat trick.

The GHHT is not a rare occurrence. Wayne Gretzky only had a couple of fights, but he had a GHHT on December 22, 1982, when he had a goal, two assists, and a fight against Minnesota North Stars center Neal Broten. Lady Byng winner Pavel Datsyuk registered a GHHT on October 8, 2010, when he had a goal, an assist, and a third-period fight against Anaheim's Corey Perry.

Although Howe was considered tough and ruthless, he only picked up 22 fighting majors during his NHL career. Three of Howe's fights came against Hall of Famer Fern Flaman. Most opponents chose to stay away from Howe, fearful of his wrath.

The GHHT record holder is former Red Wings Hall of Fame winger Brendan Shanahan, who had 17 during his career.

"It was later in my career before I even knew anything about it," Shanahan said. "It's only been over the last few years that you started to hear more about it."

It's certainly an interesting twist that Shanahan would own a record associated with fighting, because he went on to become the league's discipline guru.

62 The 1977–78 Red Wings Were Respected Like Champions

The 1977–78 Red Wings didn't win the Stanley Cup, but they did win the hearts and minds of their Detroit fans.

Led by Dale McCourt, Reed Larson, Dan Maloney, and others, this Red Wings squad is a candidate for the title of the most beloved sub-.500 team in NHL history.

"In all sports, there is a time when a team comes together and no one knows when it will happen or why it will happen," said former Red Wings player Paul Woods, who was on that team. "That's what happened to this team. And once that happens, you can go beyond what your problems are. You think, *We are just going to go out and win*, and you believe you can."

The Red Wings were 32–34–14 in 1977–78, but they were 22–11–7 at home.

"You could really feel, especially in the second half of the year, that the fans were really into it too," Woods recalled.

Detroit had missed the playoffs for seven consecutive seasons and fans were starved for something to cheer about. From March 4 to March 28, the Red Wings went on a 7–1–4 run that created a buzz around the NHL about this feisty team.

"You could see great improvement under new coach Bobby Kromm," said longtime Red Wings statistician Greg Innis. "Fans were excited about youngsters like McCourt and Larson."

Larson had a nuclear-powered slap shot, and McCourt was a classy scorer who never celebrated a goal. The Red Wings also boasted aging Dennis Hull, who could still shoot the puck; and Czech star Vaclav Nedomansky, who had been a dominant player in international hockey; plus Errol Thompson, who still had an exceptional backhander. Defenseman Greg Joly was a former No. 1 draft pick.

Given the misery fans had endured following the Red Wings, it was easy to understand why fans were smitten with this team. It was like these Red Wings were the Little Engine That Could. When the Red Wings qualified for the playoffs and earned the right to play the Atlanta Flames in a three-game postseason series, it felt as if the Red Wings had already had a successful season.

"The Stanley Cup playoffs is what happened for other teams like the Canadiens, Flyers, Bruins, or Rangers—not the Red Wings," said sports journalist Larry O'Connor, who was an ardent Detroit fan in those days. "So to have the Wings—the miserable god-awful Wings whose fortunes once rested on the vastly unfulfilled talents of Barry Salovaara, Mike Bloom, Rick Foley, and Mike Wong—actually make the playoffs was a wonderful shock to the system. It was like the hockey gods took pity on us for one brief moment to remind us what a great franchise the Red Wings once was."

Fans stood in line all night at Olympia for playoff tickets. In what turned out to be poor judgment, the Red Wings allowed the hundreds of waiting fans to come inside the arena.

"Then, in an inspired moment of capitalism, they also decided to sell beer," O'Connor remembered, noting that the whole experience was "surreal."

At one point, the inebriated masses marched onto the ice and began to play a game of foot hockey, using a crushed beer can for a puck. O'Connor recalls one participant falling and splitting his head open on the ice.

"The lawlessness took an ominous turn around 4:00 AM, when another drunken sod commandeered a high-lo and proceeded to drive it through the corridor and into the line of people, who scattered out of harm's way," O'Connor said. "As daylight broke, all hell broke loose and there was the predictable rush on the ticket window."

When the mess was sorted out, O'Connor said he ended up with standing-room tickets for Game 2.

The Flames, boasting a big, physical team with high-powered offense, were favored against Detroit. Atlanta boasted Tom Lysiak, Eric Vail, Bob MacMillan, Guy Chouinard, and Willi Plett, among others.

But the Red Wings won Game 1 by a score of 5–3 in the Omni Center in Atlanta and then came home to play what has to be considered one of the most memorable games in Red Wings history.

The Red Wings had not won a playoff game in Detroit since 1966, but there was a positive aura around the city about the Red Wings' chances of ending the series in Olympia. An Olympia-record crowd of 16,671 showed up, and those in attendance said the feeling was similar to what fans felt when watching the Red Wings during their glory years in the 1950s. The building was alive with optimism.

Lysiak and Nedomansky both scored to make a 1–1 game, and then Bill Lochead scored to give Detroit a 2–1 lead in the third period. Five minutes later, Bobby Lalonde tied the game.

That set the stage for Lochead to score one of the most memorable goals in Red Wings history.

With overtime looming, the speedy Lochead took a pass from Woods as he scooted out of his zone. Playing on his off-wing, the right-hand shooting Lochead flew down the left-wing boards and skillfully avoided an attempted hip check by defenseman Dick Redmond.

As Atlanta goalie Dan Bouchard drove out of the crease to meet him, Lochead looked like he was going to go around the net. But instead he pushed the puck in front of the net and then reached back over the crossbar and flicked the puck in the net one-handed.

"It just startled everyone," Woods recalled. "I don't blame Bouchard because I thought he was going around the net too. I thought he was going to pass it out front, and I was getting ready for a pass."

Woods said what was remarkable about the play was that it was accomplished at full speed. Lochead didn't stop to flick the puck in the net. "He was still skating," Woods said. "This was all done on the momentum of the rush. It was one of the most amazing goals I've ever seen."

Because Woods and Lochead were going at full speed when the goal was scored, Woods continued on toward Lochead to celebrate and knocked the wind out of him when he went to hug him.

"When Lochead scored, it was the loudest noise at Olympia in years," Innis recalled. "…Fans finally had something to cheer about. Outside, people were dancing, horns were honking. It seemed like the Stanley Cup had been won."

Lochead, a former first-round draft pick, had scored 20 goals that season, and that turned out to be the best season of his NHL career. He never quite lived up to the expectations the Red Wings had for him, and ended up playing much of his hockey career in Germany.

By beating the Flames, the Red Wings earned the right to meet the Scotty Bowman–coached Montreal Canadiens. That Montreal team had scored 107 goals more than the Red Wings during the regular season and gave up one fewer goal per game.

But the Red Wings shocked the Canadiens by winning the first game of the series in Montreal. Detroit lost Game 2, and then came back and had a 2–1 lead in Game 3, only to end up losing 4–2.

"If you look at the lineups of the two teams, it's not even close," Woods said. "But if we won that Game 3, we would have gone at least six games and then I don't know what would have happened."

The Habs blew out the Red Wings 8–0 in Game 4, but a strange thing happened in that game. With Montreal leading 7–0, Red Wings fans in Olympia stood and gave their team a standing ovation for the effort they had put in just to get that far.

"It was one of the most amazing things I've ever seen in sports," Woods said. "We're down 7–0, but we kept playing, and then it happened…. I don't think there has ever been a team down 7–0 in a playoff game that got a standing ovation game. It was an amazing feeling."

Fans simply wanted to salute one of the most popular teams in Red Wings' history. Although no one knew it at the time, that ended up being the last playoff game ever held at Olympia.

63 Howe and Bower: Friends and Foes

Johnny Bower's best friend was frequently his worst nightmare.

When Bower was a young goaltender in his hometown of Prince Albert, Saskatchewan, his youth team would often travel to Saskatoon to play the local club there. Most nights, the team would come back with their tails between their legs due to one fellow on that Saskatoon club—a lad by the name of Gordie Howe.

"We did alright when we played against Flin Flon or Battleford or Moose Jaw, but Saskatoon was too powerful for us," Bower recalled in his book *The China Wall.* "We just couldn't beat Gordie Howe and his teams. One game we lost 8–2 and we were lucky to get two goals against them. Howe, he got more than a hat trick on me. I think he ended up with five goals."

Little did the two boys know at the time that someday they'd both grow to be NHL stars and, perhaps even more surprising, fast friends.

Playing in the American Hockey League with the Cleveland Barons, Bower opened a restaurant in the summer months in the northern Saskatchewan resort town of Waskesiu. Bower's Big Boy was known to serve the best burgers in town.

At the same time, Howe was establishing himself as the NHL's most dominant player with the Red Wings, but in those days, even superstars didn't make so much money that they didn't require summer employment.

"I decided I'd maybe go up to Waskesiu and work on the golf course there," Howe recounted in the foreword to *The China Wall.* Howe and his wife, Colleen, found a summer cabin not far from where Bower and his wife, Nancy, were living. The wives hit it off almost immediately, and the men also soon developed a friendship.

They fished and played sports together—such as tennis and soft-toss with the baseball—and thanks to Gordie's ingenuity, they also got in plenty of time on the links.

"Every second day, I was required to change the water in the ball washers, rake the sand, and put new holes on the greens," Howe explained. "So I'd tell Johnny, 'I'm starting at 7:30 in the morning. Meet me at the second hole.' Then I'd play out of his bag…. I'd get all of my work done, and we'd get a round of golf in at the same time."

One day, Howe and Bower were spotted teeing it up on a hole by one of the course's members, who reported Howe to the club pro. "He told the member, 'Just relax. The guy who did it before him took the whole morning and two hours in the afternoon to do it. He gets it all done in four hours,'" Howe said. "They let me alone, and we played a lot of golf that summer."

The friendship garnered an added twist in the summer of 1958, when the Toronto Maple Leafs claimed Bower from Cleveland in the NHL intra-league draft. Suddenly, Bower was the No. 1 goalie for Canada's most popular NHL team and Howe was the league's preeminent scorer, a relationship that would normally mesh together about as well as fire and water. In this case, though, nothing could spoil the bond between Howe and Bower.

"We were such good friends that Gordie always used to have me over to his house for dinner whenever the Leafs played in Detroit, even though the NHL had a strict no-fraternization policy in those days," Bower said.

Howe insisted the first goal he ever scored in a Red Wings uniform was in a preseason game against Bower and Cleveland, and it turned out to be a habit-forming experience. In the NHL, Howe scored 49 regular-season and 11 Stanley Cup goals against Bower.

"There's no doubt that he's Mr. Hockey, the best player in history," Bower said in his book *The China Wall*. "I'd put his shot and Bernie ["Boom Boom"] Geoffrion's shot down as the hardest to get a read on, but I'd have to put Gordie down as the most dangerous opponent I ever faced.

"He gave me fits. He could switch hands and shoot just as hard left-handed as he could right-handed. Howe had the strongest, fastest wrists in hockey. A goalie never knew whether he'd shoot straight or try for the angle. He would change direction when you were positive he couldn't."

Howe allowed that Bower got the best of their one-on-one showdowns over the years.

"He was so good, he could make saves in his dreams," Howe said. "There was a lot of kidding that went on between us during games. I'd go in on him and I'd score, then I'd circle the net and I'd say, 'Thank you.' But when he'd stop me, all he'd do was grin.

"One time, he stopped me in the playoffs, and I let him know that I was going to throw him in Waskesiu Lake that summer."

Even when they found themselves at opposite ends of the ice on hockey's biggest stage, nothing could shake their friendship. Toronto and Detroit met four times in Stanley Cup series during the time Bower and Howe were opponents. Three times, Bower's Leafs emerged victorious, including triumphs in the 1963 and 1964 Stanley Cup Finals.

After the Leafs wrapped up a five-game victory in the 1963 Cup Finals, Howe and Bower stood arm-in-arm on Maple Leaf Gardens' ice conducting an interview with *Hockey Night in Canada*'s Frank Selke Jr., a moment that was captured in a famous photograph exhibiting the ultimate in sportsmanlike behavior.

"I felt it was the right thing to do," Howe explained. "He was an old friend, and I had to go congratulate him.

"After they beat us in the 1964 Finals series, I wanted Johnny's stick, and I asked him for it as we shook hands. I've often done that after a series or at an All-Star Game, asked somebody whom I respected for their stick. I've got over 50 sticks from people I think very highly of. Johnny is certainly one of those players."

The friendship continues to this day and was most recently renewed when Bower and Howe were both on hand for the Toronto-Detroit alumni showdown that was part of the 2013 Hockeytown Winter Festival at Comerica Park.

64 Gadsby Doesn't Buy the Entire Bobby Baun Legend

Every time Hall of Fame defenseman Bill Gadsby ran into Bobby Baun through the years, he would jokingly tell Baun that he still doesn't believe his leg was broken in 1964.

Gadsby is half serious when he says it.

"Maybe he had a hairline crack in his bone," Gadsby said. "But it wasn't any compound fracture. He's gotten a lot of ink with that story."

Gadsby remembers that 1964 Stanley Cup Game 6 well, and not because of Baun's heroics to score on a broken leg in overtime. Gadsby remembers his shot that didn't go in.

"What nobody remembers is that less than a minute before Baun fired the shot that made him famous, I took a shot that haunts me to this day," Gadsby said.

Early into the overtime, Gadsby carried the puck into the Toronto zone. He spotted Floyd Smith on the right wing. He moved the puck to Smith, who returned it immediately to complete the give-and-go. Gadsby shot the puck immediately.

"The play developed so quickly that [Toronto goalie Johnny] Bower never even reacted to the shot," Gadsby said.

The puck seemed to be on course to zoom past Bower's shoulder. "I was already raising my stick to celebrate," Gadsby said.

With Detroit leading 3–2 in the series, the Red Wings were the Stanley Cup champions if Gadsby's shot found the net.

Instead, the puck struck the upper shaft of Bower's goalie stick and deflected harmlessly away from the net.

The puck quickly turned the other way, and Gadsby found himself in his defensive position facing Baun, who had carried the puck into the Detroit zone.

Earlier in the game, Baun had been carried off the ice in the stretcher after injuring his right leg blocking Gordie Howe's shot.

When Baun shot the puck, Gadsby recalled, "it fluttered toward me like a Hoyt Wilhelm knuckleball…. Baun's shot struck my stick, and the puck deflected up, just missing my head, and went past Sawchuk. In hindsight, I wish that shot would have hit me square in the bean. Given all the stitches that had been sewn into my face by that time, what would a few more have mattered?"

That goal gave Toronto a 4–3 win, and then the Maple Leafs won Game 7 by a 4–0 decision. Baun played in that game as well. After the series, it was revealed that Baun was playing on a broken leg. The legend was born. For 50 years, Gadsby has listened to stories about Baun's heroics. He would love to see those X-rays.

They Took the Shirts off Their Backs

The Red Wings old-timers were playing the Quebec old-timers at the Montreal Forum the night of January 21, 1966, the night before the Wings tangled with the Montreal Canadiens at the same locale, so Detroit trainer Lefty Wilson packed both home and away uniforms for the trip. But after the Old-Timers Game ended and everyone had gone for the night, thieves worked their way into the

Red Wings' dressing room, making off with both sets of sweaters, 45 of them in total.

Luckily for the Wings, their junior affiliate, the Hamilton Red Wings, were slated to play the Montreal Jr. Canadiens at the Forum on January 23, so the Hamilton jerseys, which were identical to the Detroit sweaters, were shipped by airplane to Montreal a day early, avoiding postponement of the game and allowing the Wings to skate against the Habs wearing the outfits of their junior squad.

The different apparel did require some alterations, since not all players wore the same size sweater. 6'3" Ab McDonald was forced to switch from 15 to 22. Alex Delvecchio wore his usual No. 10 but had to do without the *C* indicating he was the captain. For that night, Floyd Smith wore the *C*, as the Hamilton captain Nick Libett wore No. 17.

By the end of the night, after Roger Crozier made 31 saves and Paul Henderson, Gordie Howe, and Ron Murphy tallied for a 3–0 Detroit win, the Canadiens probably wished that the burglars had also made off with the Detroiters' skates. Luckily for the Wings, they had another set of red sweaters back in Detroit that they wore at Olympia Stadium when facing the New York Rangers the following night.

When he first learned of the missing sweaters, Detroit coach/GM Sid Abel suggested that maybe the Habs had pulled a fast one on the Wings. "If it's a joke, we're not laughing," Abel said.

Within a couple of days, the whereabouts of the Detroit sweaters became apparent, because the shirts seemed to be everywhere in Montreal. It turned out that the robbery was a prank engineered by University of Montreal students as part of their winter carnival celebrations, part of an inter-faculty competition to see who could steal the most original object.

After Montreal's 4–2 home-ice loss to Chicago on January 26, students invaded the ice surface, all wearing Red Wings sweaters, and 44 of them were arrested.

People were showing up around town wearing Detroit sweaters, and physical education department queen Suzanne Dupras, 17, was photographed by the *Montreal Gazette* wearing Howe's white No. 9 sweater at the carnival.

Along with the sweaters, the students also stole four Tex Coulter paintings, valued at $200 each, from the Forum lobby. Among other objects purloined were two brewery trucks, a city of Outremont municipal truck, a six-foot-high painting of Queen Elizabeth, a radio station cruiser, and a black bear taken from the Garden of Wonders Zoo. The bear, which was also seen wearing Howe's No. 9 sweater, was safely returned to his pen.

David Molson, president of the Canadiens, did not see the humor in what the students pegged as harmless pranks.

"We are going through with the charges of destroying public property and I hope the Detroit Red Wings also press charges so that those responsible will feel the full consequences," Molson told the *Gazette*.

On January 27, 1966, three women and 30 men were brought before Judge Armand Chevrette and charged with possession of property, obtained by crime, a charge that carried a maximum term of 10 years imprisonment.

Though the Wings and Canadiens quickly dropped the charges once their missing items were returned, Montreal police continued with criminal proceedings, but on January 18, 1967, all 33 students were acquitted by Judge Irenee Lagarde, though according to the *Gazette*, she did give a verbal dressing-down to law student Andre Belisle, the apparent ringleader of the escapade.

"It seems to me that you are the party principally responsible for the affair, although you are not accused," Lagarde said. "I wonder what kind of lawyer you will turn out to be?

"If you are going to be a lawyer, you are going to have to change your notions of the law. As a future lawyer, how do you condone a violation of the law? Do you people consider yourselves a caste apart?

"You might find it funny, but I don't. Everyone, no matter his station in life, is bound by the laws of the land. I hope you will reflect before repeating such an act."

Apparently, the pleas fell on deaf ears. The same day, four University of Montreal students were arrested attempting to steal a Montreal Police anti-riot truck, part of that year's winter carnival prank contest.

66 Red Wings Robbed by Pocket Rocket's Sleight of Hand

Montreal Canadiens center Henri Richard is credited with scoring the game-winning, series-clinching overtime goal against the Detroit Red Wings in Game 6 of the 1966 Stanley Cup Finals.

Almost a half century later, the players from that Detroit team would argue that Richard should not be credited with anything except getting away with an undeserved victory.

"Most of the players knew he had gloved the puck into the net with his hand," said former Detroit defenseman Bill Gadsby.

The OT tally, giving Montreal a 3–2 win, came at 2:20 after a Dave Balon centering feed from the left wing.

Gadsby said the late Roger Crozier, playing goal for Detroit, was clear that Richard pulled the puck into the net with his glove as he was sliding into Crozier.

That's not what Richard told the media. In the May 16, 1966, *Sports Illustrated*, Richard's version was this: "[Dave Balon] passed the puck out from the corner, and as I was going to hit it, someone tripped me. The puck hit my knee and went in."

Detroit defenseman Bert Marshall didn't buy Richard's version, telling *Sports Illustrated*, "I know one thing. Richard didn't shoot it in. [Balon's] pass from the corner hit my stick and dropped in front of the goal—right in front of Richard."

Gadsby said Crozier's anger was directed more at referee Frank Udvari than Richard.

"Crozier believed Udvari wasn't in a position to make the call," Gadsby recalled.

The Red Wings were only a fourth-place team in 1966, finishing just four games above .500. But they upset the Chicago Black Hawks in the first round, thanks to brilliant goalkeeping from Crozier, who gave up only 10 goals in six games.

Montreal was highly favored in the Stanley Cup Finals, but the Red Wings grew confident when they defeated the Canadiens in the first two games at the Montreal Forum. The acrobatic Crozier was impressive to the point that the Red Wings believed they could win the series.

Even after the Canadiens won the next three, Gadsby said the Red Wings' confidence was still high.

"They hammered us 5–1 in Game 5, but we really felt like we would win Game 6 and force a Game 7," Gadsby said.

In Game 6 in Detroit, Floyd Smith had scored at 10:30 of the third period to tie the game 2–2.

Gadsby had played Game 6 with a broken toe, suffered in Game 5 when he blocked a shot by J.C. Tremblay.

When the Cup had been awarded to Montreal after the controversial goal, no one took it harder than Gadsby. When Detroit had been up 2–0 in the series, the media had focused heavily on the story line that he was the only 20-year NHL veteran who had never won a Stanley Cup. Dit Clapper and Gordie Howe, the only other 20-year players at the time, had won the Stanley Cup.

Gadsby was 38 then, which made the loss more difficult to accept.

"If Richard rifled the bastard into the net you don't mind," Gadsby told *Sports Illustrated*. "But you hate to lose like that. Well, what the hell, it's not the end of the world."

But it was the end Gadsby's career. Before he had left the ice after Game 6, Gadsby had skated over to the stands and told his wife, Edna, that she had seen her husband play his last game. He fulfilled a promise he made that she would be the first to know when he decided to retire. He played 1,248 games without winning a Stanley Cup.

67 Wings Fans Hate the Leafs More Than the Habs

Sid Abel, who captained, coached, and served as general manger over a 26-year stint with the Red Wings, was once asked which of the so-called Original Six NHL teams the Wings despised the most.

"They paid us to play the rest of the league," Abel responded. "We played the Leafs for free."

On the flip side, the feeling was mutual.

"I used to enjoy playing against Montreal," Red Horner, Toronto defenseman from 1929 to 1940 and one of the NHL's toughest customers, remarked in a 2001 interview. "Those Detroit teams, that was no fun. We'd be scrapping all night."

On their route to glory, no two teams stood in the path of the Red Wings more frequently than the Toronto Maple Leafs and the Montreal Canadiens. The Wings have played in more Stanley Cup Finals against the Leafs (seven), but have won more Cups at the expense of the Canadiens (three) than any other team.

In those days, with NHL sponsorship of junior clubs and far less player movement than there is in today's game, the feuding was born at a young age.

"It was an organization thing," former Wing Johnny Wilson once explained to Jack Dulmage of the *Windsor Star*. "It started in the sponsored junior clubs and stayed with a player into the NHL. There wasn't much trading except at minor levels. On the trains we didn't even speak to the opposition.

"For that matter, we had nothing to do with them from the end of one season to the start of the next. By the time a new season started, we were ready to hate them again. You don't see that now.

"I remember on the trains when they had the dining car and when we went past the other guys, we snarled at each other."

Still, as much as both are strong rivals of the Red Wings, there's a lingering nastiness between the Leafs and Wings that doesn't seem to exist in battles between the Canadiens and Wings.

Even old Leafs see it that way in terms of their own rivalry with the two teams. "Montreal-Toronto was the traditional rivalry," explained former Leafs forward Bob Nevin. "Detroit-Toronto was the bitter rivalry."

Much bad blood has been spilled, both literally and figuratively, over the years between the Wings and Leafs. The first time Detroit ever hit double-digits on the scoreboard was a 10–1 rout of Toronto at Olympia Stadium on Christmas Day 1930. Toronto's record shutout win and Detroit's record shutout setback came when the Leafs drubbed the Wings 13–0 on January 2, 1971, at Maple Leaf Gardens.

Detroit won the first Stanley Cup in franchise history at the expense of the Leafs in 1935–36. But in six Cup Finals meetings since, the decision has gone Toronto's way every time.

In the opening game of the 1950 Stanley Cup Semifinal series against Toronto, Detroit right-winger Gordie Howe suffered a near-fatal head injury in a collision with Leafs captain Teeder Kennedy.

Once he regained consciousness, Howe exonerated Kennedy from blame, but old-time Wings fans held a grudge against him

Most Wins by Wings vs. NHL Opponents

Team	Wins
Chicago Blackhawks	364
Toronto Maple Leafs	278
New York Rangers	261
Boston Bruins	252
Montreal Canadiens	203
St. Louis Blues	119
Dallas Stars*	108

*Includes games as Minnesota North Stars

regardless. Likewise, Leafs fans still gloat to their Detroit rivals over Nikolai Borschevsky's Game 7 overtime winner in the 1993 opening-round series between the two teams, the most recent playoff series between Toronto and Detroit.

In the 1942 Finals, the Leafs rallied from a 3–0 deficit to beat the Wings in seven games, the only time that's ever happened in a Cup Finals series.

The cross-pollination of Toronto and Detroit Stanley Cup–winning rosters with ex-Leafs and former Wings also has served to ramp up the rivalry. Red Kelly won four Stanley Cups with the Leafs after being dealt to Toronto by Detroit. Goalie Turk Broda, shipped to Toronto when he was still a Detroit farmhand, beat the Wings in three Stanley Cup Finals series.

Toronto's most recent Cup winner in 1966–67 featured five former Wings—goalie Terry Sawchuk, defensemen Larry Hillman and Marcel Pronovost, and forwards Larry Jeffrey and Kelly. In more recent times, former Leafs such as Larry Murphy, Jamie Macoun, Dmitri Mironov, and Bob Rouse found Stanley Cup glory in Detroit after coming up empty with Toronto.

The Leafs failed to sign Kelly and left-winger Ted Lindsay when both were in the Toronto junior system. They ended up in Detroit, combining to produce four Stanley Cups, three Lady

Byngs, an Art Ross Trophy, a Norris Trophy, and 17 All-Star selections for the Wings.

"It was always such an intense rivalry," said Hall of Famer Pronovost, who won Cups with the Wings and the Leafs. "People always talk about Toronto-Montreal, but Toronto-Detroit was just as much of a battle."

Detroit-Montreal was the NHL's biggest battle in the 1950s. The two franchises won nine of 10 Stanley Cup crowns during the decade, meeting four times in the Cup Finals series.

"It was quite a rivalry," former Detroit captain Alex Delvecchio said of the feud with the Habs. "Montreal was our biggest obstacle to winning the Stanley Cup.

"They were a powerhouse. It made you play better, because you wanted to beat them so badly."

Certainly, there was an element of bitterness in the rivalry. "I hate that club," Montreal superstar Maurice "Rocket" Richard once remarked of the Red Wings.

While playing for Detroit, Pronovost lived across the border in Windsor, Ontario, and recalls that there wasn't much fondness for the Wings in Canada at the time.

"When I first played in Detroit, everyone in Windsor was either Montreal or Toronto fans," recalled Pronovost.

That was when *Hockey Night in Canada* first hit the airwaves and lingering bitterness developed amongst Canadian-border hockey fans because Detroit utilized its territorial rights to black out the Saturday night games.

"We used to joke that whenever we played the Canadiens or Toronto [at the Olympia], there were more fights in the stands than on the ice," Pronovost said.

There have been ebbs and flows in the rivalry between Detroit and Montreal over the years, but the distaste between the Wings and Leafs never gears down, and the intensity was reborn in 2013, when both moved into the NHL's Atlantic Division.

"It's great to see the old Norris Division kind of getting back together with the Leafs and the Red Wings back in the same division," former Toronto captain Wendel Clark said. "The rivalry was always great. Friday in Detroit, Saturday in Toronto.... It was always an exciting time, and it's great to be part of that again."

There was bitterness with Montreal, but it reached its apex decades ago. But the Leafs-Wings rivalry will live on forever.

68 Take in a Game at Gordie Howe Bowl

Several former Red Wings have arenas named in their honor. There's the Steve Yzerman Arena in Nepean, Ontario; the Centre Marcel Dionne in Drummondville, Quebec; and the Martin Lapointe Arena in Lachine, Quebec.

But Gordie Howe is the only Red Wings great who can boast of a football stadium bearing his name.

"It says something about the respect he holds in Saskatchewan," said Red Wings coach Mike Babcock, who as a youngster in Saskatoon, Saskatchewan, skated at Kinsmen Arena, part of the Gordie Howe Park complex in the city.

On July 22, 1966, the city of Saskatoon held Gordie Howe Day to recognize, as *Montreal Gazette* writer Vern DeGeer called Howe, "its mightiest ambassador." He wrote, "This native son has been the greatest thing that has happened to Saskatoon since the Barr colonists pitched tent here in 1903."

Actually, Howe was born in Floral, a tiny railway stop just southeast of the city, easily spotted by the solitary Co-Op grain elevator bearing the town's name.

Ab and Grechen Howe moved their brood into Saskatoon a few months later, and it was where Gordie was raised.

You could say Howe put Saskatoon on the map, even that he had a hand in building the city.

"I helped lay the foundation for the Bessborough Hotel," Howe said during one visit to Saskatoon, noting one of the city's famous landmarks.

Representatives from every NHL team—including captains Alex Delvecchio (Detroit), Pierre Pilote (Chicago), and John Bucyk (Boston)—were on hand to salute Howe as he was paraded through town and then honored during a ceremony held at Saskatoon Arena. Howe's good friends Johnny Bower of the Toronto Maple Leafs, John Ferguson of the Montreal Canadiens, and Garry Peters of the New York Rangers were also present.

Testimonials offered to Howe included a life-size oil painting and a university scholarship in his name to go to a deserving player from the Saskatoon Kinsmen Club Pee Wee Hockey League, where Howe got his start in organized hockey in 1940.

Most significantly of all, the 350-acre sports complex in the city that first opened on September 23, 1960, and was known as Holiday Park was renamed Gordon Howe Park. And the football stadium within its confines was rechristened Gordie Howe Bowl.

Curiously, Howe knew the site well. It wasn't far from his childhood Saskatoon home, which used to be adjacent to the farmland that was utilized to construct the park.

"I got my first job there when I was 12 years old," Howe recalled. "The farmer who owned the land paid my brother and I to hunt the gophers and keep them out of his crops."

Gordie Howe Bowl is home to the Saskatoon Hilltops—15-time Canadian junior football champions—and also plays host to the city's high school football league.

There was talk of replacing the stadium in recent years, but instead, a fund-raising campaign was launched to raise $11 million and renovate the venerable complex. Upgrades will include a 12,000-square-foot two-story clubhouse, field turf to replace the current natural grass field, and a new scoreboard.

Those behind the renovation plans insist the changes will make Gordie Howe Bowl a viable facility for the next 30 years, ensuring that Howe's legacy will carry on for many decades to come.

69 Gadsby's Firing Remains an Unsolved Mystery

It's been more than four decades since Bill Gadsby was fired as coach of the Detroit Red Wings, and yet he still finds himself wondering why it happened.

The Red Wings had posted an 8–1 record during the preseason and then won their first two games of the 1969–70 season. When the late former Red Wings owner Bruce Norris summoned Gadsby to his office before a home game against the Minnesota North Stars, Gadsby believed he was going to receive a pat on the back, not a pink slip.

"The whole conversation lasted 60 seconds," Gadsby recalled. Norris told Gadsby he was relieving him of his duties and installing Sid Abel as the new coach. "It was the most shocking moment of my life," Gadsby said.

He pressed Norris for a reason, but he offered none that made any sense to Gadsby. "He said, 'I run a lot of corporations, and sometimes I just have a feeling of when I need to make a change,'" Gadsby said.

Did Abel talk Norris into the move because he wanted the job? Did Jim Bishop, serving as a right-hand man to Norris, shove Gadsby out the door? Was Norris resentful of the relationship

Portrait of Bill Gadsby from the 1965–66 season, Gadsby's last as an NHL player, though he went on to just more than one season as coach of the Red Wings before being unceremoniously—and mysteriously—fired.

Gadsby had with the veterans? Did Norris believe Gadsby was too independent-minded? It was well established that Norris liked to micromanage, and Gadsby was not a yes-man.

There were many theories floating around Detroit, but no one to this day knows officially why Gadsby was fired on October 16, 1969, with a 2–0 record.

The Red Wings had beaten the Chicago Black Hawks 4–1 the night before, and Gadsby remembered that Norris put his arm around him and said, "Bill, you really got these guys going."

As Gadsby walked out of the dismissal meeting with Norris, he wondered what had changed in less than 24 hours.

Gadsby was able to tell his wife, Edna, before she heard elsewhere. But news of the firing spread around Olympia like a raging brush fire, and Gadsby's daughters, sitting in the stands, heard before he could reach them. They were in tears.

The Detroit players were the last people in Olympia to hear what happened. Gadsby headed down to the dressing room during the warm-up, and Frank Mahovlich was still receiving treatment for a charley horse. He had not been told that Gadsby was fired.

Gadsby said he was looking for Abel because he just wanted to know if he had any information on why he had been fired.

According to Gadsby, before he said a word, Abel immediately blurted out, "I had nothing to do with this. It was Bruce's decision."

News accounts of the game said the Red Wings looked disorganized that night during a 3–2 loss to the North Stars.

At one point, fans began to chant, "We want Gadsby! We want Gadsby!"

After the game, Detroit defenseman Ron Harris said the players had been badly shaken by the firing.

"It just makes me sick," Gordie Howe told reporters that night. "There was no inkling this was coming. No warning. I just wonder if I still have a job on this team."

Howe and Gadsby were close friends then, and remain close friends to this day. Howe and his wife, Colleen, sat with Gadsby and his wife until 5:00 AM that night discussing what had happened.

The media reported that Norris had been "vague" about his reasoning for the coaching change. He mentioned that he didn't believe Gadsby had been a good communicator with players, a strange comment given that Gadsby was viewed as a players' coach.

In the previous off-season, Norris had hired former lacrosse executive Bishop to serve in a management role that was never clearly defined.

During training camp, there had been some tension between Bishop and Gadsby over how Gadsby had handled team discipline.

Bishop wanted Gadsby to be tougher, and Gadsby wanted Bishop to mind his own business. It was established that Bishop answered to Norris, but it was written nowhere that Bishop had any power with the team. Gadsby believed it was his job to decide how to deal with players.

Gadsby recalled that Bishop was always talking about how coaches from other sports conducted their business. "When I was fired, I half-expected Vince Lombardi to replace me," Gadsby said.

Abel had the same issue with Bishop. He didn't like how Bishop was always trying to call meetings to discuss what should be done with the team. Abel was the general manager, and he believed that Bishop was overstepping his bounds. His arguments with Bishop were more heated than Gadsby's exchanges with Bishop.

Gadsby admitted that he didn't enjoy having Norris meddling into coaching decisions. Norris had a habit of telling coaches what to do. He recalled Norris coming up to him between periods of a game against the Pittsburgh Penguins and demanding that veteran Dean Prentice be benched.

Prentice had no idea why he was being benched, and Gadsby said he didn't believe it was appropriate to tell him about the conversation he had with Norris. "[It] just tore me up, actually haunted me for years because of the respect I had for Dean as a player and a man," Gadsby said. "Through the years, I've said consistently that I thought he should have been in the Hall of Fame. Everyone in hockey understood how valuable he was."

Gadsby admitted that Norris used to call him on the bench during games. One night after Norris called him four times, he yanked the phone off the wall. But that happened the season before Gadsby was fired.

Norris never confronted Gadsby about those issues, but probably they played a role in his decision to fire him. However, Gadsby doesn't know for sure because he could never get Norris to discuss it.

After the firing, Gadsby left the hockey world to become a sales representative. He assumed he would never see Norris again. He was wrong. Gadsby was in Key Largo, Florida, visiting his boss, John Curran, who had a home down there. Gadsby and his wife were out for supper with Curran and his wife at the Ocean Reef Lodge. "Imagine my astonishment when [Norris] walked into the Ocean Reef Lodge," Gadsby said. "Better yet, imagine his astonishment."

By coincidence, the maitre d' parked Norris and his entourage at a table near Gadsby's table. Gadsby's wife, Edna, asked him not to make a scene, but Gadsby stood and asked Norris if they could talk. "[He] had that same look of dread that opponents used to get when they realized they had ticked off Black Jack Stewart in Chicago or Gordie Howe in Detroit," Gadsby recalled.

Gadsby said Norris first tried to say he didn't want to leave his guests, and then realized that Gadsby wasn't going to go away. He motioned for Gadsby to meet him in the hallway. When they get into the hall, Gadsby loudly tried to convince Norris to tell him why he fired him when the team was playing well. Norris again tried to offer the same speech about his experience in running corporations and trusting his instincts. Gadsby didn't accept that, and demanded that Norris provide more detail.

According to Gadsby, Norris said it wasn't the place to have that conversation. He offered to meet Gadsby the next day on the Norris family yacht. That angered Gadsby even more. "I don't want to go on your boat," Gadsby said. "I don't want to see you again. I just want to know why I was fired."

Gadsby said he was loud, and by then, the meeting had attracted a crowd. Finally, he saw his wife, pleading for him to back off. "I just pushed [Norris'] head against the wall and said, 'You're not a man,'" Gadsby recalled.

Gadsby believes that 1969–70 Red Wings team could have won the Stanley Cup had he stayed behind the bench. He believed he had a strong rapport with that team that still boasted Mahovlich, Alex Delvecchio, and Gordie Howe as its top line.

The Red Wings finished third that season, four points out of first. They were swept by the Black Hawks in the playoffs.

Bishop convinced Norris to hire Ned Harkness as the team's coach. The next season, Abel resigned as general manager, saying Harkness didn't know how to coach. Norris made Harkness general manager.

The Gadsby firing seemed to be the start of a dark period in Red Wings history.

70 Ned Harkness Was Ahead of His Time

They called it the Darkness with Harkness, the point at which the Red Wings hit bottom during what long-suffering faithful fans of the team refer to as the Dead Wings era.

Ned Harkness, hired as coach of the team in 1970 and general manager of the Wings from 1971 to 1974, takes much of the heat for the failures that saw the franchise plummet to the depths of the NHL, but hindsight—always 20/20—suggests that perhaps he was just a man who was ahead of his time.

The first US college coach to go directly to the NHL, Harkness arrived in Detroit after guiding Cornell to an NCAA title and a perfect 29–0–0 season. But his new way of thinking met almost immediate resistance from the NHLers of whom he now found himself in charge.

Alex Delvecchio, Detroit captain at the time and the man who would ultimately replace Harkness as GM, still shudders at the first meeting with his old coach, who stopped by Delvecchio's home in the summer to introduce himself.

Delvecchio offered Harkness a beer, but Harkness informed him that he didn't drink and that he felt it was bad for the NHL's image if the players drank. Things took a turn for the worse when Delvecchio lit up one of his trademark stogies. "I don't smoke, and I don't think athletes should, either," Harkness told Delvecchio. "There will be no smoking in the team's dressing room this season."

As soon as Harkness departed, Delvecchio got on the phone and dialed Red Wings superstar right-winger Gordie Howe. "Fats called me that afternoon and he didn't even say hello," Howe recalled in a *Toronto Star* interview, invoking Delvecchio's nickname. "He said, 'Nine, we've got one hell of a problem on our hands.'"

An old friend of Red Wings executive Jim Bishop, Harkness was a harsh departure from his immediate predecessors behind the Detroit bench, Bill Gadsby and Sid Abel. And that didn't sit well with the pros he'd suddenly be coaching.

There was no question that Harkness was a stern taskmaster and someone who paid attention to detail. When Cornell was asked to appear as one of the teams to play against Ryan O'Neal's

Harvard in the 1970 film *Love Story*, Harkness agreed on one condition—that Cornell win the fictional game against Harvard.

He was equally stern with the Red Wings, and just as inflexible. Harkness took young center Garry Unger out to lunch and, on a napkin, drew a sketch to display to Unger how much hair should be trimmed from his flowing blond locks.

Ken Dryden's college coach, Harkness was looked upon as a man who could bring a new way of doing things to the NHL, but his players bristled at his views on the game and especially at his edicts for personal grooming and behavior.

"I want guys who go both ways, guys who forecheck, guys who back-check, guys who do it all," said Harkness, who stressed the value of work ethic in practice and games.

Harkness operated with eyes in the sky, spotters working in the press box and relaying messages to the bench via walkie-talkie. He was among the first coaches to put a forward on the point on the power play, a common practice in today's game. He believed in constant communication and held frequent team meetings to discuss special teams and systems play, also commonplace in the modern game. He sought to switch Howe to defense to prolong his career, but the plan didn't work, simply because there was no other forward capable of making up for Howe's lost production up front.

But his players did not see into the future and butted heads with Harkness at every turn. "We've had more meetings than the negotiators who settled the strike at General Motors," veteran Detroit defenseman Gary Bergman told *Sports Illustrated*.

Harkness realized quickly that he didn't have the same power or control over his players that made him such a success at the college level. "I think now that no coach, no owner, no general manager can control his destiny in the pros," Harkness told *Sports Illustrated*. "The players are excellent athletes. But the player associations take over. Motivation is gone and money takes over. If you

Detroit's Worst Coaches*

Coach	Season	G	W	L	T	PCT
Larry Wilson	(1976–77)	36	3	29	4	.138
Ted Garvin	(1973–74)	12	2	9	1	.208
Brad Park	(1985–86)	45	9	34	2	.222
Ted Lindsay	(1980–81)	29	5	21	3	.224
Duke Keats	(1926–27)	11	2	7	2	.272
Harry Neale	(1985–86)	35	8	23	4	.286
Doug Barkley	(1971–72; '75–76)	77	20	46	11	.331
Art Duncan	(1926–27)	33	10	21	2	.333
Ned Harkness	(1970–71)	38	12	22	4	.368
Wayne Maxner	(1980–82)	129	34	68	27	.368

*Minimum 10 games coached

like being a puppet, great. Not me. If I am going to be blamed for a decision, I want it to be my decision."

The new coach was also hampered by the loss of No. 1 goalie Roger Crozier, who was traded to Buffalo, and All-Star defenseman Carl Brewer, who opted to retire.

"[Detroit GM] Sid [Abel] says that I inherited a third-place team," Harkness complained, "but without Crozier and Brewer, last year's club would never have made the playoffs."

Early season injuries to goalie Roy Edwards (fractured skull), defenseman Ron Harris (shoulder), and forwards Frank Mahovlich (knee) and Howe (ribs) further weakened his club.

Detroit was 12–22–4 and coming off the worst defeat in franchise history, a 13–0 loss to the Toronto Maple Leafs, when the players, with the aid of NHLPA executive director Alan Eagleson, attempted to stage a mutiny to have Harkness removed.

They got their wish—in a sense. Harkness was promoted to GM, Sid Abel was fired, and Doug Barkley took over as coach. In complete control, Harkness set out to remove those he felt had sought to undermine him. He traded Unger to St. Louis, Mahovlich to Montreal, and Bruce MacGregor and Pete Stemkowski to the New York Rangers.

Harkness came in and started making all these changes," Mahovlich told the *Vancouver Province*. "Garry Unger wouldn't cut his hair, so he traded him. Stemkowski disagreed with Harkness about something, so he traded Stemkowski. He got nothing for these guys. He was doing all these ridiculous things, and I got very upset."

Had he come along a few years later, it's likely players would have been more open to Harkness' suggestions on how to do things. The close call Team Canada suffered at the hands of the Soviet Union in the 1972 Summit Series convinced the narrow-minded types that the NHL didn't hold a patent on hockey knowledge and that other schools of thought were worth considering.

"These days, all barriers are down in the game of hockey, and everyone learns from everyone else," said New Jersey Devils GM Lou Lamoriello, a former college coach at Providence. "That's why we have the best sport there is."

Even some of those who butted heads with Harkness now look back and wonder whether perhaps they should have listened.

"I don't think I was so much a rebel as just acting my age [23]," said Unger, who feels he was traded more for participating in the secret players' meeting to plot a strategy to deal with the hated Harkness than the issue of his hairstyle.

"Young guys were beginning to wear their hair long, but the NHL was a league of older guys still in crew cuts. It was really a generation gap thing with Harkness.

"What I learned was it's never just one person's fault. I was young and immature and didn't handle it well."

Even Howe believes that Harkness takes far too much of the blame for the failures that put Detroit at the bottom of the NHL standings. "People can talk all they want about the bad coaches and Harkness, but they just got rid of so much great talent," Howe said. "They made bad trades, the people didn't come up through the system to replace them, and they made more bad trades trying to fill the holes. It was the old case of two wrongs not making a right."

Harkness left the Wings for good following the 1973–74 season and returned to his first love, taking over as coach at Union College in 1975.

He may have been ahead of his time, but the passage of time didn't leave him bitter about his lone NHL experience. "I made a lot of close friends in Detroit, people who are still close to me now," Harkness told the Associated Press in 1982. "I learned a great deal. Regardless of the ups and downs, I would never exchange my years in the NHL.

"The experience of the NHL made me a better college coach when I went back there than I ever was before."

Wings fans might not like to hear it, but to place the entire blame for the Dead Wings on Ned Harkness is dead wrong.

71 The End of Newfoundland's Stanley Cup Drought

While many players have been joined by close friends and family on the ice to celebrate their Stanley Cup triumphs, Daniel Cleary may be the only NHLer who can boast that his Stanley Cup celebration featured a head of state.

When Cleary and the Red Wings captured the Stanley Cup with a 3–2 victory over the Pittsburgh Penguins at Mellon Arena on June 4, 2008, Newfoundland premier Danny Williams was on hand to share in Cleary's big moment.

That's because it was also a big moment for Newfoundland. Cleary was the first player born in the Canadian province to have his name inscribed on Lord Stanley's mug.

Red Wings from Unusual Locales

Player	Birthplace	Seasons
Ed Hatoum	Beirut, Lebanon	1968–70
Xavier Ouellet	Bayonne, France	2013–14
Poul Popiel	Sollested, Denmark	1968–70
Jan Mursak	Maribor, Slovenia	2010–13
Jim McFadden	Belfast, Northern Ireland	1947–51
Nelson Debenedet	Cordenons, Italy	1973–74
Ivan Boldirev	Zrenjanin, Yugoslavia	1983–85

"I had visions of lifting the Cup. I finally lifted it, and it was unbelievable," Cleary said. "I'm a Stanley Cup champion, and they can't take it away from me."

A 20-goal scorer for the Wings during that Cup–winning campaign, Cleary, born in Carbonear, Newfoundland, was a hero to an entire province that spring, single-handedly turning the Wings into Newfoundland's team.

The place whose fans Foster Hewitt used to personally welcome to his *Hockey Night in Canada* broadcasts was thrilled to welcome a first-time famous hockey visitor to its shores—Lord Stanley's mug—and it was Cleary who made it happen.

"That will always be something that I'll be proud of," Cleary said. "I was the first guy who got the Cup and got to bring it back home."

Decades earlier, another Newfoundlander also made Stanley Cup history with the Red Wings, though his story didn't come equipped with a fairly-tale ending.

In the springs of 1963 and 1964, center Alex Faulkner of Bishop's Falls became the first Newfoundland-born NHLer to play in the Stanley Cup Finals when he suited up for the Wings in back-to-back series against the Toronto Maple Leafs.

"I was less than 10 minutes away from winning the Stanley Cup," Faulkner said. "We were up 3–2 in the series and ahead in the third period of Game 6."

The Leafs tied it, then won in overtime on Bob Baun's goal, following up with a 4–0 shutout win in Game 7.

"That's my sad story," Faulkner said.

Individually, Faulkner's best playoff was in 1963, when he scored five goals—two of them in Detroit's five-game Finals series setback against the Leafs, including the winner in Detroit's only victory. The following spring, Faulkner played just one game of the heartbreaking seven-game Finals loss to Toronto.

A year later, he was back playing senior hockey in Newfoundland and never played another NHL game.

Faulkner, who broke into the NHL with the Leafs in 1961–62, was the first native Newfoundlander to play in the league, and he understands that when you're first, you'll always be foremost.

"Nobody remembers the second guy to walk on the moon," said Faulkner. "You ask someone who the second Newfoundlander in the NHL was, and they won't have any idea. That's just the way it works."

The Red Wings weren't the only commonality that connected the two Newfoundlanders. Cleary played his youth hockey in nearby Harbour Grace, since there was no rink in his hometown. Faulkner played senior hockey in Harbour Grace.

Faulkner, who still makes his home in Bishop's Falls, remembered how the island of Newfoundland got caught up in Red Wings fever in the spring of 2008.

"There was quite a buzz out here," Faulkner said. "Everywhere you looked, people had Red Wings sweaters hanging in their windows."

Another native Newfoundlander familiar to NHL fans agreed it was a tremendous boon to the province.

"It was very exciting for all of us," said *Hockey Night in Canada* play-by-play man Bob Cole of St. John's. "They were all very excited and hoping it would be a win for the Red Wings so they could see the Stanley Cup."

72 Read Sawchuk Biography to Understand His Tragic Tale

Hall of Fame goaltender Terry Sawchuk was such a troubled man that he even viewed compliments as veiled forms of attack.

"He hated for people to pat him on the back," said Red Wings Hall of Fame defenseman Marcel Pronovost. "He would say, 'SOBs are just looking for a place to put the knife.'"

Sawchuk's tragic life is presented in stunning detail by Canadian author David Dupuis in his book *Sawchuk: The Troubles and Triumphs of the World's Greatest Goalie.*

Patrick Roy reportedly read the Dupuis book when he was chasing Sawchuk's NHL wins record.

Although the book is 16 years old, it remains a fascinating read. Dupuis presents Sawchuk as a moody athlete, womanizer, violent alcoholic, and sometimes abusive parent.

Pat Sawchuk Milford, his former wife, admitted that she filed for divorce four times before following through on a petition. In the book, Milford also tells a story of Sawchuk demanding she have an abortion when she became pregnant with their seventh child.

Pronovost was Sawchuk's closest friend in hockey, and he has admitted that he had no idea what was happening in Sawchuk's home life.

"Terry was someone who compartmentalized his life," Dupuis said. "His teammates were his teammates, his family was his family, his friends were his friends, and he never let someone from one compartment gain entry to another." Sawchuk's mood swings were pronounced enough that it is now clear that he suffered from untreated depression. It's easy to conclude that if Sawchuk played today, he probably would have benefitted from the more advanced

Terry Sawchuk—considered by many to be the best professional hockey goalie of all time—here bats the puck away in a 1958 contest. Sawchuk's undiagnosed clinical depression made his behavior paranoid, erratic, and sometimes violent.

and accepted psychological therapy that is available. It would have been unthinkable for an athlete to see psychiatric help in those days.

Teammates often did not know how to deal with Sawchuk. His personality was unpredictable. Hall of Famer Bill Gadsby started rooming with him in Detroit and thought he had wronged Sawchuk because Sawchuk never replied when he would say "Good morning."

It was Gordie Howe who informed Gadsby that Sawchuk didn't speak for the first two hours he was up.

Sawchuk could be cruel or very kind. When Sawchuk played in Los Angeles, he paid to have a truckload of crushed ice poured on his lawn to ensure that his children could have a "snowy" Christmas.

One night in Toronto, a child in the stands was struck by a puck during a game. Sawchuk had him brought into the dressing room and had all of the players sign a stick for him. He turned to Pronovost and said he would "kill" Pronovost if he told the media about it.

"He liked to present himself as this moody, aloof person, because then people would leave him alone," Pronovost said.

Although he retired with a record 447 wins and 103 shutouts, Sawchuk was an athlete with more demons than confidence. He was riddled with insecurities.

Sawchuk died under tragic circumstances on May 31, 1970. He was only 40. Sawchuk had succumbed to internal injuries suffered in a scuffle with Rangers teammate and roommate Ron Stewart. They apparently were arguing over the debts occurred over the renting of a house during the 1969–70 season.

Sawchuk took responsibility for what had happened, and Stewart was exonerated of any wrongdoing. Sawchuk died of a pulmonary embolism after undergoing a second surgery. His gallbladder had been removed in his first surgery.

Shirley Fischler was the last journalist to interview Sawchuk at a Long Island Hospital. In an interview shortly before her death, Fischler said, "When I walked into his room, he had two female groupies and a full bottle of whiskey on his nightstand."

Three days later, Fischler said, Sawchuk's condition had deteriorated, and he died.

"There were rumblings and mumblings about what really happened," Fischler said. "One of the reasons why I went to see him in person was because one of the big rumors was that Ron had beaten him to a pulp. They hated each other. But when I went to see him, there was not a bruise on him. He just looked a little pale and thinner. It had to have been his liver that killed him."

73 When the Wings' Farmhands Skated Across the Pond

The Czech border guards, the open-air rinks of Sweden, and Amsterdam's red-light district. The memories remain fresh whenever Dennis Polonich reflects back on his season playing in Europe for the London Lions.

The idea was the brainchild of Red Wings owner Bruce Norris, who envisioned a European pro league with franchises sponsored by NHL clubs and invested $300,000 in his British squad in 1973–74, playing exhibition games throughout Europe.

Future plans called for the Toronto Maple Leafs to ice a team in Sweden and slated the Montreal Canadiens to place a farm club in Finland.

There was excitement in the players' minds about lacing up the skates in Europe, but there was also trepidation.

"Guys were thinking, *I'm getting further away from the NHL, not closer*," Polonich said. "We were worried we'd be forgotten. As it turned out, they kept us abreast and we were somehow able to get a little bit of news and updates on the NHL."

Doug Barkley, coach of the parent Red Wings during the 1975–76 season, was bench boss of the Lions, whose red sweaters combined London's Wembley lion with Detroit's winged wheel.

The team played in the arena at London's famous Wembley Stadium, where fine dining was offered during games in the upper bowl of the rink, the occasional meal being spilled by an errant puck.

"The first month and a half, we played all our games at Wembley Stadium," Polonich said. "Then we went on a three-month excursion all over Europe."

They played games in Holland, Wales, West Germany, Belgium, Austria, Luxembourg, Switzerland, Finland, Scotland, Czechoslovakia, Sweden, and the Baltic Island of Gotland.

They played seven February games behind the Iron Curtain, including a 6–3 loss to the Czech national team.

"The Czech border guards held us up forever," Polonich said. "We had these pieces of exercise equipment called a Bullworker, which were designed to improve your strength. The Czech soldiers were trying to figure out what they were. I got off the bus and showed them how to work it and they all started testing their strength. They let us into the country right after that."

Though they didn't visit Russia, the Lions did defeat Dynamo Moscow 2–1 during the Ahearne Cup tournament in Sweden. They also dropped the Swedish club Handen 8–4 on an outdoor rink in Stockholm. Overall, the Lions finished 52–13–7.

Although the plug was pulled on the plan after one season, several Lions skated on hockey's biggest stage.

Polonich, today an NHL player agent, played 390 games for the Wings, and London teammates Terry Richardson, Rick McCann,

Tom Mellor, Earl Anderson, Brian McCutcheon, Tord Lundstrom, Brian Watts, Nelson Pyatt, Murray Wing, Mike Korney, Rick Newell, and Bill McKenzie also skated in the NHL with Detroit.

"It was my first year pro," Polonich remembered. "To have the opportunity to go play in Europe, it was fascinating, really."

74 Rutherford Was Not Trying to Make a Fashion Statement

When goalie Jim Rutherford donned his famous mask with the Red Wings logo painted around each eye hole in 1974, everyone loved it except the man wearing it.

Famed mask designer Greg Harrison had created the artwork without Rutherford's permission.

"I was upset about it because I had asked him just to paint the mask white," Rutherford recalled.

On January 17, 1974, the Pittsburgh Penguins had traded Rutherford back to the Red Wings in a deal for defenseman Ron Stackhouse. Defenseman Jack Lynch also went to Detroit in the transaction.

Rutherford had started his career in Detroit, but he had established himself as a regular in Pittsburgh. He was not pleased with the change of address, and he certainly wasn't looking to be a fashion trendsetter.

"When you are traded, you are emotional and you don't want to think about other things," Rutherford said. "My mask had been [powder] blue in Pittsburgh, and when we went into Toronto after the trade, I met Greg Harrison and I said, 'Make sure you paint it white.' The next day he came down to the morning skate and he had a big smile on his face."

Who Is That Masked Man?

Claude LaForge was the first Red Wing to wear a goalie mask in a game, which in itself wouldn't be big news, until you realize that LaForge played left wing. Called up from Hershey of the AHL, LaForge had suffered a fractured cheekbone earlier in the month but wasn't going to miss his NHL chance, so he donned a goalie mask and played against Chicago on December 28, 1961, at Olympia Stadium, beating a maskless Glenn Hall for the tying goal in a 2–2 draw.

When Harrison pulled the mask out of the box, Rutherford was mortified to see it had Red Wings logos surrounding the eyeholes.

"I said, 'I don't want that,'" he recalled.

The game was going to be telecast on *Hockey Night in Canada*, and Rutherford envisioned everyone talking about his mask. The eyeholes were wheels in the winged wheels. No goalies had art on their masks in those days.

Rutherford only wore the Harrison-designed mask because he had no other option. He had no spare mask that made him comfortable. "There wasn't enough time to do anything else," Rutherford said.

He never guessed that 40 years later he would be remembered as the goalie who helped introduce artwork to goalie masks. "I kept it because we tied the game and everyone liked the mask," Rutherford said. "It was kind of the start of design works on masks."

Rutherford once had three consecutive shutouts for the Red Wings, but that's not what fans want to discuss when they meet him. "Lots of people have talked to me through the years about that mask," Rutherford said.

75 Jim Riley Turned a Unique Double Play

By the time he arrived in Detroit following a January 31, 1927, trade with the Chicago Black Hawks, left-winger Jim Riley had already assembled an impressive and unique résumé.

In the spring of 1917, his second year in pro hockey, Riley was part of the Seattle Metropolitans team that downed the Montreal Canadiens to become the first American-based club ever to win the Stanley Cup.

It was Riley's other pro sport that brought him to the state of Washington in the summer of 1916. He played baseball with the Tacoma Tigers of the Northwestern League, beginning an odyssey that would make the Bayfield, New Brunswick–born Riley the only man to play in Major League Baseball and the National Hockey League.

Riley was a star on the ice in Seattle. He played in another Stanley Cup Finals series in 1920, coming up short against the Ottawa Senators that spring. In both 1920–21 and 1921–22, he finished second in the Pacific Coast Hockey League in goal scoring. He was a three-time All-Star selection in the PCHA, his run of success disturbed only by a one-year stint in the Canadian Army during which he saw duty during World War I.

Serving as an engineer, Riley was promoted to the rank of sergeant but couldn't find anywhere to skate while across the pond. There were plenty of baseball games, though, and he was able to hone his skills on the diamond to the point where he was considered among the top third basemen in the military leagues.

Playing for Vancouver of the Pacific International League in the summer of 1921, Riley, a second baseman, was batting .303 and turning heads, with no less than three major league teams—the

St. Louis Browns, Brooklyn Robins, and Chicago White Sox—all negotiating with Vancouver owner Bob Brown in order to purchase Riley's contract.

"Jim Riley, the famous Seattle hockey star, is another slated for promotion," noted the *Sporting News*. "Riley is the Babe Ruth of the circuit, and let it be mentioned also that at the keystone bag, he has no peer in this company. Riley started the season batting just above the pitchers. Today he's in the cleanup hole on the Vancouver squad and delivering all the time."

On June 28, 1921, the Browns acquired Riley, and on July 3 he made his major league debut against the White Sox. He played both ends of a July 4 twin bill against the Detroit Tigers and was in the lineup again the next day versus the Tigers, but after going 0-for-11 at the plate, Riley was shipped back to the minor leagues.

Two years later, he was back in the show, playing alongside future MVPs Walter Johnson and Roger Peckinpaugh with the Washington Senators, again going hitless in three at-bats. In August 1923, Riley informed Seattle manager Pete Muldoon by mail that he was giving up hockey to focus on baseball, but he relented and joined the Metropolitans in mid-January of 1924, playing 13 games. At the end of the season, though, Riley again hung up his blades and picked up his glove.

A steady .300 hitter in the minor leagues, Riley never got another shot at the big leagues, and when Muldoon became the first coach in Chicago Black Hawks history when the franchise joined the NHL for the 1926–27 NHL season, he began wooing his old left-winger to try and convince Riley to don his skates once again.

On January 19, 1927, Riley agreed to terms with the Black Hawks, making his NHL debut that night against the Toronto St. Patricks, becoming the first and so far only player to perform in the NHL and in Major League Baseball. But after just six games in a Chicago uniform, Riley was shipped to the Cougars, where several of his old Seattle teammates, including goaltender Hap Holmes and forwards Frank Foyston and Jack Walker, were entrenched.

Riley made his Detroit debut on February 1, 1927, in a 4–3 overtime victory over the Black Hawks, adding more firsts to his résumé.

He was an original with both the Chicago and Detroit NHL franchises and is also the only guy who can claim he played for Detroit in the NHL and against the Detroit Tigers.

Another unique Riley feat—he went hitless as a big-leaguer (0-for-14) and goalless in nine games as an NHLer.

Deion Sanders or Bo Jackson he wasn't, but Riley was, and is, the only two-sport athlete to reach the big time on the ice and the diamond.

76 Up Steve Yzerman Drive, Through the Gordie Howe Entrance

Gordie Howe was thrilled to be made an entrance.

"It's a lot better than an exit," joked the Detroit Red Wings legend.

It could be said that the path to Hockeytown was cemented with Howe's elbows.

In 2006 they made it official. Thirty-three years after previous ownership essentially shoved Howe out the door, the Wings named one after him.

The west entrance to Joe Louis Arena was officially christened the Gordie Howe Entrance prior to Detroit's November 22, 2006, game with the Vancouver Canucks.

The move recognized Howe's contribution to the establishment of Detroit as one of the top National Hockey League centers in the United States, and it also honored the 60th anniversary of his debut as a Red Wing.

Still, there was plenty of irony in the announcement. The last thing Howe ever did as a player was roll out the welcome mat.

One of the oversized photos that greet fans as they come into the building through Howe's entrance offers a window into what it was like to visit his house on game night. Mr. Hockey is crashing the St. Louis Blues' net. Blues center Red Berenson is desperately trying to hold Howe back with an arm lock, while St. Louis defenseman Bob Plager is coming at Howe from the other side with a shoulder block. Neither is enjoying much success at derailing this train.

Howe retired in 1971 after a league-record 25 seasons as a Detroit right-winger. He played in 1,687 games and scored 786 goals, including 121 game-winners, all club records.

Howe was given a title in the front office, but the position was a facade. He was offered virtually no input into the direction of the team. He called it getting the mushroom treatment. "They'd keep me in the dark, and every once in a while come in and throw manure on me," Howe explained, blaming then–Wings owner Bruce Norris.

"He was a drunk, and he had enough money to stay drunk," Howe told the *Montreal Gazette* of Norris. "We had no choice but to do what he said; this was the man who signed the cheques."

Basically, the Wings pushed him out the door and into a 1973 comeback with the World Hockey Association's Houston Aeros, where he teamed with his sons Mark and Marty. "We didn't run off to the WHA," Howe said. "It was almost an escape clause."

Being the name that rolls out the welcome mat suits Howe much better than being treated as a floor mat.

"I like the entrance better," Howe said. "My exit wasn't on a high note. The team wasn't going anywhere, and I didn't just want to hang on…. Then somebody put the love back in the game, when they got Marty and Mark to play with me."

Howe played seven seasons alongside his sons, the last in the NHL with the Hartford Whalers in 1979–80, allowing him to return to Detroit and play three times that season at JLA—twice with the Whalers and once during the NHL All-Star Game, where he was afforded a lengthy, thunderous ovation from the Detroit faithful, offering evidence that Howe will never be forgotten.

His name on the entrance to Detroit's hockey home ensures that this will be the case forever. Long after Howe is gone, his likeness will continue to welcome fans to the rink. A statue of him is also situated at his entrance.

To get to the Gordie Howe Entrance, just walk up Steve Yzerman Drive to No. 19, the new address for the JLA. Third Street was officially renamed Steve Yzerman Drive by the city of Detroit in 2007.

77 The Hanson Brother Who Became a Red Wing

Whenever Dave Hanson meets the masses as his alter ego Jack Hanson, the middle sibling of the fictional Hanson brothers, those thugs with the horned-rimmed glasses who raised mayhem in the 1977 cult film *Slap Shot*, it's one of the facts that leaves most in disbelief: He didn't merely play a hockey player on the big screen. He actually played the game on hockey's biggest stage.

"Two of the things that people are always surprised to learn about all of us is that we're American—everyone assumes we're from Canada—and that all three of us did play hockey," Hanson said.

Born April 12, 1954, in Cumberland, Wisconsin, and raised in St. Paul, Minnesota, Hanson played defense in 33 National

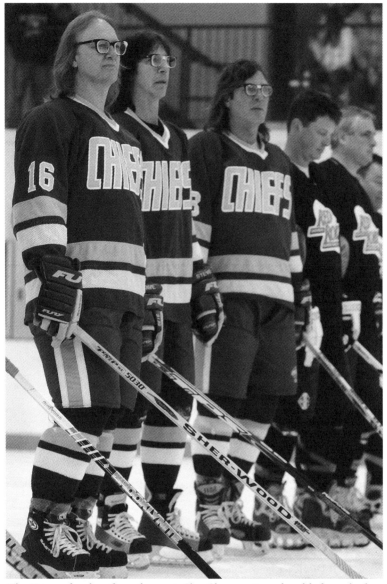

The Hanson brothers from the movie Slap Shot *are introduced before a hockey game to benefit the Pennsylvania Breast Cancer Coalition on April 28, 2012, at Klick Lewis Arena in Palmyra, PA. The Hanson brothers are, from left, Dave Hanson, Steve Carlson, and Jeff Carlson. Few people realize that all the fictional Hanson brothers played very real professional hockey, including Dave Hanson's brief stint with the Detroit Red Wings.*

Hockey League contests, 11 of them with the Red Wings during the 1978–79 season.

In theory, it should have proven to be a match made in heaven. Here were the revamped Wings, coming off their first playoff campaign in eight seasons, led by general manager "Terrible" Ted Lindsay, the former Wings tough guy who borrowed the club's marketing slogan—"Aggressive hockey is back in town"—from the fictional Charlestown Chiefs, the goon squad the Hansons toiled for in the equally fictional Federal League.

Instead, it was a marriage that ended in bitter divorce.

The Wings selected Hanson in the 11th round of the 1975 NHL amateur draft, the 176th overall selection, but he opted instead to sign with the Minnesota Fighting Saints of the rival World Hockey Association.

Detroit finally got Hanson into the fold in the fall of 1977, signing him to a five-year contract, and then loaned him to the WHA's Birmingham Bulls, where he established the WHA's single-game penalty-minute mark, garnering 48 minutes in a February 5, 1978, game against the Indianapolis Racers. Hanson didn't just play a tough guy in the movies. He lived the life.

The next season, Detroit decided to keep Hanson around, and the possibilities excited him. "Coming to the Wings, playing at the Olympia for Ted Lindsay, I thought it was going to be a great chance," Hanson recalled. "The opportunity to go with such a storied franchise as the Red Wings was at that time for me just a great feeling, thinking there was going to be a shot for me to play in the National Hockey League."

There was just one fly in the ointment. Wings coach Bobby Kromm wanted nothing to do with a player of Hanson's ilk.

Kromm came to Detroit from the WHA's Winnipeg Jets, where he loaded his team with skilled Europeans—the first North American pro team to do so—and was against fighting. In one of the more infamous playoff games in WHA history, Hanson's Bulls

Tell Detroit Bullshit!

Dave Hanson wasn't the only Hanson brother with ties to the Red Wings. Steve Carlson, who played Steve Hanson, was selected 131st overall by Detroit in the 1975 NHL amateur draft, but opted to jump to the WHA instead.

brawled with Kromm's Jets, and during the scuffle, Hanson accidentally ripped the toupee off the head of Winnipeg star Bobby Hull.

While Hanson's previous coaches such as Glen Sonmor and John Brophy encouraged a rugged, intimidating brand of hockey, Kromm was a completely different cat.

"He wanted the game played a different style," remembered Hanson. "It didn't take long to see that I didn't fit into his plans."

The Wings won just 23 games that season, missing the playoffs. "It was a tough time to be a Red Wing," Hanson said. "That's when everyone was calling the team the Dead Wings."

On December 4, 1978, Hanson was dealt back to Birmingham by the Wings. Picked up by the Minnesota North Stars after the 1979 NHL-WHA merger, Hanson scored his lone NHL goal at Joe Louis Arena against Detroit goalie Rogie Vachon.

Claimed on waivers by the Wings in 1980, Hanson spent two seasons with the club's Adirondack farm club, winning a Calder Cup title in 1980–81.

At the conclusion of his five-year deal, Wings GM Jimmy Skinner advised Hanson not to worry. They liked how he worked with the kids in their farm system and intended on keeping him in Adirondack, envisioning coaching in his future.

Shortly thereafter, Mike Ilitch purchased the Wings, and the situation changed under new GM Jimmy Devellano. Instead of signing a new contract that summer, Hanson was advised he was being released.

He played two more seasons in the minors and retired in 1984.

78 Willie Huber Was More Talented Than You Remember

Anyone who attended many games at Olympia Stadium in the 1970s will remember the fan in the lower level who would occasionally rise up and yell, "Hit him with your purse, Willie."

Willie Huber was a skillful 6'5", 230-pound defenseman who preferred to use his hands more to make plays than punch someone.

"He was really a gentle giant," said his former Red Wings teammate Jimmy Rutherford.

Huber's only problem was that he was playing in the Broad Street Bullies era when fans expected a Huber-sized player to be a human bulldozer.

"Willie Huber was a fearsome body-checker when he was a rookie," said Red Wings fan Larry O'Connor. "He'd lay some hits that rocked Olympia...then perhaps through injury or desire to become a more complete player, he stepped away from that part of the game, and fans never forgave him."

After being drafted ninth overall out of Hamilton of the Ontario Hockey League in 1978, Huber amassed more than 400 penalty minutes his first three NHL seasons. He had a career-high 164 minutes his second season. He had 10 fights over his first two seasons and then never had more than one or two fights per season.

"He had a hard shot, and he was a good teammate," said former Detroit player Paul Woods.

What's forgotten about Huber is how much skill he had. He scored 17 goals in his second NHL season. He averaged 15 goals and 44 points over a four-year span in Detroit. "If he were playing today, he would be appreciated a lot more," said former New York Rangers defenseman Tom Laidlaw, who played with Huber later in his career. "Because he was so big, everyone expected him to hammer everyone. The reality was, he was a skilled player in a big man's body."

When Jim Devellano took over as general manager in Detroit, he was not among Huber's fans. He traded him on June 13, 1983, to the Rangers along with Mark Osborne and Mike Blaisdell for Eddie Johnstone, Ron Duguay, and Eddie Mio.

"He could play physical, and he did," Laidlaw said. "But what he could really do was run a power play, make a good breakout pass, and he had a great shot. He could read the play well. He was a smart player."

Laidlaw viewed Huber as "a Larry Murphy" kind of player "only with a different kind of body."

"He was the big, goofy kid that all of his teammates absolutely loved," Laidlaw said.

Laidlaw said Huber was tougher than everyone realized. "I saw him fight Bob Nystrom once," Laidlaw said. "He wasn't standing there like Clark Gillies throwing punches, but he could fight.

Other Red Wings Who Shouldn't Be Forgotten

1. Defenseman Gary Bergman: He was picked to play for Canada in the Summit Series against the Soviet Union in 1972.
2. Left wing Danny Grant: He scored 50 goals for the Red Wings playing on a line with Marcel Dionne in 1974–75. Plagued by injuries, he never was able to score more than 12 in a season after that.
3. Left wing John Ogrodnick: He averaged almost 40 goals per season for Detroit in one six-season span (1980–81 until 1985–86). He scored a career-high 55 in 1984–85.
4. Left wing Marty Pavelich: He played on all four Detroit Stanley Cup championship teams in the 1950s. It was his job to check Maurice "Rocket" Richard. Pavelich scored a game-winning short-handed goal during the 1955 Finals.
5. Bryan "Bugsy" Watson: He is remembered most for checking Bobby Hull during the 1960s. Hull hated him.

He wasn't the toughest guy on the ice, but he would not allow someone else's toughness to stop him from playing his game."

It seemed as if Huber never caught any breaks when he was playing. He was also only 52 when he died of an apparent heart attack in 2010.

79 Paiement Attack Changed Polonich's Career

When Colorado Rockies winger Wilf Paiement connected on his stick-swing to Dennis Polonich's face on October 25, 1978, the aftermath looked like a crime scene.

"I remember Polo going down in a heap, and the circle of blood quickly emerged," said Red Wings fan Larry O'Connor, who was at the game. "I swear the pool of blood was as big as the faceoff circle."

O'Connor, now a sports journalist, called it one of the most "horrific things" he has ever seen.

"I vividly recall ushers mopping up blood in the corridor between periods where they had carried him off on a stretcher," O'Connor said.

Not many witnesses were available because the Polonich-Paiement encounter happened away from the play. But Greg Innis, who has been the Red Wings' statistician for four decades, saw the incident from start to finish.

"I used to really love to watch Polo," Innis said. "He was only 5'6", and I loved the way he would skate around and aggravate the opposing players. He didn't care who they were. He drove Dave Schultz nuts all of the time. He was always yapping. You could hear him in the press box."

Innis saw Polonich and Paiement yapping at each other and anticipated there would be trouble.

"Polo did give Paiement a little cross-check across the face. He didn't swing his stick, but I thought, *Oh wow, I don't like to see that,*" Innis remembered. "And then Paiement turned around and took a baseball swing."

Polonich suffered a shattered nose, facial lacerations, and a concussion. He needed reconstructive surgery to repair his nose.

Paiement received a 15-game suspension for the attack. Had that happened in today's game, he may have faced a lifetime ban.

"What he did is beyond me," Polonich said in the book *What it Means to be a Red Wing*. "You would have to ask him, but he probably doesn't have an answer either. Obviously he just snapped. He maintains 'til this day that he was provoked, that when I went to ice the puck I high-sticked him. Because I was knocked unconscious, I don't know if I did or I didn't."

There's no video available of the incident. Polonich was awarded an $850,000 settlement through a lawsuit because he had permanent breathing problems and disfigurement.

Polonich said if Paiement or someone from the Rockies would have called and apologized, he may never have sued.

"I have some unbelievable pictures where my eyes were swollen shut," Polonich said. "I looked like death. I remember [Detroit general manager] Ted Lindsay coming to the hospital, and I was squeezing his hand so tight he had to let go."

At the time of the incident, Polonich was among the Red Wings' most popular players.

"He was our pint-sized answer to the Broad Street Bullies," O'Connor said. "For that, fans loved him. As a player, he'd get those little legs churning and chase the puck like a bull terrier would chase a rabbit. When he got the puck, though, he had hands of cement and would often shoot wide of the net."

Polonich missed a month and a half of the season.

"Certainly it hurt my career," Polonich said. "Look at my stats: I had 11 goals, 18 goals, 16 goals, and after that my play dropped. I was never the same type of player. Was I black-balled because I sued another player? I don't know. I can live with it."

He wasn't the same player the following season. His penalty minutes and offensive production were down. In 66 games, he had just two goals and 10 points. He had 127 penalty minutes, compared to 208 the previous season.

From that point, he played only 43 more NHL games and he was only 30 when he played his last NHL game. He toiled in the minor leagues until 1986–87, finishing his career with the Muskegon Lumberjacks in the International Hockey League.

80 Howe Had a Memorable Moment Playing at the Joe

The loudest ovation Gordie Howe ever received from Detroit fans may have come almost nine years after he played his final game with the Red Wings.

Coach Scotty Bowman selected the 51-year-old Howe, then playing for the Hartford Whalers, for the Prince of Wales Conference All-Star team. When he was introduced to the Joe Louis Arena crowd, he received a thunderous greeting that seemed to go on forever.

"I don't remember seeing a longer standing ovation," said former Red Wings defenseman Reed Larson, who was standing next to Howe during player introductions. "Five minutes is forever for a standing ovation; this one was at least 10 minutes. Sometimes it's difficult to judge, but it was a long one."

NHL All-Star Games Played at Detroit
October 8, 1950—Detroit 7, NHL All-Stars 1
October 5, 1952—NHL First All-Stars 1, NHL Second All-Stars 1
October 2, 1954—Detroit 2, NHL All-Stars 2
October 2, 1955—Detroit 3, NHL All-Stars 1
February 5, 1980—Wales Conference 6, Campbell Conference 3

Based on the YouTube video, the crowd probably applauded for four to five minutes after public-address announcer John Bell introduced Howe with the phrase, "Representing all of hockey with great distinction, Number Nine."

Bell never said Howe's name, simply calling him "Number Nine."

The decibel level climbed exponentially as Howe skated next to Larson, who was the Red Wings' only representative.

"Gordie was so humble," Larson said. "I remember him shuffling his feet and saying, 'We've got to get this game going.'"

On the Hughes Television broadcast of the game, host Dick Irvin Jr. asked analyst Gary Dornhoefer and play-by-play guy Dan Kelly whether they had ever heard such a loud ovation. Kelly opined that it would get even louder if Howe could score a goal in the game. Howe had scored 10 previous All-Star goals.

It was Howe's 23rd NHL All-Star appearance, and it seemed as if fans wanted to thank him one final time for all that he had accomplished in a Detroit jersey.

Larson recalled that Howe joked with his teammates that he was too old to keep up with the league's top players.

"At his age he was playing like Jean Beliveau, never making a mistake," Larson recalled.

Howe set up the Wales Conference's final goal by Quebec Nordiques forward Real Cloutier in a 6–3 win against the Campbell Conference.

"He played very well in that game, and that's pretty wild when you consider how old he was at the time," Larson said. "What I remember is that he never bobbled the puck, always made the right play at the right time."

Joe Louis Arena was only 45 days old when the All-Star Game was played there.

Marcel Dionne, five years removed from leaving Detroit through free agency, was booed by fans. Wayne Gretzky also made his first All-Star appearance in that game.

81 Swedish Invasion in Detroit Started with Thommie Bergman

Borje Salming is considered a pioneer by many older NHL fans for enduring considerable physical abuse to create a path for Swedish players to follow to the NHL. Detroit fans consider Nicklas Lidstrom as the player who established the Red Wings' trust in Swedish players.

But the reality is that Swedish defenseman Thommie Bergman probably deserves credit as a Swedish pioneer and a player who showed Detroit fans that the Red Wings could benefit from foreign players.

"Thommie was a big Swedish defenseman," said his former Red Wings teammate Paul Woods. "He had skills and he could really shoot it. He was really an underrated player."

Lidstrom was only two years old when Bergman played his first game with the Red Wings in 1972–73. That was also the season before Salming played with the Toronto Maple Leafs.

The Red Wings signed Bergman after watching him play well for the Swedes at the 1972 Olympics in Sapporo. In his first season with the Red Wings, Bergman posted nine goals and 12 assists for 21 points. He did that in an era when opponents weren't very open-minded about accepting foreign players in the NHL. The 1970s-era hockey was known for lawlessness, brawling, and violence.

"When it comes to being an ambassador for Swedish hockey, there's no question that Borje Salming was the most important guy," former NHL and World Hockey Association star Anders Hedberg told Swedish journalist Linus Hugosson of *Pro Hockey Magazine*. "But it was Thommie Bergman who began to tear down the wall for us Swedes."

In his first month in the NHL, Bergman, who was 6'2", 200 pounds, fought Dave Schultz and Steve Durbano, two noted NHL heavyweights. Later that season, he fought Philadelphia's Bobby Clarke, who was just establishing himself as a prickly presence on the ice.

Bergman told Hugosson that he had no idea who Schultz was when he fought him on October 14, 1972. "[But] after that fight, I was sort of accepted," he said.

Hedberg said when you evaluate the Swedes who came over to the NHL in the 1970s, Bergman "was probably the toughest of us all."

"He never hesitated to throw off his gloves," Hedberg said. "He took a lot of beatings, but he also gave a lot of beatings."

Bergman was highly respected by his teammates. "He could take whatever was thrown at him," remembered former Detroit goalie Jim Rutherford. "He was mentally tough. He always had a big smile on his face. He let everything roll off him."

Already 25 when he signed with Detroit, Bergman played three seasons before the Red Wings sold him to the Winnipeg Jets, who already had Swedish players Ulf Nilsson and Hedberg.

But the Red Wings re-acquired him late in the 1977–78 season when it appeared the team had a chance to make the playoffs.

Bergman had a goal and six assists for seven points in 14 games during the stretch run. "He played through a lot of injuries that other players couldn't," Woods recalled.

Bergman played for the team in the playoffs. He scored 10 goals the next season.

"He was just a real good player with a very heavy shot," Rutherford said. "And he was one of the most likeable guys you would ever want to meet."

Bergman wrapped up his professional career in Sweden in the 1980s, and today scouts for the Toronto Maple Leafs.

82 Mike Ilitch Was a Game Changer for the Red Wings

Little Caesars Pizza owner Mike Ilitch paid $8 million for the Detroit Red Wings in 1982, and a case can be made that he overpaid.

The Bruce Norris–owned Red Wings had missed the playoffs 14 of the 16 previous seasons. In 1981–82, they won 21 of 80 games and gave up an average of almost 4.5 goals per game. The team's leading scorer was Mark Osborne. Detroit fans were apathetic or angry about their hockey team.

When Jim Devellano was hired as Ilitch's first general manager, he asked co-owner Marian Ilitch how many season-ticket holders the franchise had. "Marian told me that Bruce Norris had told her that we had about 5,000," Devellano recalled.

At that point, Devellano and Marian Ilitch decided to talk to Bob Kerlin, who was head of the team's ticket office, to get an accurate count.

"He said, 'Marian, I hate to tell you this, but it is only 2,100 season tickets,'" Devellano recalled.

Hockeytown, like Rome, wasn't built in a day. Ilitch family members worked the phones that summer and rebuilt the season-ticket base to 5,000. The Red Wings gave away a car to one fan at every Red Wings home game. Still, the team averaged an attendance of only 7,000 in the first season of Ilitch ownership.

More than three decades later, Mike and Marian Ilitch are considered among the top owners in all of professional sports.

"You could say they are like the O'Malleys were with the Dodgers and the Griffiths were with the Washington Senators," Devellano said.

The Philadelphia Flyers' Ed Snider (1967) and Boston Bruins' Jeremy Jacobs (1975) are the only two NHL owners with longer tenures than the Ilitch family.

Detroit fans have benefitted significantly from Ilitch ownership because of their unwavering commitment to winning. "Money has never been an issue for Mike Ilitch," Devellano said. "He made it very clear to us if we needed something, or wanted to sign a player, money would be no problem. You could see it every year at the trade deadline."

In 2003–04, the last season before the NHL salary cap was introduced, the average NHL payroll was $44 million, and the Red Wings spent $77 million on players. By contrast, the Pittsburgh Penguins were spending $23 million.

Everyone wanted to play in Detroit in those days, because the Red Wings offered top dollars and royal treatment. Mike wrote the checks, and Marian wrote hand-signed cards and notes that made everyone feel like their bosses cared.

"Mr. and Mrs. Ilitch treated players like family," said former Detroit goalie Kevin Hodson. "The Ilitches always cared about who you were, who your wife was, and who your kids were."

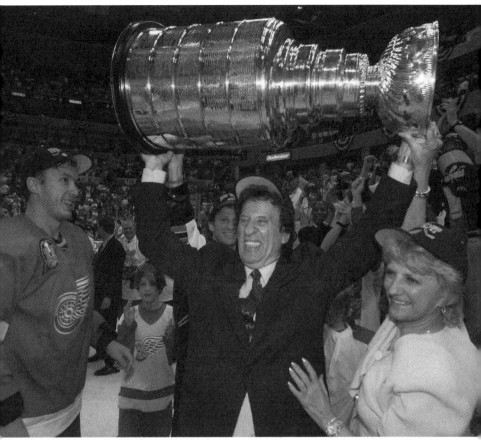

Detroit Red Wings owner Mike Ilitch (center) hoists the Stanley Cup on June 17, 1998, after the Red Wings won their second consecutive NHL championship. Slava Kozlov (No. 13, left) looks on.

Mike Ilitch hired coach Jacques Demers and then fired Demers. "But I still love the man," Demers said. "He handled my firing with so much class and respect that I couldn't be mad at him."

Demers tells the story of being broke when he was hired to coach the Red Wings, and the Ilitches deciding to pay for his honeymoon as a gift.

"Mr. Ilitch was like a second father to me," Demers said.

As it turned out, the Ilitch purchase of the Red Wings was a wise investment. In 2013–14, *Forbes* magazine listed the value of the Detroit franchise at $470 million. The Red Wings were ranked ninth in the NHL in franchise value.

Those numbers, and the ranking, are simply projections. If the Red Wings were ever put up for sale, there might be a lengthy line of potential buyers. The selling price could be higher. This franchise has a romance and aura that has been lovingly nurtured by the Ilitches for more than three decades.

"They love the city of Detroit and made us feel like we were playing for the city of Detroit," Hodson said.

In professional sports, owners often seem to get in the way of success. In Detroit, ownership has been a primary reason why the team has won four Stanley Cup championships, advanced to the Stanley Cup Finals two other times, and has made the playoffs every season since 1991.

83 Detroit's 1983 Draft Produced Hockey's Toughest Class

There are those teams that have tough drafts, and there are those teams that draft tough. But if you're looking for the toughest draft in NHL history, consider some of Detroit's selections in the 1983 NHL entry draft.

The Red Wings got Bob Probert from the Ontario Hockey League's Brantford Alexanders with the 46th pick, then they selected Joey Kocur 91st overall from the Western Hockey League's Saskatoon Blades, and took Stu Grimson of the WHL's Regina Pats 193rd overall.

"We'd been pushed around a lot the year before and decided we needed to get bigger and tougher," recalled Detroit senior vice president Jimmy Devellano, who as GM of the club back then called the 1983 class his first draft.

Oh, yeah. Detroit also got Steve Yzerman with the fourth overall pick that year, and Yzerman remembers the first time all of that year's draftees got together to mingle and get to know each other. "They brought us all to Detroit for the [July 4] Freedom Festival celebrations," Yzerman recalled. "We had dinner together at Carl's Chop House and then all went to see a Detroit Tigers game together.

"I remember looking around and thinking that we'd drafted a pretty good football team. They drafted me in the first round, Lane Lambert in the second round, and then after that, it seemed like they just went for guys with 300 penalty minutes. Jimmy D was looking for his Clark Gillies."

Kocur viewed things a different way: "It was like Jimmy D was looking for his weapon of mass destruction."

In 1985–86, Kocur racked up 377 penalty minutes to lead the NHL and set a new Red Wings single-season record.

"Detroit adores guys like him," former Montreal Canadiens defenseman Serge Savard said.

Two years later, Probert obliterated that mark, sitting out 398 minutes to also lead the NHL and top Kocur's team mark.

"He could score and play," Devellano said of Probert.

Even opponents admired what Probert brought to the table. "I don't know how you couldn't admire him," former Toronto Maple Leafs coach John Brophy said. "He was 6'4" and the heavyweight champion of the NHL as far as I could see.

"I never saw him to be a goon. He did his job with the big guys, clean as a whistle. He didn't use the stick and other advantages he could have."

Red Wings Who Led the NHL in Penalty Minutes

Season	Player	PIM
1930–31	Harvey Rockburn	118
1940–41	Jimmy Orlando	99
1942–43	Jimmy Orlando	99
1945–46	Jack Stewart	73
1962–63	Howie Young	273
1985–86	Joe Kocur	377
1987–88	Bob Probert	398

Grimson was also making a statement with his fists in the NHL, though originally he'd made it elsewhere.

"They didn't even make me an offer," Grimson said of the Wings. "I had a really bad year with Regina that [following] season."

Grimson posted 8–8–16–131 numbers in 63 games for the Pats in 1983–84. Since he wasn't made an offer by Detroit, under NHL rules, the 6'4" 220-pounder went back into the draft pool two years later and was tapped 143rd by the Calgary Flames.

Grimson spent two seasons playing for the University of Manitoba Bisons before signing with Calgary. After collecting 397 penalty minutes with Salt Lake City of the International League in 1988–89, he got his first taste of the NHL with the Flames that season.

The Grim Reaper, as Grimson was known, went on to fill the enforcer's role with Chicago and Anaheim before he was acquired by the Wings in a 1995 deal.

"I was responsible for the physical well-being of the other people on my team," Grimson said. "That was my job, and I took a great deal of pride in it."

Even the guys who didn't make it to Detroit could deliver a payload. Defenseman Craig Butz (146th overall) of Kelowna led the Western Hockey League in penalty minutes with 307 in 1982–83.

Lambert might not have been in that class of tough guys, but he was no shrinking violet. Seven times he topped 100 penalty minutes and in 1991–92 led the Swiss B League in penalty minutes with Ajoie.

While Yzerman gave the rebuilding Wings a much-needed injection of skill, the presence of the toughness acquired through the 1983 draft gave blue-collar Detroit fans another reason to flock to Joe Louis Arena.

As far as former Detroit coach Jacques Demers is concerned, Probert was a significant catalyst in the turnaround of the team.

"I think he did a lot for the franchise," Demers said. "Bob Probert changed the dynamic of the building. If you want to come play in Detroit, there's [Bruise Brothers] Probert and Kocur. That won us a lot of games. Yzerman was great, no question, but those two guys, they helped us a lot."

84 Nick Lidstrom Should Have Won the Lady Byng 20 Times

One of the great mysteries of NHL history is how Nicklas Lidstrom could have played 20 seasons in the NHL without winning the Lady Byng Trophy.

The Byng, according to the award's description, goes to the player "adjudged to have exhibited the best type of sportsmanship and gentlemanly conduct combined with a high standard of playing ability."

Has any NHL player ever been a better fit for that description than Lidstrom?

The man played 20 seasons and averaged 26 penalty minutes per season. He was one of the NHL's top stars, and he treated everyone with respect, including referees and opponents who didn't deserve his respect.

Over two decades, Lidstrom had one roughing penalty and one fighting major. Even Wayne Gretzky, who won the Lady Byng five times, had two fights.

As a rookie in 1991–92, Lidstrom fought Buffalo's Brad Miller. Lidstrom was even assessed an instigator in that brawl. Maybe that's what hurt his Byng candidacy through the years.

Leaving aside the numbers, how about the fact that Lidstrom was simply regarded as one of the nicest athletes the NHL has ever known?

"I don't think I know anyone who doesn't like Nick Lidstrom," Red Wings defenseman Niklas Kronwall said.

Members of the Professional Hockey Writers' Association vote on the award, and Lidstrom came close to winning it in 2001 when he lost by four voting points to Colorado Avalanche center Joe Sakic.

Lidstrom had more first-place votes than Sakic (21–15), but Sakic had more second-place votes (18–7). Plus, Sakic appeared on 43 ballots and Lidstrom only appeared on 41.

In 1999–00 Lidstrom totaled 18 penalty minutes in 82 games. But that wasn't his career low. He had 14 in 81 games the season before. That was during a four-season span when he only had 68 penalty minutes in 324 games.

The primary reason why Lidstrom never won the Lady Byng is hockey writers have long discriminated against defensemen when it comes to Lady Byng consideration. Before Florida Panthers defenseman Brian Campbell won the Lady Byng in 2012, no defenseman had won it for 58 years.

It would have been fitting for Lidstrom to have won that award at some point because the last defenseman to win it before Campbell was Detroit Red Wings star Red Kelly. He is the only defenseman to win the Lady Byng more than once. He won it three

Free Men

The longest penalty-free streak in NHL history posted by a defenseman and a forward are both held by former Red Wings players.

Defenseman Bill Quackenbush was the first defenseman in NHL history to win the Lady Byng Trophy when he went through the entire 1948–49 season without being assessed a penalty. Quackenbush played a record 138 consecutive games without taking a seat in the sin bin. The streak began on March 10, 1948, and extended through January 26, 1950, when he was playing for the Boston Bruins. Quackenbush was called for tripping Chicago's Jim Conacher by referee Hugh McLean in the third period of a 5–1 loss to the Black Hawks.

Left-winger Val Fonteyne came to the Wings in 1959–60, and for three straight seasons—from 1965–66 through 1967–68—he did not serve a single penalty minute. His NHL-record streak of 257 penalty-free games ended when Fonteyne was playing for the Pittsburgh Penguins on December 1, 1968, when referee John Ashley called him for hooking Norm Ferguson in the first period of a 4–4 tie against the Oakland Seals.

Fonteyne served just 26 minutes in the penalty box during an 820-game NHL career and was never assessed a major foul.

times as a defenseman (1951, 1953, and 1954) and once as a center (1961).

Kelly only had eight penalty minutes the season he won in 1953, and 18 when he won it in 1954. Kelly and Lidstrom were similar in that they were both humble, unassuming superstars.

"I never thought of the Lady Byng being about penalty minutes," Kelly said. "People look at the penalty minutes aspect, but to me, it's an award which goes to a player who displays sportsmanship. That's what matters. Not that he doesn't get penalties, but that he doesn't get penalties and still gets the job done."

Bill Quackenbush, the other defenseman to win it before Campbell, was also a Red Wing. He won in 1949.

Given Lidstrom's reputation, it's unfathomable that he has no Lady Byng Trophy. He probably doesn't let it bother him, considering he has seven Norris Trophies, a Conn Smythe Trophy, and four Stanley Cup rings to fill his trophy case.

Lidstrom should also own a Masterton Trophy, which is awarded for perseverance and dedication to the sport. He played until he was 42, hardly ever missed a game, and once played a game with a testicle injured severely enough that doctors considering removing it.

How did Lidstrom not win the Masterton? That's a story for the next book.

85 Top of the Sears Tower in a Wings Jersey

One of the oddities of the smash-hit film *Ferris Bueller's Day Off*, which is set in Chicago, is that Bueller's best friend, Cameron Frye, played by actor Alan Ruck, spends the majority of the movie cavorting through the Windy City in a Gordie Howe No. 9 Red Wings jersey.

The reason behind this seeming faux pas is that it was in fact a deliberate move. Although he lived in Illinois and set the majority of his films in the state, John Hughes, the director of this and several other iconic 1980s movies, was a huge Red Wings fan.

"I grew up in the Detroit area," Hughes told NHL.com while attending the Red Wings–Blackhawks Winter Classic Game at Wrigley Field in 2009. "Gordie Howe was my hero growing up. We listened to games on the radio…. [That's why] I used the [Red Wings] No. 9 [in *Ferris Bueller*]."

After the film debuted, Howe shipped Hughes an autographed sweater. Hughes responded in kind, sending Howe the official *Ferris Bueller's Day Off* T-shirt, emblazoned with the phrase *Leisure Rules*, and in Howe's case, with a No. 9 added for good measure.

Howe returned to Hughes a photo of himself wearing the shirt and signed it with the message, "To John Hughes: Here's to more days off."

"That was a big thrill," said Hughes, who died in the summer of 2009.

Hughes was born in Lansing, Michigan, and spent much of the first 13 years of his life living in the upscale Detroit suburb of Grosse Pointe. Even though his film career took him to Hollywood and later to a decision to settle within the anonymity of the Chicago suburbs, where he became a Blackhawks season-ticket holder, Hughes never quite cut his ties to the Red Wings.

When Detroit won the Stanley Cup in 1997 for the first time since 1955, Hughes was there, seated in a second-row seat at Joe Louis Arena as Wings captain Steve Yzerman paraded Lord Stanley's mug in a victory lap around the ice.

So the next time you're in Chicago, go to the top of the Sears Tower, don your Wings jersey, press your forehead against the glass like Cameron, and let Detroit tower over that toddlin' town.

86 Demers Would Like a Do-Over on Joe Murphy

Former Detroit Red Wings coach Jacques Demers says if he bumped into Joe Murphy today he would apologize for not being more patient with him in his first few seasons in the NHL.

"There were things I did right and things I did wrong in my NHL coaching career, and I think that's one of the things I did wrong," said Demers, who was Detroit's coach from 1986 to 1990. Murphy, a Michigan State University player, was drafted No. 1 overall by the Red Wings in 1986. He scored 14 goals in 90 games for the Red Wings before being traded to the Edmonton Oilers in 1989–90.

"I didn't need to be on him all the time," Demers said. "If he made a mistake, I put him at the end of the bench. I wasn't as patient as I should have been."

Now a Canadian senator, Demers said he has often reflected on his career in Detroit and concludes he didn't handle Murphy properly.

"Maybe I was too pumped with the idea that I was getting a special player," Demers said. "Honestly, I thought I could get him to be a 40-goal scorer."

It probably didn't help Murphy that he arrived in Detroit three years after Steve Yzerman was drafted. "Steve Yzerman could do what he wanted because Steve Yzerman came to play every single night," Demers said. "Maybe because Yzerman had blossomed so quickly, I expected too much from Joey."

When Murphy showed up in 1986, Demers played the role of bad cop with him. Now, Demers thinks he should have been the good cop. "He had an attitude that rubbed his teammates the wrong way a little bit," Demers said. "But he wasn't a bad kid. He was a little cocky because he had been a star at his university, but I've seen a lot of cocky players."

Maybe what Murphy needed, Demers now says, was to know that Demers was going to be on his side and that he was going to stick with him. "Players always said I was a players' coach," Demers said. "I wasn't a players' coach with Joe Murphy. A players' coach is supposed to work with the players and be patient. I had him on a shorter leash, and I don't know why. He didn't do anything to me."

When Murphy didn't progress quickly enough, Demers said, he grew frustrated. "That wasn't how I wanted to coach," Demers said. "I've never discussed this before with anyone. But I've thought about it. I don't know what Joey is doing now, but if I saw him I would tell him this. I would say I should have coached him better."

Because Murphy was drafted No. 1 overall and never became a superstar, he is generally listed among the most disappointing top draft picks. But most NHL teams would have drafted him No. 1 if they had the chance. He was the consensus No. 1 pick because he could skate, shoot, and make things happen on the ice.

"He was pure, pure, pure talent," Demers said. "I looked at him as someone who could help take us to the Finals. I thought he would come in, and it would be like, boom, he would be ready. That was wrong of me to think like that."

In hindsight, the 1986 draft crop was weak. Brian Leetch was chosen ninth overall by the New York Rangers, but teams didn't have him rated as highly as Murphy.

The Red Wings traded Murphy on November 2, 1989. They gave up Petr Klima, Adam Graves, Jeff Sharples, and Murphy to acquire Jimmy Carson and Kevin McClelland and Edmonton's fifth-round pick. Carson was a Michigan native who was taken No. 2 overall behind Murphy in the 1988 draft.

While never becoming the superstar that Demers hoped he would be, he did have a significant career. He helped the Oilers win the 1990 Stanley Cup championship, and he was a 35-goal scorer one season in Edmonton. He scored 20 or more goals seven times in a career that lasted until 2000.

"One thing that Kenny Holland and I always laugh about is our timing," said former Detroit general manager Jim Devellano. "In 1984 the Pittsburgh Penguins finished dead last and got Mario

0

Lemieux. In 1986 the Detroit Red Wings finished dead last and got Joe Murphy. What would the Detroit Red Wings have been like if we had been last in 1984 and got Mario Lemieux to go with Steve Yzerman?"

87 Jiri Fischer, the Wing Who Came Back from the Dead

In nearly a decade since the night of November 21, 2005, when defenseman Jiri Fischer collapsed on the Detroit Red Wings' bench at Joe Louis Arena and went into cardiac arrest during a game against the Nashville Predators, he has learned much about the value and quality of life.

There's one aspect of Fischer's ailment that remains uncertain to this day—the cause of his cardiac arrest.

"We know exactly what state I was in before I got shocked [by the portable defibrillator], and that was ventricle fibrillation," Fischer said. "My heart was beating close to 300 beats per minute. It needed to be stopped by the defibrillator and restarted by the chest compression."

Within an hour, Fischer was resting comfortably at a Detroit hospital. In the span of 15 days, though, he suffered three further heart episodes.

"It happened on a Monday [at Joe Louis Arena], then [at home] the next Monday, and then the next Monday again," he said.

Fischer was wearing a defibrillator vest the last two times, and readings again indicated ventricle fibrillation as the cause.

With medical personnel unable to solve the riddle behind these episodes, instead of cowering in fear from the uncertainty, Fischer decided that knowledge would be his best companion. He's read and traveled extensively in the years since, devouring information relating to the heart and its conditions.

"I've met the best cardiologists in the country," Fischer said. "Cardiologists that have their own clinics around the country who have their own philosophies of cardiac health and the whole picture of health, from the environmental aspect, to the emotional, to the physical."

Shortly after his cardiac arrest, he began therapy for his condition at a rehabilitation center in Troy, Michigan. He was by far the youngest among the group, and Fischer quickly learned how wise his elders were.

"One thing everybody had in common was how excited everyone was to be there and just to walk on the treadmill, or lift that extra weight on the dumbbell," he recalled. "That's where my priorities literally started to change, from interacting with people who'd been through things far more severe than I [had]. There were people there who'd had several heart attacks. Their appreciation for things was remarkable. It was really fun to be around. It was life-changing—it really was."

He started his own nonprofit organization, Healthy Hope: The Jiri Fischer Foundation, with a concrete goal of raising funds to put portable defibrillators in every public facility and convince more people to learn CPR.

His message to the public is simple—listen to what your body is telling you. Be aware of the symptoms of heart disease and pay attention for the often subtle signs. And get regular checkups and heart screening. Most of all, never give up.

"What we want to share most as part of our foundation is hope," Fischer said. "There're many patients that don't have hope anymore. They just survive. It's not fully living. If someone wants to be healthy, they've got to keep their hope up. It's the most important thing of it all. Keep the passion for life.

"I don't believe that cardiac arrest changes people. I believe it's the life after. At least that's what it's been like for me. The cardiac arrest was the starting point of some sort of a change. A change from the physical standpoint, but mostly from the psychological standpoint. A lot of rethinking, a lot of reprioritizing. A shift in the values that I had that has been pretty dramatic."

Currently the Wings' development coach, Fischer was Detroit's top pick in the 1998 NHL entry draft and was just hitting his prime at 25 and becoming the All-Star–caliber rear guard the Wings envisioned when he suffered his career-ending heart episode.

"I was career-oriented, driven," he said. "I didn't care about anything else but hockey, and I wanted to be the best hockey player I could possibly be. Today, I'm actually enjoying everyday life, enjoying my family."

88 Nobody Messed with the Red Wings in the Late 1980s

The Red Wings were not a championship-caliber hockey team in the late 1980s. But they were the heavyweight champions of the NHL.

With Bob Probert and Joe Kocur leading the way, the Red Wings packed a punch in those days.

"My approach was: 'I don't know how many games we are going to win, but nobody is going to fool around with us,'" Jacques Demers said. "We were going to let Stevie Yzerman do his thing."

Demers remembered the turning point. It came before an afternoon game in Boston.

"Bob said in the room, before the game, 'Stevie, go out and dance today, because no one is going to touch you,'" Demers recalled.

Probert played nine seasons in Detroit and is considered one of the toughest fighters in NHL history. Some say Kocur was even scarier because he had a knockout punch that frightened everyone he faced.

"Teams feared us," Demers recalled.

In addition, the Red Wings had light heavyweights and welterweights such as Harold Snepsts, Jim Nill, Gerard Gallant, Mel Bridgman, Steve Chiasson, Dave Barr, and Lee Norwood, among others. All of them could, and would, fight.

"Not everyone was a heavyweight, but we were like a pack of wolves," Nill recalled.

It had a positive impact on Detroit's ability to compete. Yzerman got the room he needed to skate and score. The word around the NHL was that if you touched Yzerman, there would be a high price to be paid. Chicago's Gary Nylund clipped Yzerman's skates and sent him tumbling into the boards in one game. A few shifts later he had a meeting with Probie, who brought him to his knees with an uppercut. That was how the Red Wings handled things in that era.

"We used it to our advantage," Nill recalled. "There would be a faceoff by the bench, and Probie would be telling the guy on the other team, 'Hey, I'm going to get you on the next shift.' I don't care who you were. If you heard Probie say that, you couldn't be sure what was going to go on."

Probert totaled 398 penalty minutes in 1987–88, and Kocur had 263 minutes. The greatest fear for any heavyweight in that era was that they might have to fight Probie and Kocur in the same game.

"Guys would fight Probie," Nill recalled. "But no one wanted to fight Joey, because if he hit you, you were done."

Detroit players still talk about how badly Kocur hurt Brad Dalgarno on Long Island or how he KO'd Jim Kyte. He had to be carried off on a stretcher.

"Guys were afraid to go to Detroit," Probert said in an interview before his death of a heart attack in 2010. "Teams were intimidated to come into our building. You could kind of tell. You'd go out there and run a couple of guys, and you could sense a feeling from the other team that they weren't going to respond at all."

Kocur said the Red Wings believed their best chance of winning came from taking away the opponents' will to win.

"If somebody hit Petr Klima, or Gerard Gallant or Brad Park, you knew there was going to be a fight," Kocur said. "It was like Roger Clemens throwing high and hard at a batter. You just wanted to back them up. And that's what Probie and I did. It was either a fight or taking a run at a goalie, just something to let them know, 'Hey, we're not sleeping tonight.'"

The Red Wings were not a great team in the 1980s, but they could put on an entertaining show for fans, who were excited by the Red Wings' roughhouse tactics. Probert's popularity rivaled Yzerman's popularity.

"I grew up watching the Dead Wings, so I know what it was like before," Probert said. "The place started coming alive after we started fighting and roughing it up. You could see that."

The Red Wings were a 40-point team when Demers took over, and he took them to 78 and the Western Conference Finals the following season.

"These guys made a difference," Demers said. "I never liked the guys who just sat on the bench until they fought. Bob Probert was an All-Star one year, and Joey Kocur could play."

The team just didn't have enough skill to reach the Stanley Cup Finals. "We were a difficult team to play against," Nill said. "But I think Jacques got all that he could out of us."

89 Detroit's One-Hit Wonders

Perhaps it should come as no surprise that the hockey team from the town that brought the world the Motown sound should spawn its share of one-hit wonders.

In total, 26 players have skated their only NHL game in a Detroit uniform since the team was first born as the Detroit Cougars for the 1926–27 NHL season, the most recent being defenseman Ryan Sproul, who debuted against the St. Louis Blues in Detroit's 2013–14 regular-season finale.

"You're never guaranteed a career in the NHL," said right-winger Mitch Callahan, who made his Detroit debut on March 25, 2014, in a game against the Columbus Blue Jackets. "This could be my only game I ever have, so I'm going to take it all in and try to remember the most I can of it."

It's good advice that he could have easily received from those who came before him. Some simply faded away into nothing more than agate type at the back of the team's yearbook. Others, though, managed to leave a mark in franchise history, no matter how brief their stay in Hockeytown turned out to be.

In the case of Gord Haidy and Doug McKay, their lone turn as Red Wings came in the Stanley Cup Playoffs during Detroit's successful run to the 1949–50 title, and in McKay's case, he became the first player in NHL history to skate his only NHL game during a Stanley Cup Finals match playing for the team that won the Cup.

Others made history the moment that they stepped on the ice. When Gerry Abel made his NHL debut on March 8, 1967, versus the New York Rangers, he became the first and only player in franchise history to play for his dad. Sid Abel was coach/GM of the Wings at the time.

KEVIN ALLEN AND BOB DUFF

Likewise, when defenseman Bill Mitchell took part in his lone Red Wings game on February 23, 1964, against the Montreal Canadiens, he also made NHL history. It was the day after his 34th birthday, and Mitchell became the oldest rookie in the league.

The Ones Who Only Played One
The 26 Players Who Skated in Their Lone NHL Game as Red Wings

Player	Position	Date	Result
Gerry Abel	LW	March 8, 1967	Detroit 3 at New York Rangers 1
Mitch Callahan	RW	March 25, 2014	Detroit 2 at Columbus Blue Jackets 4
Harrison Gray	G	November 28, 1963	Montreal Canadiens 7 at Detroit 3
Gord Haidy	RW	April 1, 1950	Detroit 0 at Toronto Maple Leafs 2
Galen Head	RW	March 21, 1968	Toronto Maple Leafs 5 at Detroit 2
Rich Healey	D	January 4, 1961	Detroit 4 at Toronto Maple Leafs 6
Earl Johnson	C	March 20, 1954	Detroit 1 at Montreal Canadiens 6
Ken Mann	RW	February 25, 1976	Detroit 0 at Toronto 8
Alexey Marchenko	D	January 4, 2014	Detroit 5 at Dallas Stars 1
Tom McCollum	G	March 30, 2011	St. Louis Blues 10 at Detroit 3
Doug McKay	LW	April 15, 1950	Detroit 4 New York Rangers 0*
Bill Mitchell	D	February 23, 1964	Montreal Canadiens 2 at Detroit 3
Dean Morton	D	October 5, 1989	Detroit 7 at Calgary Flames 10
Brian Murphy	C	November 28, 1974	Detroit 2 at Buffalo Sabres 5
Ed Nicholson	D	March 21, 1948	Toronto Maple Leafs 5 at Detroit 2
Bert Peer	D/RW	March 15, 1940	Chicago Blackhawks 4 at Detroit 3
Chris Pusey	G	October 19, 1985	Chicago Blackhawks 6 at Detroit 2
Dave Rochefort	C	March 28, 1967	Detroit 2 at Chicago Blackhawks 7
Pat Rupp	G	March 22, 1964	Toronto Maple Leafs 4 at Detroit 1
Bjorn Skaare	C	November 29, 1978	Detroit 2 at Colorado Rockies 2
Ryan Sproul	D	April 13, 2014	Detroit 3 at St. Louis Blues 0
Frank Steele	C/RW	December 25, 1930	Toronto Maple Leafs 1 at Detroit 10
Barry Sullivan	RW	February 3, 1948	Detroit 4 at Chicago Blackhawks 1
Joe Turner	G	February 5, 1942	Toronto Maple Leafs 3 at Detroit 3
Murray Wing	D	April 7, 1974	Detroit 4 at Chicago Blackhawks 7
B.J. Young	RW	November 28, 1999	Phoenix Coyotes 4 at Detroit 3

*Game played at Toronto's Maple Leaf Gardens

Though his mark was later surpassed by 38-year-old St. Louis defenseman Connie Madigan, the unique circumstances surrounding Mitchell's only NHL appearance are still worth talking about. He was skating for the defending Allan Cup–champion Windsor Bulldogs and had actually played for them earlier in the day. When Sid Abel discovered injuries to Marcel Pronovost and Junior Langlois would prevent them from playing for the Wings that night, the Detroit coach called Mitchell and asked him to suit up.

"He did a good job," Abel told the *Windsor Star*'s Jack Dulmage. "That was a tough spot to put a guy in [in] his first pro game, but he didn't look out of place at all."

Mitchell paired with future Hall of Famer Bill Gadsby in Detroit's 3–2 victory and remembered Gadsby's pregame advice: "It's just a hockey game. No different than playing out on the pond."

"It was a little strange being up here for the first time, but I wasn't nervous in making my big bow," Mitchell told the *Windsor Star*'s Jim Nelson.

Later that season, Pat Rupp, goalie for the US Olympic team at the 1964 Winter Games in Innsbruck, Austria, also made a one-game appearance for Detroit on an amateur tryout basis. Rupp returned to the amateur ranks after losing 4–1 to the Toronto Maple Leafs in his only NHL game on March 22, 1964, playing again for the USA at the 1968 Winter Olympics in Grenoble, France.

Five of the one-game wonders were goalies, including Joe Turner, tragically killed in action in World War II, whose lone NHL game was a 3–3 tie with the Leafs on February 5, 1942. On March 30, 2011, against the St. Louis Blues, Tom McCollum surrendered three goals on eight shots in 15 minutes of work in relief of starter Joey MacDonald, leaving him with a career goals-against average of 12.00, the highest in franchise history.

Others gained notoriety for where they were from. Center Bjorn Skaare (1978–79) was the first NHLer from Norway. Right-winger

B.J. Young (1999–2000) was the first Red Wing born in Alaska. Curiously, both men later died in car accidents.

Then there was defenseman Murray Wing, whose lone Detroit game came on April 7, 1974, against the Boston Bruins. Wing and Dwight King of the Los Angeles Kings are the only players in NHL history to share a surname with their team's nickname.

Perhaps the most memorable one-hit wonder in Detroit history was defenseman Dean Morton. Part of the opening night lineup on October 5, 1989, as the Wings fell 10–7 at Calgary to the Flames, Morton scored Detroit's first goal.

"When a grinder like myself scores the first goal of the season in a game you lose 10–7, which is essentially a lacrosse score, you know you're in trouble," Morton told the *Globe and Mail*.

He was correct on two counts. Morton was sent to the minors a few days later, and the Wings went on to miss the playoffs in 1989–90, the last time the franchise has failed to qualify for postseason play.

Though he'd never play in the league again, Morton has skated in more than 400 games since earning his stripes as an NHL referee in 2000. "If I'm working in a game where some rookie gets his first goal, I'll skate over to the kid and say, 'Been there, done that,'" Morton joked.

90 Five Decisions That Altered Red Wings History

1. Naming Devellano GM

When Mike Ilitch bought the Detroit Red Wings in 1982, it was not a foregone conclusion that Jim Devellano was going to be his general manager.

"He told me his list included David Poile, Red Berenson, Ron Mason, and Pat Quinn," Devellano recalled.

Mason was Michigan State's coach then, and Berenson had just been fired as coach of the St. Louis Blues. Poile was a rising young star as an assistant general manager for the Atlanta Flames. Pat Quinn had just been fired as coach of the Philadelphia Flyers.

In an interview for this book, Poile said he remembers his Detroit interview well because he came away thinking that Ilitch was more interested in Poile's ideas for changing the team than he was in actually hiring him.

Always the shrewd businessman, Ilitch undoubtedly chose to interview several people to get a cross-section of ideas and solutions for the team moving forward.

Lou Nanne, then general manager of the Minnesota North Stars, had strongly recommended to Ilitch that he hire Devellano, who had been Bill Torrey's protégé with the New York Islanders.

Years later, Devellano said he talked to Ilitch about the interview process, and noted that he had been up against an impressive group.

"Yeah, but none of them have won the Stanley Cup," Ilitch said.

Not long after that, the Washington Capitals hired Poile. Mason stayed at Michigan State. Red Berenson ended up at Michigan, where he has been ever since. Pat Quinn did eventually end up a general manager in Vancouver.

Devellano built through the draft in the early years, and supplemented with free agents. "I said it would take eight years to win the Cup, and it actually took 15," Devellano said, laughing.

However, Devellano also built the organization and structure that has allowed Detroit to win four Stanley Cups and reach the Stanley Cup Finals two other times during Ilitch's ownership. Who knows what would have happened if Ilitch would have hired one of the other guys?

2. Mike Keenan vs. Scotty Bowman

At one point, Ilitch wanted to hire Mike Keenan to coach the Red Wings.

"I said I didn't think he was the right guy," Devellano said. "And then, he asked, 'Well, who is?'"

Devellano said he thought the right guy would be either Al Arbour or Scotty Bowman. "Can you get one of those guys?" Ilitch asked.

Devellano assured Ilitch that he could secure one of those coaches. The opportunity came when Detroit told coach/GM Bryan Murray to focus solely on his role as GM after Toronto upset Detroit in the 1992–93 playoffs on a Game 7 overtime goal by Nikolai Borschevsky.

He called Arbour first because he knew him well from their days together with the Islanders. He said he was not interested in coaching again.

That opened the door to hire Bowman in 1993.

Keenan was hired by the New York Rangers, and they won a Stanley Cup in 1993–94. But who knows what would have happened in Detroit if Keenan had been hired?

What we do know is that Bowman transformed Steve Yzerman and the Red Wings into champions.

3. Roenick Chooses Flyers Over the Red Wings

When Jeremy Roenick was a free agent in 2002, he came very close to signing with the Red Wings.

His wife, Tracy, believed he was leaning in that direction. He was in a Detroit hotel mulling the decision, when his good friend Rick Tocchet called and convinced him to go to Philadelphia.

Here is the rest of the story: Had the Red Wings signed Roenick, they probably would have been done buying free agents that summer. They probably would not have signed Luc Robitaille. The Red Wings definitely would not have signed Brett Hull, who ended up scoring more goals that season than Roenick.

Would Pavel Datsyuk have played as much that season if Roenick had signed in Detroit?

4. Curtis Joseph vs. Ed Belfour

After Dominik Hasek retired in 2002, the Red Wings needed a No. 1 goalie. Belfour and Joseph were both unrestricted free agents.

The Red Wings went after and signed Joseph, who turned out not to be a good fit. He never seemed to find his comfort level in Detroit.

Meanwhile, Belfour went on to be a Vezina finalist for Toronto in 2002–03. He posted 17 shutouts over the next two seasons with the Maple Leafs.

If the Red Wings had signed Belfour, would they have re-signed Hasek when he wanted to come out of retirement? It's a fair question.

5. Fred Williams vs. Bernie Federko

In 1976 the Red Wings owned the fourth pick in the draft.

General manager Alex Delvecchio took center Fred Williams, who had registered 31 goals and 87 assists for 118 points for the Saskatoon Blades in the Western Hockey League.

Scouts, curiously enough, thought he played a similar style to Delvecchio during his Hall of Fame career.

But Williams turned out to be a bust. He played just one season in Detroit, scoring two goals in 44 games. It didn't seem like he could handle the pace of the NHL game.

One of the players Delvecchio spurned to take Williams was his Saskatoon linemate Bernie Federko, who had scored 72 goals in 72 games for the Blades. Some scouts believed he was the better player, and he was drafted three picks later by the Blues.

The drafting of Williams seemed to epitomize the nightmarish quality of the Red Wings managerial decisions in the 1970s. Meanwhile, Federko went on to a Hall of Fame NHL career, registering 1,130 points in 1,000 games. He scored 20 or more goals for 11 consecutive seasons.

Had the Red Wings drafted Federko, they might have been a much better team in the late 1970s. Would Bruce Norris have sold the team then? Would they have ended up with Steve Yzerman? It's impossible to know.

91 Coming to the Defense of Fedorov

One of the beautiful qualities of sport is the ability to debate, to wonder *what if?*

In Detroit they still wonder what might have transpired if Wings coach Scotty Bowman had stayed with his brief experiment to turn center Sergei Fedorov into a defenseman.

"I'm convinced," Red Wings vice president Jimmy Devellano said, "that Sergei could have won a Norris Trophy if he had played there for a season."

In need of a defenseman during the 1995–96 season with Viacheslav Fetisov still en route from Moscow following the death of his mother, Detroit coach Scotty Bowman didn't turn to the farm club for help. He just turned to Fedorov.

"We didn't call up a defenseman, because we knew we had him," recalled Bowman, who'd also employed Fedorov on the blue line in a similar emergency situation in Dallas earlier in the season and had used him there sporadically ever since.

Bowman jokingly suggested that he'd move Fedorov to the back end in order to appease his father, Viktor.

At the time, Fedorov didn't seem to mind. "The coaches asked me to play defense, and I did it," Fedorov said. "It's okay. I like it."

Sergei Fedorov skates past the Colorado Avalanche bench after scoring the Red Wings' second goal in Game 6 of the Western Conference Finals series at Joe Louis Arena on May 26, 1997. The Red Wings beat the Avalanche 3–1 to win the Western Conference championship.

Imagine the excitement at the time in the marketing department at Nike, which provided Fedorov with his skates back then, and already had built an ad campaign around Deion Sanders, who was playing on both sides of the ball for the NFL's Atlanta Falcons.

Certainly they considered all of the possibilities and the commercial dynamics.

DEION: I play offense.

SERGEI: I play offense.

DEION: I play defense.

SERGEI: I play defense.

If only Fedorov had embraced the concept.

Long-term, Fedorov expressed no desire to join the back end on a full-time basis, which some felt was too bad, because they agreed with Devellano's assessment that Fedorov could have blossomed into an All-Star rear guard.

"He won a few Cups, he was MVP in the league, and won the Selke," veteran Russian goalie Nikolai Khabibulin said. "He was the best all-around player."

Fedorov certainly wasn't the first great Wing to attempt the transition from forward to defense. Wings GM Ned Harkness briefly experimented with right-winger Gordie Howe on his blue line in 1970–71, Howe's final season in Detroit. It failed, not because Howe couldn't handle the position, but because the Wings could find no one capable of filling the void on the offensive side of the game without Howe playing up front.

In a much earlier era, Ebbie Goodfellow, a high-scoring center for Detroit, was moved to the blue line by Detroit coach Jack Adams, and stayed there. He was part of two Stanley Cup winners for the Wings and earned NHL All-Star and Hart Trophy recognition as a defender.

Hockey people feel similar honors could have come Fedorov's way had he stuck out the switch.

"I talked to Wayne Gretzky, and he said to me, 'I couldn't play forward and defense,'" Bowman said. "Mario [Lemieux] couldn't do it. [Jaromir] Jagr couldn't play defense, but Sergei could. He was a hell of a player.'"

It's easy to visualize the machinations that went on inside Bowman's unique and clever hockey mind when he contemplated Fedorov as part of his blue-line crew. Fedorov's ability to make a clean, crisp first pass, the essential element to becoming a puck-moving defender, was astounding, as was his mobility. At 6'1" and 200 pounds, Fedorov possessed the necessary strength to win battles for pucks and space.

Hockey Canada president and CEO Tom Renney felt that it was Fedorov's willingness to commit to a 200-foot game that made him capable of patrolling the blue line so effectively.

"He embraced the two-way game, the commitment away from the puck, the wherewithal to anticipate the defensive game," Renney said. "He did things in a game on both sides of the puck. Fedorov was very, very complete.

"That's why the Red Wings have some banners hanging at the Joe [Louis Arena], because of his efforts."

St. Louis Blues coach Ken Hitchcock followed Bowman's lead, also toying with Fedorov as a defenseman when he coached him with the Columbus Blue Jackets.

"His greatness was that he's a cerebral player," Hitchcock said. "He plays with limited emotion, but tremendous positional play with and without the puck.

"He managed the game for us. He organized the line he played with, and he organized the defense pair. He was always in a position to get you out of trouble.

"At that stage of his career he was never going to score at the level he used to, but he was still a really effective player. He was always there. He was there for wingers, he was there for the *D*. He'd go in and pull it off the boards when you're in trouble. You'd get spinning, and he'd just go in and settle it down in our zone."

Fedorov's Detroit teammates, especially those who already played defense, seemed far less impressed by his ability to make the move to the rear guard.

"The great players, they all play good styles and good systems, so they can play all positions," defenseman Vladimir Konstantinov said at the time. Years earlier, he'd made the change from center to defense, and suggested it wasn't all that difficult to master his position of choice.

"If you can skate backward, you can play defense," he said.

If Fedorov had taken to the back, many in hockey feel he would have moved to the front of the list among elite NHL defensemen.

92 Ebbie Was a Goodfellow

The first of four Red Wings to win the Hart Trophy as most valuable player of the NHL had much in common with the most recent winner. Like Sergei Fedorov, Detroit's Hart Trophy winner in 1993–94, Ebbie Goodfellow made the switch from center to defense. Only in Goodfellow's case, it was a permanent move.

Goodfellow owned one of the hardest and truest shots in the NHL, accurate from long range. When he first broke into the big time with the Detroit Cougars in 1929–30, Goodfellow was a slim athlete, but after about six or seven years in the league, he began to bulk up. Goodfellow put on muscle in the right areas—over the back and across the shoulders—and when Detroit coach Jack Adams needed help on his back end, he moved Goodfellow to the Detroit rear guard, and the result was a stalwart defender who became an NHL All-Star selection at the position.

He was selected to the NHL's First All-Star team alongside Boston's Aubrey "Dit" Clapper in 1939–40, the season he became the first Wing to garner the Hart, the 11-year veteran anchoring a rebuilding Detroit club with his savvy and experience. Goodfellow never lost his offensive touch when he moved to the blue line. In that season, only forward Syd Howe (14–23–37) collected more points on the Red Wings roster than the 11–17–28 numbers posted by Goodfellow.

That the Wings got Goodfellow at all was a story in itself.

Adams played his final NHL season with the Stanley Cup–champion Ottawa Senators in 1926–27 and made plenty of friends in the area who became bird dogs for him in his search to assemble the Detroit club after he was named coach and general manager of the team in 1927.

Nate Abelson, who managed Abelson's haberdashery on Bank Street, was one of Adams' Ottawa contacts, and he highly recommended Goodfellow, who'd led the Ottawa City League in scoring during the 1927–28 campaign, skating for the Ottawa Montagnards.

Wanting to protect his hometown interests, Abelson contacted Senators owner Frank Ahearn, strongly advising they sign Goodfellow, but when his suggestion was ignored, he called Adams.

Adams acted fast, trading $4,000 to Saskatoon of the Prairie League—which had signed Goodfellow to a contract he'd chosen not to honor—to acquire his rights. Adams then got Goodfellow's name on a contract.

In his first season as a pro with the Canadian Professional League's Detroit Olympics, he led the loop in scoring with 26–8–34 totals in 42 games. Goodfellow moved up to the big club the next season, working in the middle of the Cougars' top

KevIN ALLEN AND BOB DUFF

forward line between Carson Cooper and George Hay. During the
1930–31 season, Goodfellow established club single-season offensive marks with 25 goals, 23 assists, and 48 points.

On January 2, 1934, with the Wings in a three-game losing
skid in which they'd been outscored 17–4, Adams opted to shake
things up. He benched veteran goalie John Ross Roach and
acquired Wilf Cude on loan from the Montreal Canadiens and
shifted Goodfellow back to defense, where he went on to play the
remainder of his NHL career. The moves paid dividends when
Detroit finished first in the NHL's American Division and made it
to the Stanley Cup Finals for the first time in history, losing a best-
of-five series in four games to the Chicago Black Hawks.

Detroit won back-to-back Stanley Cups in 1935–36 and
1936–37, and the Goodfellow shift received the ultimate stamp of
approval when he was named to the NHL's first All-Star team in
1936–37, garnering 13 of a possible 23 votes. No other defender
received more than five votes.

Named Detroit's captain in 1938, all the praise and attention
seemed a shock to the quiet Goodfellow, known as "Poker Face"
due to his serious expression. "There's nothing sensational about
me," Goodfellow told the *Altoona Tribune*. "I just go out there and
play the best I know how."

Considered the first stud defender in Red Wings franchise
history, Goodfellow shares another common trait with Nicklas
Lidstrom, Detroit's most decorated defenseman.

Both wore No. 5.

93 Why Scotty Bowman Was a Hockey Genius

Scotty Bowman looked at hockey the way Albert Einstein viewed physics. The numbers, rules, and laws that looked one way to us looked vastly different to him.

"His mind was like no mind I was ever around," said Detroit general manager Ken Holland. "His mind goes 100 different directions at the same time."

Holland remembers sitting down in a coffee shop to talk to Bowman on the morning of a 1996 playoff game in St. Louis and getting up two hours later "marveling" at how prepared Bowman was for that game.

"He was so concerned about everything, whether it was the schedule, travel arrangements, or whether the benches were too high or too low," Holland recalled.

He recalled Bowman calling him down during the 1998 playoffs to tell him that ESPN had installed a camera hanging under the scoreboard that was against NHL regulations. "What's the difference?" Holland asked.

Bowman explained that Dallas always cleared the puck along the glass, and his team liked to lift the puck high through the neutral zone. Bowman was worried one of his players would hit the camera.

"He thought the camera was a one-in-a-million advantage for Dallas, and he didn't want to give the Stars that advantage," Holland remembered.

By the time the game started that night, ESPN had removed the camera.

Another time, Bowman called Holland in the middle of the night because he didn't believe the food service on the team's jet was what the players should be fed.

Bowman won nine Stanley Cups as a coach. He won five in Montreal, one with Pittsburgh, and three more as Red Wings coach. Here are reasons why Bowman is generally regarded as the greatest coach in league history:

1. Attention to detail: Throughout Bowman's career, he was known as someone who knew everything about his players and his opponents. "He would talk to the cook to see which players were coming in, or he would talk to the parking attendant to see who was arriving with whom and what time they were coming in," Holland said.

2. Changed with the times: Although he was known as a tough coach, Bowman certainly didn't coach the Red Wings the same way he coached the Montreal Canadiens. He was clearly not as overbearing in Detroit as he was in Montreal.

   "Scotty coached in five different decades," said NBC's Pierre McGuire. "He was wise enough to study trends."

3. Master of the match-ups: Bowman had a knack of knowing how to maximize the effectiveness of his stars.

   "He would get his star players more free ice away from match-ups," McGuire said. "His philosophy was the head coach had a responsibility to make his star players perform at a higher level. He felt that the role players could cancel one another out. The stars needed to make a difference. One way he could help was to get them into positive match-up situations."

4. Passion: He loved being at the rink, and still loves talking the game.

   "No man has ever watched as many games at any level as Scotty," McGuire said. "He watches hockey at all levels, and he never gets tired doing it. His eye for talent is amazing, and his ability to understand the team-building process is second to none. He also studies coaching trends and ways to make the game better."

5. Boundless energy: Former Red Wings pro scout Bill Dineen used to say he never saw Bowman yawn. He stayed up late watching games and got up early to start acquiring information. Even today, octogenarian Bowman has the energy of a younger man.

6. Fountain of information: Bowman had to know everything that was going on in the NHL. He usually pulled more news from members of the media than they pulled from him. He was all hockey, all of the time.

"As soon as the Internet became popular, he learned how to use it, because he wanted every bit of information he could get," Holland said.

94 Bryan Murray Deserves More Credit

When Jacques Demers was deposed as coach of the Detroit Red Wings following the 1989–90 season after the club missed the play-offs for the most recent time, he tipped his cap to his successor, Bryan Murray, who was named coach and general manager of the Wings.

"They're in good hands with Bryan Murray," Demers said at the time. "He's a good man."

A man who would, in fact, put the Wings on a path toward the top but wouldn't be around when the team finally collected the silver chalice at the end of the journey.

Scotty Bowman gets acknowledged as the genius who led the Wings to consecutive Stanley Cups in 1996–97 and 1997–98, ending Detroit's 42-season title drought, and deservedly so. He is, after all, the greatest coach in hockey history, winning nine Stanley Cups while working behind NHL benches.

But while handing out kudos, save a few for Murray, because although he wasn't around for Detroit's Stanley Cup glory, Murray's fingerprints were all over that silver mug during the assembly of the NHL's last back-to-back championship victories.

"I think anytime, whoever's involved [in building a championship team] should feel some sense of accomplishment," Murray said.

During Murray's Detroit tenure, seven-time Norris Trophy winner Nicklas Lidstrom, Vladimir Konstantinov, 1993–94 Hart Trophy winner Sergei Fedorov, and Slava Kozlov made their NHL debuts. Murray was deeply involved in helping spirit Fedorov away from the Soviet national team while in Seattle for the 1990 Goodwill Games, as well as getting Kozlov's release from Red Army.

He acquired Kris Draper, who went on to play in more than 1,000 games as the center on Detroit's famed Grind Line. His drafts produced right-winger Martin Lapointe, goaltender Chris Osgood, and right-winger Darren McCarty, all of them multiple Stanley Cup winners. Both McCarty (1997) and Lapointe (1998) scored Stanley Cup–winning goals for the Wings.

Murray takes pride in the role he played in Detroit's development as the NHL's powerhouse club. "I felt that we did a lot of the right things, brought in some good kids," he said.

When Toronto's Nikolai Borschevsky scored in overtime of Game 7 to eliminate Detroit in the first round of the 1993 playoffs, Murray was replaced behind the bench by Bowman. A year later, when the eighth-seeded San Jose Sharks engineered a stunning seven-game upset of top-seeded Detroit in the opening playoff round, Murray was handed his walking papers as GM.

"In my last year, I felt we were on the verge of becoming a championship-caliber team, and that proved true," Murray said. "When I left [Detroit], I felt very good about that."

Murray has rebuilt teams wherever he's stopped along the NHL trail. He was the first coach to take the Washington Capitals into the playoffs and as GM of the Florida Panthers assembled a squad that reached the Stanley Cup Finals in their third year of existence in 1996. He later moved to the Anaheim Ducks and in 2003 as their GM engineered a first-round sweep of the defending Cup-champion Red Wings en route to a Stanley Cup Finals appearance, where Anaheim lost to the New Jersey Devils in seven games.

The Wings became the first reigning Stanley Cup champions since the 1951–52 Toronto Maple Leafs to be the victims of a first-round sweep.

Four years later, with Brian Burke now the GM, he reaped the benefits of the groundwork laid by Murray as the Ducks captured the Stanley Cup, defeating the Red Wings in the Western Conference Final en route to the title.

These days, Murray is again stockpiling solid young talent as GM of the Ottawa Senators, building another team from within.

"I have no questions in my own mind about anything I've done, or the record I have," Murray said. "I think anybody who understands hockey knows how well my teams were always prepared, and how well they played."

Murray didn't get his name on the Stanley Cup with the Wings, but his signature was on their success.

95 No Sales Job Was Required to Keep Holland in Hockey

In 1985 Ken Holland was not contemplating a career in hockey management. He was thinking he was going to clean up as a vacuum salesman.

He was 29, retired from hockey, living in British Columbia, and his mother convinced him his personality would be perfect for a vacuum sales job she saw advertized in the newspaper.

"These vacuums were going for over $320, and 10 or 20 percent of all sales went to the salesperson," Holland recalled. "My mom said, 'I need a new vacuum, and I'll be your first sale.'"

Then Holland's grandmother said she also would buy one. "I'm thinking, *This job is great, I haven't even gotten the job yet, and I've sold two vacuums*," Holland recalled, laughing. "Then it hit me, *Who was I going to sell to after that?*"

A week later, Red Wings general manager Jimmy Devellano called and offered him a job as a scout in Western Canada. Twelve years later, Holland succeeded Devellano as GM of the Detroit Red Wings. Today, he's one of the most respected GMs in the game.

"Sometimes I wake up and pinch myself to make sure I haven't been dreaming the opportunity I've had as general manager of the Detroit Red Wings," Holland said. "This franchise has been around for many years and has had so many great players that you feel an obligation to keep it strong. Everywhere we go, we play in a sold-out building. This franchise means so much to so many people, you don't want to screw it up."

In addition to winning three Stanley Cup championships (1998, 2002, and 2008), here are the five most important moves Holland has made as Detroit's GM:

1. Hired Mike Babcock as Coach

After promoting Dave Lewis didn't work, Holland tried to catch a rising star and did with Babcock.

Babcock's chief strength is his ability to prepare his team to compete at its highest level. He seems always to get the most out of his players.

2. Acquired Defenseman Chris Chelios

Holland gave the Blackhawks two first-round draft picks and defenseman Anders Eriksson. It was considered a steep price, but Chelios ended up being a valuable addition for many years.

Chelios may be considered a Detroiter now, as much as he is considered a Chicago native.

3. Acquired Dominik Hasek

Holland dealt Slava Kozlov and a first-round pick to the Buffalo Sabres in 2001. It was like adding a Picasso painting to a museum that already had a room full of Rembrandts. It was the perfect move.

Hasek is one of the top 10 goalies in NHL history, and he played a major role in the 2002 Stanley Cup win.

4. Signed Brett Hull and Luc Robitaille

They were both free agents in the summer 2002, and both played significant roles on that team.

That 2002 team will go down as one of the most talented teams in NHL history. Hall of Famers, or potential Hall of Famers, on that roster include Holland, Coach Scotty Bowman, plus Steve Yzerman, Chris Chelios, Nicklas Lidstrom, Brendan Shanahan, Hull, Robitaille, Pavel Datsyuk, Hasek, and Sergei Fedorov.

5. Mentored Yzerman and Jim Nill

Before taking the job of general manager in Tampa Bay, Yzerman worked for Holland. Nill was Holland's right-hand man for years.

It was like learning chess from a master or studying politics under the Bush family. When Yzerman accepted the job in Tampa Bay and Nill went to Dallas, they were more than ready for those challenges.

96 Tomas Holmstrom: Toughest Red Wing of Them All

You wouldn't want to work where Tomas Holmstrom worked. You wouldn't want to live where he's lived.

Holmstrom's hometown of Lulea, Sweden, is near the Arctic Circle and gets about 90 minutes of light per day during the winter months.

It's barren, cold, and often unforgiving—much like life in the slot, where Holmstrom made his living for 15 seasons and 1,026 games as a Red Wing.

"I had no problem to go to the net, to stay around the net, to take a beating for the team and draw those penalties so we could score on the power play," Holmstrom said.

"I would do it all over again. That was the best part of my game. I cannot be like [teammates] Pavel [Datsyuk] and Hank [Henrik Zetterberg] and be so skilled. But I think you need a good mix to be a successful team."

The elements that Holmstrom brought to the mix exacted a terrible price on his body. Two hernia surgeries and countless knee operations are the price for Holmstrom's career choice.

"After a while, it wears on you," Holmstrom said. "Getting out of bed in the morning and stumbling to make it to the bathroom, and all of the medication they give you [for the pain], it can't be good for you."

It wasn't so much the punishment he took that impressed people. Many players absorb their share of welts and contusions during the course of their career. It was that Holmstrom would absorb the abuse, shrug it off, and go right back to the area where it would hurt the most again without giving the pain a second thought.

"A lot of guys can stand there and deflect the puck in the net when no one's cross-checking you," Wings coach Mike Babcock said. "But most guys are trying to find out who's cross-checking them, and not worried about the puck.

"The good guys don't worry about getting cross-checked, they can always find the puck. That's what he was real good at.

"He had great hockey sense. He knew how to play, he knew to protect the puck, knew how to get it back, he knew where to stand. He wasn't an elite skater, and yet he was an elite competitor."

Tomas Holmstrom celebrates after scoring past San Jose Sharks goalie Antti Niemi (No. 31), during the third period of Game 5 of an NHL hockey Stanley Cup Western Conference semifinal playoff series on May 8, 2011, in San Jose. Detroit won 4–3.

The role he filled isn't taught as much as it is accepted. A coach can request of a player to take abuse and not hit back for the good of the team, but in the heat of battle, it's the player who must choose to suffer the punishment in silence.

In Holmstrom's case, retaliation for the red welts on his body came when his team lit the red lamp.

"You score the goal and you make your point," he said.

His bravery and tough exterior won Holmstrom many fans inside the Detroit dressing room.

"He had bad knees when he first joined the league," said former Wings captain Nicklas Lidstrom, Holmstrom's best friend. "Seeing him battling through those things and knowing he was in pain, just his determination and his willingness to battle through it to be on the ice, it showed a lot about his character."

"It's got to be a little bit tearing on the body to play the way he did," Wings defenseman Jonathan Ericsson said. "It's pretty amazing that he could play as many games as he did."

Holmstrom left the game in 2012 third all-time in Red Wings history in power-play goals, sixth in regular-season games played, and fourth in playoff games played, and even his enemies acknowledged their admiration for what he was willing to tolerate to ensure team success.

"What a true warrior," said former Edmonton Oilers forward Ryan Smyth, who also earned his living in front of the other team's net. "I'm sure his body ached a lot after games.

"He was one of the best, if not the best, in my opinion. I watched him over the years, and I picked up a few things.

"I have tremendous respect for him."

Sticks and stones may have broken Holmstrom's bones, but nothing was ever able to break his will.

97 McCarty's Stanley Cup Goal Was Assisted by a Swede

When Darren McCarty roared around Philadelphia Flyers defenseman Janne Niinimaa to score the Stanley Cup–clinching goal in 1997, Detroit captain Steve Yzerman greeted him with a hug and profanity.

"He screamed, 'What the fuck was that?'" McCarty recalled. "And I said, 'I don't know, but who gives a fuck?'"

McCarty swears that his sweet move around Niinimaa marked the only time in his NHL career that he ever beat a defenseman one-on-one. He might be exaggerating, but it is true that McCarty was known more for using his hands for fighting. Stickhandling was not considered his forte.

The play started in Detroit's defensive end with defenseman Vladimir Konstantinov making the first pass to Tomas Sandstrom. He head-manned the puck to McCarty, who was knifing through the neutral zone.

"We were yelling for Mac to dump the puck into the offensive zone," center Kris Draper recalled.

McCarty knew his role, and he usually played it safe. However, he didn't this time. The Flyers were in the midst of a line change, and perhaps McCarty, one of the Red Wings' most popular players, sensed his destiny was upon him.

"It was like my automatic pilot engaged," McCarty said.

Over the past two summers, McCarty had traveled to Sweden to work with noted stickhandling coach Tomas Storm.

"We worked on moving my hands back and forth with the idea that stickhandling would become second nature," McCarty said.

McCarty spent hours upon hours in Storm's camp, working on controlling the puck. Often, McCarty would be on the ice with

12-year-olds and teenagers who were all there trying to learn the art of stickhandling. The first time it was clear to McCarty that the training was paying dividends occurred when he saw Niinimaa in the path in front of him.

"I thought, *Holy shit, I've got him beat,*" McCarty recalled.

Storm had taught McCarty that stickhandling was simply muscle memory. He made McCarty think about moving the puck north-and-south, instead of side-to-side. "If you watch Pavel Datsyuk, that's how he moves the puck," McCarty said.

Apparently, Finns weren't allowed in Storm's camp, because when Niinimaa dove in to steal the puck away, McCarty suddenly pulled it back like he was working a yo-yo. Niinimaa seemed shocked. McCarty engaged his warp drive. Quickly, McCarty was around Niinimaa, in the blue paint, and then around goalie Ron Hextall. Suddenly the puck was in the net to give the Red Wings a 2–0 lead.

"What I was thinking was, *Don't miss the fucking net,*" McCarty recalled.

No member of the Red Wings had ever seen McCarty make an offensive move like that. It was a scorer's move.

"Yzerman's eyes were as big as plates," McCarty said.

Everyone on the ice, and in the crowd, could sense that this goal was the backbreaker for a Flyers team that was already down 3–0 in the best-of-seven Finals. The Flyers did eventually score, and Detroit ended up a 2–1 winner.

"Tomas Storm was at the game, and no doubt he was analyzing what I did with my hands on that play," McCarty said.

McCarty scored 23 playoff goals in his career, and none were more memorable, or prettier, than that one.

"Timing is everything in life," McCarty said.

98 Wings Camp at Traverse City, AKA Hockeytown North

What began as a one-year experiment has grown into a three-pronged staple of the Red Wings' season.

In the fall of 1997, following their first Stanley Cup triumph since 1955, the Wings trekked from Detroit to the shores of Lake Michigan, holding their training camp in the northern resort town of Traverse City, Michigan.

The move was an immediate hit, and much like a successful Broadway show, the run appears to be never-ending.

"They put a great production on in Traverse City," said Kris Draper, who first experienced training camp there as a player and now as a member of the club's front office.

Tickets to Detroit's training camp workouts are hot commodities and generally are sold out early in the summer. Fans come from all over the state of Michigan to get a close-up look at the Wings and cram into the Centre Ice complex in Traverse City like sardines.

"It's fun to see the energy in the stands," Wings captain Henrik Zetterberg said. "We have fun up there."

That influx of rabid fan support makes it easy for the players to keep up the tempo-during what can be a grind at times as a new season gets under way.

"When we're up there, we know the practices and games will be hard," said Draper, who believes the atmosphere also creates plenty of opportunities for team-bonding activities that didn't exist when training camp was held at Joe Louis Arena.

"Afterward, you grab a group of 15 or 16 guys and hit the golf course and then go out for dinner. If we stayed in the city, you'd obviously go home to your families. It's unique in that way."

On the links, the players have created their own version of the Ryder Cup with an original Red Wings twist.

"It's Sweden against everybody," former Detroit captain Nick Lidstrom recalled.

Other players find different activities to partake in with teammates.

"I love fishing," former Wing Tomas Holmstrom said. "I'd work hard on the ice and then I'd go have a nice time on the lake."

The brainchild of Detroit GM Ken Holland, the plan to take the team away from it all for an early season get-acquainted opportunity has come together even better than he could have imagined.

"The people of Traverse City and everyone associated with Centre Ice do a tremendous job to make our camp there so successful," Holland said.

More than 300 locals volunteer their time to ensure all runs smoothly during the camp sessions.

"It's huge for us at the rink," Terry Marchand, executive director of Centre Ice told the *Traverse City Record-Eagle*. "For the city itself it's millions of dollars in income during those two weeks."

For those who attend the sessions, it's a chance to get up close and personal with Wings players they'd normally only see on a television screen.

"There's people who come for the first time, and they see it, and they can't believe how close they can get to the players," Marchand said.

Away from the ice, situated in such a small town, it's not uncommon to run across some Red Wings players out for dinner or checking out the sights around town.

"How lucky we are in Traverse City that the Wings pick[ed] us," Marchand said. "It's very cool."

In 1998 the Wings added a pre–training camp rookie tournament to the festivities. What started as a four-team event has grown to involve eight NHL franchises, and in 2013, for the first time, the Red Wings rookies won the tourney.

More than 400 players who've skated in the rookie tournament have gone on to play in the NHL, offering up a who's who of NHL talent from Red Wings stars like Zetterberg, Pavel Datsyuk, and Jimmy Howard, to opponents such as Ilya Kovalchuk, Dany Heatley, and Erik Johnson.

In recent years, the Wings have also moved their post–NHL draft summer prospects camp to Traverse City, giving the newcomers to the organization a chance to get away and begin the process of developing team chemistry.

Even other NHL teams have come to learn how significant the Wings are in Traverse City.

St. Louis Blues coach Ken Hitchcock got married in Traverse City and learned that the city might as well be called Hockeytown North.

"It was June 27, and there were signs all over town welcoming the Red Wings," Hitchcock said.

Camp wasn't scheduled to open until September.

99 Jimmy Orlando, Detroit's Draft Dodger

A youngster arriving for a Red Wings game at Olympia Stadium during the 1941–42 season with a free pass was asked by an usher where he'd like to sit.

"Put me next to the penalty box," the boy eagerly responded. "I want to be somewhere where I can see Jimmy Orlando."

Detroit defenseman Orlando was a man with a reputation. For three straight seasons from 1940–41 through 1942–43, Orlando led the NHL in penalty minutes. He once suggested that the best way to improve the game of hockey would be to eliminate all penalties from the rule book.

"He's tough," Detroit captain Sid Abel said of Orlando. "That's the only way he can get his name in the papers."

Orlando established himself as the bad man of the league but tried to convince people he was really an okay guy.

"I'm greatly misunderstood," Orlando told the *Boston Traveler* during the 1942–43 season, while claiming in the article that he, as all NHL players who skated for American-based teams were required to be during World War II, was employed in an occupation away from hockey that aided the war effort.

"I'm a defense worker in more ways than one, but I'll be ready when they want me," Orlando suggested of whether he'd follow the lead of many of his teammates and enlist in the Canadian military at season's end.

Soon, the worst deed of this NHL bad man would come to light.

On March 29, 1943, Orlando pled guilty to a charge of obtaining draft deferment by posing as an essential war worker. He'd been arrested by the FBI at the Michigan Central Depot as the team was preparing to board a train for a playoff game in Toronto.

John S. Bugas, chief of Detroit's FBI office, indicated Orlando faced two charges in violation of the Selective Service Act—failure to notify his board of a change in his occupational status and falsification of later information provided the board.

Orlando had misrepresented himself as a machinist employed by the Lincoln Tool and Die Company of Detroit. He actually worked as a machinist for only two weeks, and then transferred to office work.

David Ferguson, part owner of Lincoln Tool and Die, was also charged with aiding Orlando to establish an erroneous selective service classification, though the charge against Ferguson was later dropped.

Orlando, a Canadian citizen, was freed on $2,000 bond and left for Toronto to join his team, claiming he misunderstood the affidavit he was accused of falsifying.

"I was working at the time," Orlando told the Associated Press. "The only thing I didn't know was that I had to notify my draft board when I started playing hockey."

Based on the documents he was accused of falsifying, Orlando was given a 2-B draft deferment as an essential war worker by the Detroit draft board.

On April 16, 1943, Orlando was indicted by a federal grand jury on four counts of violating the Selective Service Act and one count of perjury. After a three-day trial in US federal court, on July 30, 1943, a jury of nine women and three men found Orlando guilty. Judge Edward J. Monet sentenced Orlando to four years in prison and fined him $2,000 for violating the Selective Service Act.

Freed on bond while his lawyer appealed the sentence, Orlando was granted permission in December 1943 to go to Montreal for his mother Santa's funeral. He opted to live with his father while appealing the sentence and was considered a fugitive from justice by the United States.

Orlando enlisted in the Canadian Army on March 2, 1944, but the conviction against him as a draft dodger in the USA stood. On April 22, Orlando lost his appeal in the Sixth US Circuit Court of Appeals in Cincinnati, and he remained a wanted man in America. He forfeited his $4,000 bond by not returning to serve his sentence.

Montreal Star columnist Baz O'Meara felt that Orlando's enlistment in the Canadian Army did nothing to remove the stain that resulted from his unpatriotic dishonesty. "It seems to us that the aggressive and very alert public-relations department of the army is being unduly alert and more than usually aggressive in trying to put a heroic halo around Jimmy," O'Meara wrote.

"Pictures of him carrying a pack and smiling happily in his new uniform are not our idea of what constitutes effective army publicity.

"Our guess is that Jimmy was badly advised when he got himself tangled with American authorities. He could have enlisted any time in Canada in the last four years. The way was open to him the first time he was interrogated by Canadian authorities."

He never returned to the United States. Orlando's NHL career was over, and he played senior hockey in Quebec until 1951. Later, Orlando worked as a pro wrestling referee in Montreal and operated several nightclubs in the city that were notorious hangouts for gangsters. Police always looked upon Orlando as being loosely connected to some of the city's major crime figures.

Orlando died in Montreal in 1992.

100 Gordie Howe vs. Steve Yzerman Is No Contest

Gordie Howe has to be the greatest Detroit Red Wings player of all time because he is the greatest NHL player of all time.

There is ample testimony and evidence to support that verdict, starting with the fact that Howe's name was synonymous with the Red Wings and the sport for the better part of three decades. From 1946–47 through the 1970–71 season, there were undoubtedly many people who didn't know pucks from polka dots, but they could have told you that Gordie Howe was the NHL's best and most famous player.

Steve Yzerman will be remembered as the greatest captain in Red Wings history, and Nicklas Lidstrom is unquestionably the top defenseman in the franchise's history. But both rank behind Howe on the list of the franchise's greatest players.

Yzerman was highly gifted, extremely dedicated, and fiercely intense. Detroit fans younger than 40 believe Yzerman can walk on water.

But Howe's level of accomplishment as a Red Wing is far greater.

As the late Detroit GM Jack Adams told *Michigan Sportscene* magazine in 1967, "[Howe] is to hockey what Babe Ruth was to baseball, only more so."

The late Frank Selke was the managing director of the Montreal Canadiens in 1961 when he said Howe was "simply the greatest" after watching him play an estimated 45 minutes of a 60-minute game in the Montreal Forum.

"Howe is a composite of some mighty fine stars, including Maurice Richard, Jean Beliveau, Milt Schmidt, and many others," Selke said in an Associated Press interview.

Selke said Howe was "an inspired leader" after Howe picked up three assists on Detroit's four goals in the game.

"His big assets are his almost superhuman strength, powerful wrists, passing, playmaking, shooting, and stickhandling," Selke said. "There doesn't seem to be anything Gordie can't do, except sit on the bench."

Obviously, there were reasons that Howe picked up the nickname "Mr. Hockey."

"Howe is the greatest player ever to lace up skates," said Adams, who was no longer working for the Red Wings when he gave the *Michigan Sportscene* interview. "He's one of those athletes that come along every 50 or 100 years. He's got everything going for him: size, disposition, reflexes, and strength."

Legendary Red Wings coach Scotty Bowman saw Howe play live in the 1950s, and he has said continually that Howe was the best all-around player he saw.

"When I think about players, I consider three ingredients: the head, heart, and the feet," Bowman said. "Some players don't have any of those, and some players have one or two. But Gordie had all three in high dimensions."

Hall of Famer Al Arbour said the most fascinating aspect of Howe's dominance was his ability to make it seem effortless.

"It is like a great golfer," Arbour said. "They swing so nice and easy, and they make it seem so simple. You try to duplicate that swing, and it's impossible. No one could do it like Mr. Hockey. No matter what it was, he could do it well, whether it was penalty killing, power play, or making passes."

The golfing analogy is more interesting when you consider that Howe was known to grab any stick off the rack to score his goals. He wasn't all that picky about his lumber.

Bowman said he doesn't believe any player ever came close to matching Howe's array of talents. "Gordie was the ultimate forward," Bowman said. "He could play center. He could play wing and he could play defense."

As much as the hockey world appreciates Wayne Gretzky, Mario Lemieux, Maurice "Rocket" Richard, and Bobby Orr, Howe simply had more tools in his box. Gretzky was known for his creativity and passing, Lemieux for his goal scoring, Richard for his shot, and Orr for his puck-moving ability. Howe was known for being the complete package. Coaches around the NHL viewed him as the perfect hockey player because there wasn't a single aspect of the game he hadn't mastered.

"In all of the years I watched Gordie play, I don't think I ever saw him play a bad game," said Hall of Fame defenseman Bill Gadsby. "I've said he's not only the greatest hockey player of all time, but also the greatest athlete."

When Howe was playing in the World Hockey Association in the 1970s, his rival, Bobby Hull, described Howe as being "tougher than a night in jail."

Newspaper accounts during Howe's heyday indicate he routinely played 30 or more minutes per game. Bowman has said he believes Howe could have played all 60 minutes if a coach would have let him.

Bowman said the Montreal players viewed Howe "as being close to Superman."

Supporting evidence for how remarkable Howe was during his career:

- Won six Hart Trophies and six Art Ross Trophies
- Suffered a brain injury, requiring surgery during the 1950 playoffs, and then won the NHL scoring championship in 1950–51
- Registered 103 points in the season during which he turned 40 years old
- Played in 29 All-Star Games in 32 seasons of professional hockey
- Scored his last NHL goal at age 52, now an age when you can have an AARP membership
- In 1959 Howe fought and defeated New York Rangers forward Lou Fontinato, who was considered the NHL's top fighter. Howe won the Hart Trophy that season. That would have been like Yzerman taking on Bob Probert.
- In the 1960s it was estimated that Howe's wrist shot was well over 100 mph.
- In 26 NHL seasons he played almost 97 percent of his games during his career. From 1961 to 1970, he missed only two games, even though he played a ruthlessly rough style of play.

Harry Neale, who coached Howe in New England, believes that the night Howe scored his 1,000[th] career goal against the World Hockey Association's Birmingham Bulls, he was playing with a fractured hand. Even when he was 49, Howe wouldn't take a day off. Neale recalls Howe's hand looked like a gob of "swollen purplish" goo when he netted the historic goal.

Howe had special tricks, and he used them all. He could shoot with either hand, and he would often switch just to confuse the goalie. He could bank pucks off Olympia Stadium boards and read the caroms like a billiards shark. Hall of Fame goalie Glenn Hall recalled that Howe would drive to the net with his knee out to beat the defenseman, "and he could shoot with one hand if he needed to."

He was always faster than he looked. "I watched a lot of good skaters try to catch him from behind and never do it," Gadsby said.

Arbour said when a defender came too close to catching Howe, "he would put it into the next gear."

Howe also had a reputation for being able to send an opponent flying without the victim knowing exactly what had happened to him.

"Defensemen never liked playing against him because he always had his elbows in their kisser," said former Boston Bruins goalie Eddie Johnston.

Howe is one of the most popular athletes in Detroit's history, rivaling Al Kaline or Barry Sanders. Howe's persona was enormous to the point that it was difficult not to view the Winged Wheel and Howe as being intertwined. From 1946 until 1971, Howe was essentially the face of the Red Wings.

The establishment of the Red Wings' reputation as a hockey superpower occurred during Howe's watch. Long before anyone had heard of Hockeytown, Howe made the Red Wings popular by helping them win Stanley Cup championships in 1950, 1952, 1954, and 1955.

Throughout his career, Howe had a reputation for signing autographs until his wrist cramped. Son Mark Howe recalled when he was young that he and his brother Marty would start playing ball hockey in the Olympia corridor because they knew their father would be there an hour after the game. Howe would tell stories as he signed. It was almost as if he viewed his stardom as community property that needed to be shared.

"He was the meanest, nastiest man on a pair of skates I've ever seen," said his son Mark. "Off the ice, he was the most gentlemanly man I ever met."